ANGER
TAMING
THE BEAST
SECOND EDITION

A STEP-BY-STEP PROGRAM FOR
MANAGING ANGER CALMLY AND EFFECTIVELY

ANGER

TAMING
THE BEAST

SECOND EDITION

RENEAU Z. PEURIFOY, M.A.

LIFESKILLS PUBLICATIONS
CITRUS HEIGHTS, CALIFORNIA

Cover by Mayhem Cover Creations
Interior design by Andrea Costantine
Photo of Mr. Peurifoy by Jessica Giblin

Library of Congress Cataloging-in-Publication Data
Peurifoy, Reneau Z.
Anger: taming the beast / by Reneau Z. Peurifoy
p. cm.
ISBN   978-0-929437-00-2 (pbk)
          978-0-929437-01-9 (ebook)
1. Anger–Problems, exercises, etc. 2. Anger–Case studies
I. Title
BF575.A5P44 1999
152.4'7-dc2199-12007

CONTENTS

Author's Note

T HE IDEAS, PROCEDURES, and suggestions in this book are not intended as a substitute for consulting with either a physician or a psychotherapist. You should regularly consult a physician in matters relating to your health, particularly with respect to any symptoms that may require diagnosis or medical attention. Likewise, if you are finding it difficult to cope with daily life or stressful events, you are urged to seek help from a qualified psychotherapist.

Preface

Preface to the First Edition (1999)

DURING THE MANY years that I've worked with people struggling to manage their anger, I've often been disappointed by the published material available to them. Most books on anger don't provide effective tools for managing it, or worse yet, they lag behind the current research on emotions. Those that do have substance are usually targeted at men who are abusing their wives and children, or at women who are having difficulty expressing their anger. While this focus fits many people, other large groups "fall through the cracks." I could find nothing that dealt with the full range of the problems that both sexes face, such as men having difficulty expressing anger and women whose tempers wreak havoc on their husbands and children. Many good books are available on assertiveness, but they address only a small aspect of the problem.

As a result of my frustration, this book "brewed" for many years in the back of my mind. I am pleased now to be able to offer it both to fellow therapists as a resource, and to those who are struggling with managing anger effectively. If you are among the latter, it's my hope that this book will help you with your struggle. I know from the many letters I've received that it's possible to follow a program laid out in a book successfully. I encourage you to use this book as it's intended—as a workbook. If you do, I sincerely believe that you will succeed in taming the beast of anger and transform it into a positive force in your life.

Preface to the Second Edition (2016)

It's very rewarding to be releasing the second edition of a work that has been so warmly received. This edition has been updated to reflect the changes that have taken place in society over the past sixteen years. It has also been re-edited to make it more readable and user-friendly. I am especially pleased with the new eBook versions. My hope is that you find in it both information and tools that make a positive difference in your life.

Acknowledgments

THIS BOOK IS a direct outgrowth of work I've done with hundreds of people. I thank them for the insights they have given me and for the help that they will provide the readers of this book.

Elissa Callman, Caren Clarke, Jeannie Deskins, Tony Donato, Peggy Herrington, Andrew Peurifoy, and Debbie Roth reviewed the initial draft. They all made many suggestions for additions and changes. I would especially like to thank Lynn Maguire and Laura DaLanni, who went well beyond the call of duty in their suggestions on the initial draft. The present book has been greatly improved by all of their efforts.

Alissyn Link went through the second draft and helped shape it into its final form. She has been a tremendous help on both this and my previous two books.

Barbara-J. Zitwer, my agent, believed in my work during the early years when I was struggling to get it out to the public, and has been a tremendous source of encouragement. Nancy Cooperman Su, my editor at Kodansha, spent much time with the manuscript and offered many valuable suggestions on style and structure that greatly improved the final manuscript. Janet Biehl was the final copy editor. She did a superb job of increasing the book's overall readability.

Stefani Odak and John Simlett read the final manuscript for the second edition and made valuable suggestions. Frankie Sutton did an excellent job as copy-editor and corrected many small grammatical and punctuation errors that had crept into the revised manuscript.

I would also like to thank my wife, Michiyo, who has patiently stood by my side during the lean years, and my parents, who helped to give me the confidence and skills that made me who I am today.

Finally, I would like to dedicate this book to my children, Audric and Monique. It's a great privilege to be a parent. Many of the insights in this book are a direct result of experiencing my children as they were growing up.

Where Does the
Beast Come From?

T HE IMAGE OF anger as a beast is a familiar one. We have all experienced the transformation that can occur when the beast awakens; the momentary sense of power, the confidence that what we are doing is correct, and the over-whelming drive to triumph over whoever or whatever is op-posing us. Regrettably, we have also experienced the after-math of the beast gone wild: words and choices that we regret, damaged relationships, and a desire to erase what we have done. Some people respond to the havoc by locking the beast deep within themselves where it never again sees the light of day. Unfortunately, the price they pay of powerlessness can be just as great as the damage done by their uncontrolled an-ger. Others go through a constant cycle of anger and regret.

This book is for everyone who is struggling with anger. By following the lives of four people, each of whom is struggling with the beast in different ways, it shows you how to tame anger and make it your ally instead of your enemy.

Sharon, a divorced mother of two, often finds herself exploding over trivial matters. At work, she is overly aggressive and has a history of alienating her coworkers. Her trail of poor relationships often leaves her with feelings of deep regret.

David, a successful businessman and a good provider for his family, is often overly critical of his employees, even cruel. At home, his criticism and quick temper are distancing him from his wife and children, despite his desire to be close to them.

Carmen, a shy married woman who works as a clerk, remains silent when conflict arises. Sometimes, her silence dissolves into a flood of tears. Afterward, she dwells on how badly she handled the situation. Sometimes, she becomes so depressed that she sits and stares into space for much of the evening, replaying the conflict over and over in her head.

Alex, an intelligent and articulate single man, has what most would consider an easygoing manner. However, he often stews over minor things for days. When he feels he has suffered wrongs, he often retaliates indirectly, making hurtful comments or "forgetting" things that he knows are important to others. Afterward, he is often confused as to why he acted as he did.

As you follow each of these people on their journey to controlling anger, you will find many parallels in your own life. Along the way, you will acquire new tools for taming your own beast.

IS THERE A POSITIVE SIDE TO ANGER?

When I conduct workshops on anger, I often begin with this question, "What words come to mind when you think of anger?" Here is a sample of the words they list:

confusion	hitting	regret
destruction	hurt	rejection
disappointment	inadequacy	resentment
disapproval	loneliness	sadness
fear	loss	stress
frustration	out of control	running away
guilt	pain	tears
hate	powerlessness	trouble
helplessness	pushing	weakness

While we usually see anger in this negative way, it has another side as well. Sometimes, anger is a positive force. When I ask the group to think of times when this has been true for them, they begin to see that anger enables them to set limits and to say no to unreasonable demands. It can also help them take steps to meet important needs that they have been ignoring. As you work through the following chapters, you'll learn how to transform destructive anger into a positive source of strength.

What Is Anger?

Three words summarize the key aspects of anger:

- Threat
- Energy
- Motivation

Anger is an automatic emotional response to a real or perceived threat. It generates energy as well as motivation to eliminate that threat; the greater the threat. The higher the level of arousal and the greater the motivation there is to eliminate it.

In everyday speech, the word anger usually refers to a level of arousal somewhere between irritation and rage:

Irritation — Anger — Rage

When I refer to anger in this book, I am referring to this entire range of emotion: from low-level irritation to out-of-control rage. The only difference is the level of anger being felt.

Once a perceived threat has triggered anger, the energy and motivation generated by the anger produces actions that can range from any one of the following:

- Violent, destructive, and/or harmful actions
- Tantrums
- Hurtful or critical remarks (sarcasm/teasing)
- Sulking/pouting
- Passive-aggressive behavior (hurtful actions such as being late or cruel remarks that you don't mean)
- Withdrawal (you retreat from situations that incite anger)
- Hurtful or destructive fantasies
- Suppression (you're angry but pretend that you aren't)
- Repression (you're so good at suppressing anger, you don't even realize when something has made you angry)
- Constructive action (usually assertive behavior or problem solving)

As you read this list, you may have noticed that nearly all the items are destructive and self-defeating responses. The goal of this book is to reduce such destructive expressions and channel the energy and motivation of anger positively.

Two things cause anger to be expressed in harmful ways. First, anger can be triggered by a real or a perceived threat. The first step then, for transforming anger into a positive force is to learn to evaluate threats accurately. Because this is much more easily said than done, we will spend a lot of time developing this ability.

The second cause for anger's destructive side is its automatic and unconscious nature. Like many of our behaviors, the actions we take when angry tend to be fairly automatic and unconscious. The good news is that these actions are learned responses. This means that you can learn new ways of responding that eventually replace destructive and self-defeating expressions of anger. While this takes time and effort, you can succeed and learn to manage your anger in new and more effective ways.

HOW TO GET THE MOST OUT OF THIS BOOK

This book is designed to be used as a workbook. In order to get the most out of it, you need to read it slowly. Beginning with Chapter 2, I suggest that you spend at least one week on each chapter and do as many of the Recommended Activities as possible. While it is best to work through the book slowly, it is all right to first read through the entire book quickly to get a general idea of what it covers. Then, once you have done so, return to the beginning and work through the chapters slowly.

If your goal is to change the way that you experience and express anger, you need much more than just a general understanding of ideas. You need to internalize the information and skills presented in each chapter, to make them a natural and automatic part of your behavior. The Recommended

Activities play a key role in this process. The more time and energy you spend on them, the more successful you will be.

You might want to read each chapter several times. You may also wish to spend more than one week on a particular chapter. While it's important to be thorough, it's also important to maintain your momentum. So, as you work through the book, try not to overdo it. Instead, spend at least one week but no more than two weeks on each chapter, doing as many of the Recommended Activities as possible. You can spend additional time on those areas where you feel you need more work after you complete the program.

This probably sounds like a lot of work. It is, but it took all your life to develop your current thinking patterns and behaviors. Still, if you keep at it, you will soon find yourself taming your beast—first in small ways, then ultimately mastering it as Sharon, David, Carmen, and Alex have.

SUMMARY OF KEY IDEAS

1. Anger is an automatic, emotional response to a real or perceived threat. It generates energy as well as motivation to eliminate the threat. The greater the threat, the higher the level of arousal and the greater the motivation to eliminate the threat.
2. While anger is often a destructive force, it can also enable a person to set limits, say no to unreasonable demands, and take steps to meet important needs that have been ignored.
3. A threat that triggers anger may be either real or perceived. Our responses to threats are learned. New responses can be learned and replace old ones.
4. Use this book as a workbook. Read each chapter several times, and do as many of the Recommended Activities as you can before going on to the next chapter.

RECOMMENDED ACTIVITIES

Getting the Most out of the Recommended Activities

At the end of each chapter is a set of activities to help you learn how to manage anger in new and more positive ways. I have used them with clients I have counseled for many years. You'll find some to be easy, while others will be difficult and may make you uncomfortable. The easy activities probably involve skills that are already a part of how you usually think and act. The difficult and uncomfortable activities probably involve skills and ideas new to you or that you have never really mastered.

You might be inclined to spend less time with activities you find easy and more time with those that seem difficult or uncomfortable. That's fine, but I encourage you to do all the exercises. Even though a particular exercise might not seem to apply to you at first, the results of doing it could still surprise you.

One other point I would like to stress is that I have designed this book to produce permanent change rather than just a quick fix. This is a very difficult task, since you are trying to change deeply ingrained behaviors. It is very likely that you have already attended workshops or read books that taught you various assertive and communication skills that you have understood and been able to use in limited ways. However, the old dysfunctional behaviors continue to re-emerge. The problem is that irrational beliefs, distorted thinking, and reactions that were established during childhood are blocking your ability to use the various skills you have learned. Because of this, the early chapters of this book focus on removing the blocks that prevent you from using new skills. It is only then that you begin practicing communication and assertiveness skills.

Another thing that I have done is to introduce the various skills needed to manage anger effectively in a systematic way from those that are usually the easiest for a person to master, to those that are most difficult and dependent on earlier abilities (such as challenging distorted thinking or changing basic beliefs). So, while the order of the material sometimes may not make sense to you, it's all done based on my experience with many different people and with the goal of permanent change in mind.

Since you have spent your entire life developing your current thinking and behaviors, changing them will take time. Be patient. When an important change occurs, you probably won't even notice it until later. This is how personal growth takes place. If you have a strong commitment to use the book as it's designed to be used—to do the reading and apply as many of the suggestions as possible (even if they seem silly or pointless)—you will learn to respond and manage anger in new and more effective ways.

Keep an Anger Journal

Because most of our behavior is fairly automatic and unconscious, the first step in changing behavior is to identify our current patterns clearly. The more precisely you identify your automatic responses to various situations, the better able you will be to identify the changes you need to make. The best way to do this is to keep an anger journal.

Use your journal to not only record and analyze your behavior, but to complete the written Recommended Activities. List your problems and concerns, record your insights, and keep track of your progress. As you proceed through the chapters, you will find that your journal is an extremely effective tool for growth.

You don't need to use an expensive or fancy volume for

your journal. A simple spiral-bound notebook or electronic file on a computer is fine. Feel free to choose whatever is most comfortable for you. As you work with your journal, keep in mind that privacy is essential in order to write honestly and openly. Do not write for an "unseen audience." Attempting to please invisible watchers can cause you to lose much of the benefit of keeping a journal.

The main value of a journal is not the permanent record it represents, but the work put into creating it. The act of writing is a powerful way to learn because it involves different parts of the brain. This is why written homework is a fundamental part of formal education. Even after you complete this book, you may choose to keep your journal as a source of encouragement because of the progress it records.

As already mentioned, the first step in changing your anger patterns is to observe and identify your current patterns in detail. So, each day this week, take ten to fifteen minutes to write down a brief description of when you became angry. For each incident, rate your anger in terms of its level of intensity. Use a scale of 1 to 10, where 1 is minimal anger arousal and 10 is the most anger arousal you have ever felt. Also, using a scale of 1 to 10, rate each incident in terms of how aggressively you acted, where 1 is minimal aggression and 10 is the most aggression you have ever displayed. Then record your thoughts when you were angry and a brief description of what you did. You will use this information in the later chapters. Here are Sharon and Alex's first entries in their anger journals:

Sharon
Monday, June 2
Incident: I became angry with my son, who had not picked up his toys.

Arousal — 4, Aggression — 4

Thoughts: "Why can't he learn to pick up his toys? Why do I always have to follow him around? I feel like a maid. He's so irresponsible."

Actions: I yelled at him and told him how irresponsible he was. Then I made him pick up the toys.

Alex

Wednesday, May 7

Incident: My girlfriend went shopping with her friends instead of having dinner with me.

Arousal — 1, Aggression — 1

Thoughts: "How could she do this to me? I thought she cared but I guess her friends are more important than our relationship."

Actions: I went home, took the phone off the hook so she couldn't reach me, and watched TV.

Clarify Your Goals

If you are serious about making change, you can greatly increase your chances of success by clarifying exactly what change you wish to achieve. Think about each of the following questions, and record your responses in your anger journal.

- Why am I reading this book?
- What do I hope to achieve as a result of working through this book?
- How might I sabotage or undermine my work as I go through this book?
- How can I prevent myself from sabotaging or undermining my work?
- How do I feel about reading this book?

Establish a Regular Study Time

This book is a self-directed study program. Set aside a regular time to do the activities, and make this scheduled study time as important as your regular meals. If you use a calendar or appointment book, write down your study times in it. Having a regular study time helps you avoid the common mistake of working only when you are upset. *Remember the "good day rule": You can make the most progress when you are feeling good and your life seems to be running smoothly.* This is when it's easiest to look at yourself objectively and do the activities. Unfortunately, these times are also when you are least motivated. If you do the activities anyway, you will be richly rewarded.

Find a Study Partner

Although it is possible to work through this book on your own, you might find it helpful to have someone work through the material with you. Discussing the chapters with a study partner deepens your understanding and helps you discover things in the material that you may not see on your own.

Your study partner does not need to be a person with anger-related problems, but he or she must be someone you trust and with whom you are comfortable. People who might make a good study partner include a spouse, significant other, friend, or fellow member of a support group. The important thing is to be comfortable and honest with this person.

Consider Joining a Self-Help Group

Many people find that a self-help group is useful in helping them change. A well-run support group offers the advantages of a study partner multiplied by the number of people in the group. If you live in or near a large town, the chances are excellent that classes and structured groups that deal with anger are available. You can learn how to find one of these local self-help groups in Appendix 2. You could even start your own.

Consider Psychotherapy

While this book has been designed to be used as a self-help program, you may wish to use it in conjunction with professional counseling. This may be the case, especially if poor anger management—whether explosive or suppressed—is interfering with your life in serious ways. If you decide to seek professional help, find someone who is experienced in working with anger-related problems. Guidelines can be found in Appendix 1.

If you have served in combat and are experiencing problems with anger, or if you have ever committed domestic violence, you might find the help of a professional or a group anger management program especially beneficial.

A Word to Your Spouse or Significant Other

As the partner of a person struggling with anger, I strongly recommend that you read this book to learn more about what your loved one is experiencing and how he or she may change. If you are fearful of or scornful toward your partner's ways of managing anger, it may be difficult for you, but the rewards are well worth the effort. Since much of what is written in this book applies to anyone, you could find that you and your loved one are struggling with similar issues of which you were unaware. Sharing such a discovery can be very beneficial for both of you.

One of the best ways to educate yourself about anger management is to become a study partner and do the various exercises yourself. Working through the book as a study partner is a wonderful way to support your loved one and deepen the bond between you. If your personality or your relationship with your partner makes this difficult, simply read the book on your own and discuss what you have learned. Focus on how the material applies to you, and avoid using it as a weapon to punish your partner.

2

Facing the Beast

E XAMINING HOW YOU manage anger and the consequences of mismanaging it can be a terribly uncomfortable process. Still, if you are going to be successful in facing and taming your beast, you need to take an honest look
at how you are currently handling anger. So, while it might
be difficult, the more honestly you assess yourself, the greater
your chances of success in developing a new and more effective anger management style. Let's begin by looking at what I
mean by appropriate and inappropriate anger.

Appropriate vs Inappropriate Anger

Anger is appropriate when (1) a real threat exists, (2) the level
of your anger is proportional to the threat, and (3) your sub-

sequent actions effectively reduce the threat with the least amount of harm to yourself and others.

Anger can be inappropriate in any of three ways. First, you might become angry when there is no logical reason to become angry. For example, suppose you purchase a candy bar from a vending machine and upon opening the package, you find that the candy bar is broken instead of in one piece. Since the candy bar tastes the same and you received the full amount you paid for, you weren't cheated. Any reaction greater than mild disappointment would be inappropriate.

The second form of inappropriate anger is anger whose intensity is out of proportion to events. Say you put money into the vending machine, but you receive nothing. To become irritated or mildly angry would be reasonable, but to become enraged would be inappropriate.

The third form of inappropriate anger is inappropriate action taken in response to anger. If you receive nothing from the vending machine, it would be appropriate to try to find someone to reimburse you for the lost money, or to tap the machine firmly a few times to try to unstick the mechanism. Intentionally damaging the machine or screaming at the vendor would be inappropriate.

Inappropriate emotional responses sometimes have organic causes. Injury, disease, drugs, or an inherited genetic defect can cause your nervous system to function improperly. However, most emotions that occur when events don't warrant it or at a greater level of intensity than is appropriate, are due to some sort of distorted thinking. Likewise, most inappropriate actions are the result of learning that took place during childhood. Effective anger control requires both minimizing distorted thinking that generates inappropriate anger and learning how to respond appropriately when you become angry.

The two main goals of this book are (1) to help you experience anger at appropriate levels and (2), to channel the energy and motivation generated by your anger into constructive rather than destructive actions. The first step in accomplishing these goals is to overcome two common roadblocks to change.

Two Roadblocks to Change

Two common roadblocks keep people locked into old patterns and interfere with their ability to learn more effective anger management strategies. The first is the erroneous idea that self-control is not possible. When I first met Sharon and David and asked them about their fiery reactions, they both responded with, "I can't help myself," "It's just the way I am," and "I was just born this way." Carmen and Alex gave similar responses for their tendency to suppress anger and be nonassertive. They too believed that they were unable to act in new or different ways because it was somehow against their basic nature. As we talked, however, all four came to realize that they actually exercised much more control over themselves than they realized.

David, for example, always kept his cool at business meetings with his superiors. Likewise, Sharon usually kept her temper at church. It didn't take long for each to realize that they tended to "blow" only around people or in situations where no immediate negative consequences would arise. Likewise, Carmen and Alex could recall times when they stood up for themselves and acted assertively.

The second roadblock to change is the tendency to minimize the consequences of anger. When discussing her angry outbursts toward her children, Sharon initially commented, "Basically, I'm a pretty good mom. We have lots of fun together and you know how easily kids bounce back from things. My kids know I don't really mean it." Actually, her oldest child was beginning to mirror her mother's fiery temper, while her younger child was becoming withdrawn. Likewise, David soon admitted that his relationship with his wife and children had become distant over the years. In fact, it was his dissatisfaction with his home life that had caused him to seek help.

Alex and Carmen's nonassertive styles caused them to be quiet and do nothing in situations where others were acting inappropriately toward them or where they were losing something that they wanted. The depression and resentment they experienced when they failed to speak up was draining the joy out of their lives and slowly poisoning their relationships.

You will not be able to apply the information in this book or make any lasting changes until you acknowledge both your ability to control your behavior and the serious negative consequences of inappropriate behavior. Therefore, the first step in learning to manage anger effectively is to memorize the following two statements:

- I have the ability to control my behavior.
- Poor anger management has serious negative consequences.

ABUSIVE BEHAVIOR

Once you acknowledge these two crucial points, the next step is to distinguish clearly between appropriate and inappropriate responses. All too often, an inappropriate response to anger is abusive behavior. While people with explosive tempers like Sharon and David frequently act abusively, abusive behavior can also be a problem for those who suppress anger, like Carmen and Alex. There are five basic types of abusive behavior.

Emotional Abuse: Emotional abuse is any systematic attempt to control another person's thinking or behavior. It can take a variety of forms. One is repeated communication that causes unnecessary mental suffering, like calling someone stupid, belittling or blaming them, humiliating them, falsely and unreasonably accusing them, or threatening to abandon them, over and over again. Sharon often used this type of emotional abuse to control her children. It can also take the form of direct or veiled threats of physical violence. For example, David would occasionally become so enraged he would punch a hole in the wall of his home or break something. While this didn't happen very often, it occurred frequently enough that his wife and children were very intimidated and feared such outbursts each time David got angry.

Physical Abuse: Physical abuse is the use of physical force in any form against another person for any purpose other than self-defense. Examples include hitting someone with or without an object, slapping, grabbing, shoving, pushing or pulling, kicking, choking, scratching, or forcing someone to do something or to go someplace against his or her will. It also includes preventing someone from doing something or going somewhere against his or her will.

Sexual Abuse: Sexual abuse occurs whenever one person forces another person to engage in any type of sexual activity against his or her will. Examples include touching, kissing, forcing them to look at sexual material they don't want to see, treating a person like a sex object, and rape. Because children wish to please parents and adult caregivers and are easily manipulated, the sexual abuse of children includes enticing or encouraging them to do any type of inappropriate sexual activity.

Financial Abuse: Financial abuse is the use of money to gain power or control in a relationship. It can include only allowing a partner to have a meager allowance, denying access to money, forcing or forbidding someone to work, making someone "earn" money, stealing, refusing to work, ruining one's credit, destroying property, or getting someone fired or evicted.

Spiritual Abuse: Spiritual abuse takes two forms. The first is when someone uses religion or spiritual beliefs to justify the abuse of another. The second is when someone abuses another by demeaning their beliefs, not allowing them to follow their religious or cultural practices, or forcing them to do things against their religious beliefs. The second form involves non-religious actions that take away a person's sense of hope and meaning such as not allowing someone to take a promotion, go to school, have hobbies or friends, or to hold opinions that differ from the abuser.

In addition, three more forms of abuse are most commonly seen committed by adults against children or the elderly.

Cruel and Unusual Punishment: Cruel and unusual punishment of a child is any punishment that is extreme or inappropriate for the child's age or ability to understand: for example, punishment that results in injury, locking the child in a closet, forcing the child to toilet-train at six months, or sitting the child in a corner for hours at a time. With the elderly, an example would be withholding food or other necessities.

Emotional Neglect: Emotional neglect occurs (1) when a parent fails to be emotionally available to take an interest in, talk to, hold, or nurture a child, or (2), when an adult isolates an elderly person for prolonged periods of time without providing any kind of meaningful mental stimulation or human contact.

Physical Neglect: Physical neglect occurs when an adult fails to provide basic necessities—such as clothing, shelter, medical attention, or supervision—required by a child or elderly person. Leaving someone who is bedridden in one position on a bed for prolonged periods of time, which causes bed sores to become a problem, is an additional all-too-common form of physical neglect experienced by the frail elderly.

As children, Sharon, David, Carmen, and Alex each experienced one or more of the above forms of abuse. Sharon and David later adopted many of their abusers' behaviors. Carmen and Alex, were so intimidated that they learned to suppress their anger and be nonassertive. Abusive behavior toward others was less of a problem for them than for Sharon and David, but both Carmen and Alex found that when their suppressed anger did surface, they could become very abusive.

TIME-OUT

For individuals with explosive tempers like Sharon and David, the first step in managing anger is learning to take a time-out when anger flares. While this may sound easy, it's often difficult to do since it requires you to challenge the belief that you are helpless to do something different in the face of anger. One way to get past this is to write the phrase "I have the ability to control my anger" on a card and place it somewhere where you can see it daily. Fixing this sentence in your mind daily greatly increases the chances that you will remember it when anger begins to rise. In addition to accepting that you can control your anger, you need to accept that your current behaviors are the result of your past learning. As you learn and practice new behaviors, they eventually replace the old ones.

There are several ways to take a time-out. David, who was acting out his anger in abusive ways at home, had to use a very structured approach to time-outs. If this is also the case for you and you need to take time-outs with your partner or others you live with, be sure to follow these steps:

Step 1: Say, "I'm beginning to feel angry and I need a time-out." One problem with inappropriate behavior is that it's usually fairly unconscious. Making this statement focuses your awareness on what you are doing. It also puts you in charge of your behavior. A statement such as, "You're making me angry" or "You're making me lose control" places the responsibility for your anger on the other person. Because such statements are blaming, they also tend to escalate the conflict. By stating, "I'm beginning to feel angry," you immediately take responsibility for your emotion.

David began to practice making this statement to his wife and taking a time-out whenever they were engaged in an activity that escalated his anger.

Step 2: Leave for an hour. To gain time to cool down, leave for an hour. If your level of arousal is not too great, you might simply be able to go to a different room. In order for this type of time-out to work, the other person has to agree to leave you alone. If he or she is not able to do this, leave the house or place where you are and take a walk or go somewhere far enough away where you will be left alone. If you have children whose normal activities make it difficult to cool down in the house, you may also need to take a walk.

During your time-out, it's helpful to do something physical. This discharges the physical tension that anger produces and helps you focus on something other than what triggered your anger.

Do not drink or use drugs during this cooling-down period. You might think that they'll cool your anger and deaden any guilt or loneliness you might be feeling, however, I cannot state strongly enough how destructive this is. Using alcohol or any other drug to manage painful feelings always makes the problem worse. It is also best if you don't drive. Driving when you are angry can be very dangerous for both you and others on the road.

Step 3: Return and check in. Say, "I've completed my time-out and I'm checking back in." If you feel calm enough to continue the discussion, say so. If not, say, "I'd like to delay the discussion until . . ." Set a specific time and place such as, "Tomorrow after dinner." If you decide to resume the discussion that triggered your anger and again begin to feel angry, take another time-out.

If the topic is simply too emotionally charged for you and your partner to discuss on your own, take it to a counselor so you can get help in working it out. Delaying a discussion can sometimes be difficult, but if you are unable to discuss the issue calmly and rationally on your own, you need help. Your first priority is to stop your inappropriate and abusive behavior.

Time-outs have two purposes: (1) to help you regain control over your behavior and emotions, and (2), to help you reestablish trust with your loved ones. *Do not abuse time-outs by using them to avoid discussing difficult issues or to punish the other person.* Time-outs are not an excuse to do something that you want to do, such as visiting a friend or going shopping. If you abuse time-outs in this way, they become another form of manipulation and abuse that worsens rather than improves the situation.

Like many men who are struggling with angry tempers, David found it very difficult at first to take time-outs. He had grown up believing that it was cowardly to walk away from a fight. Whenever he began to argue with his wife, his first impulse was to stay and finish it, which meant he had to win. In order to help himself take time-outs, David made a card that read, "It's more important to control my behavior and stop abusing others than to try to live up to a phony image of what a 'real man' is."

David also realized that his reluctance to leave for a time-out stemmed in part from his fear that his wife might be gone when he returned. However, as he practiced taking time-outs and learned how to manage his anger more effectively, this fear lessened. For two people in an abusive relationship, rebuilding trust takes time. Just as it took time for David's wife to gain confidence in his ability to control his behavior, it also took time for David to trust that his wife would still be there for him.

Because time-outs were difficult for David, he found it useful to take practice time-outs during the first week of anger work. The reason for taking practice time-outs is simple. If you can't take a time-out when you don't need one, then you won't take it when you do need one. The three steps for a practice time-out are; first, take your practice time-out when you are not feeling angry. Second, announce what you are doing by saying, "I'm not beginning to feel angry, but I want to take a practice time-out." Third, leave for only a half hour. When you return, check back in by telling your partner, "I've completed my practice time-out, and I'm just checking back in."

Sharon also found time-outs to be an important tool, but because she acted out in less violent ways than David did, a more informal approach worked well for her. At work, when she began to feel angry, she would simply end her conversation by saying she had to do some work and walk away. She would then make a point of staying out of conversations until she cooled down. Usually, her anger lasted only a few minutes, but sometimes she needed as long as a half hour to cool down. At those times, she would take a break and walk around the building. Like David, she found it useful to carry a card reminding her to take a time-out when she was angry.

At home, Sharon found that her time-outs had to be more structured. This is a common phenomenon. The social pressure of being in public often helps people control their behavior, while in the privacy of their home, without that pressure, they might become more abusive. When her two children's misbehavior toward her or each other triggered excessive anger, Sharon learned to say, "We all need a time-out." This meant that if the children were playing together, they would separate, and everyone would go to his or her own room. Sharon also posted a reminder on her refrigerator and in her bathroom: a simple card that read, "Most disciplinary problems with the kids do not need to be dealt with immediately. Take a time-out and you will deal with them more effectively." Indeed, she found that as she delayed making disciplinary decisions, she became a much more effective parent. After a while, she could even wait until the next day to decide what to do about the various situations that arose between her children. A good night's sleep and some distance helped her become much more objective and less abusive.

If you are the partner of someone who has an explosive temper, there are two additional points I would like to make. Do not allow yourself to submit to physical abuse. If an incident is becoming physically abusive, get out immediately. In addition, if you see your partner's anger beginning to escalate, call for a time out. When you do, be sure to follow the above guidelines.

SUMMARY OF KEY IDEAS

1. Anger is appropriate when (1) a real threat exists, (2) the level of your anger is proportional to the threat, and (3) your subsequent actions effectively reduce the threat with the least amount of harm to yourself and others.
2. Anger is inappropriate when (1) you become angry when no real threat exists, (2) its intensity is out of proportion to the threat that triggered it, or (3) the actions you take as a result are inappropriate.
3. The two main roadblocks to changing behavior triggered by anger are (1) the idea that it's impossible to control ourselves, and (2) the tendency to minimize the consequences of inappropriate anger. The truth is,

we have the ability to control our behavior, and poor anger management has serious negative consequences.

4. The five basic types of abusive behavior are emotional abuse, physical abuse, sexual abuse, financial abuse, and spiritual abuse. In addition, three common forms of abuse with children or the elderly include cruel and unusual punishment, emotional neglect, and physical neglect.

5. The first step in changing explosive anger is to learn to use time-outs. The more explosive your temper, the more structured your time-outs should be.

Recommended Activities

Memorize These Two Truths

Write the following two statements on a card, and read them once each day for the next two weeks. Say them to yourself whenever you find yourself becoming angry.

- I have the ability to control my behavior.
- Poor anger management has serious negative consequences.

Begin Using Time-Outs

Begin using time-outs this week. Review the guidelines given in this chapter to make sure you are using time-outs effectively. If you have a problem with explosive anger, I recommend that you take at least three practice time-outs in advance, so you can rehearse the steps. That way, they will more natural when you really need them.

Make sure your loved ones understand the time-out concept before you begin using them. A good way to explain it to them is to read the section on time-outs together. It's also important for your partner to agree to back off when you take a time-out. Again, taking at least three practice time-outs is a good way for both of you to learn to do this.

Identify the Actions You Take When Angry

One of the first steps in changing any behavior is to identify exactly what you are currently doing. Use the following chart to identify how you respond when you are angry. Indicate how often you behave in the described manner, using the following scale.

Never = 0
Rarely = 1
Often = 2
Regularly = 3

Emotionally Abusive Behaviors

How often do you:

1. _____ Tease
2. _____ Belittle
3. _____ Humiliate
4. _____ Make statements intended to make another feel guilty
5. _____ Make false or unreasonable accusations
6. _____ Threaten to leave or abandon a loved one
7. _____ Intimidate someone through physical actions (hole in the wall) or by making direct or veiled threats

Physically Abusive Behaviors

How often do you:

8. _____ Shove, push, grab, or pull
9. _____ Hit, kick, scratch, or choke
10. _____ Injure another by your actions

11._____   Force someone to go someplace or do something
against his or her will

Sexually Abusive Behaviors
How often do you:

12. _____   Touch, kiss, or do anything of a sexual nature to
someone when he or she doesn't want it

13. _____   Force someone to engage in any type of sexual
activity (kissing, touching, intercourse, etc.)
against that other person's will

Financially Abusive Behaviors
How often do you:

14. _____   Use money to control someone by denying access
or making them "earn" it

15. _____   Interfere with another's ability to earn money

Spiritually Abusive Behaviors
How often do you:

16. _____   Use your religious beliefs to justify abusive
behavior toward your partner or others

17. _____   Demean, mock, ridicule, interfere with, or forbid
your partner to have beliefs or observe religious
or spiritual practices different from yours

18. _____   Do something that takes away a person's sense
of hope and meaning such as not allowing some
one to take a promotion, go to school, have
hobbies or friends.

19. _____   Have you tried to keep someone from holding an
opinion that differs from yours

Abusive Behaviors Toward Children
How often do you:

20. _____ Fail to hold or nurture your child when they want or need nurturing
21. _____ Fail to talk to or show interest in your child
22. _____ Sit your child in a chair or confine him or her to a room for more than an hour at a time
23. _____ Punish your child in a manner that results in bruises or injury
24. _____ Fail to provide the supervision your child needs
25. _____ Fail to provide basic necessities such as clothing, shelter or medical attention

Indirect Behaviors Directed at Others
How often do you:

26. _____ Withdraw emotionally from the person who made you angry (you become cold and distant and no longer express affection)
27. _____ Withdraw physically from the person who made you angry (you get busy with things that don't involve the other person or actually leave)
28. _____ Use passive-aggressive behavior against the person who made you angry (Doing something mean in an indirect way such as deliberately "forgetting" something that is important to the other person or being late on purpose)
29. _____ Pick a verbal or physical fight with someone other than the person you are really angry with

Internal or Self-Directed Behaviors
How often do you:

30. _____ Sulk or pout
31. _____ Have hurtful or destructive fantasies about others you are angry with

32. _____ Criticize or belittle yourself because of your perceived "inadequacy" or "failure"
33. _____ Act in a dangerous manner that you don't do
when you are not angry (such as driving recklessly or taking risks in a sport that you usually
don't take)
34. _____ Drink or take other drugs
35. _____ Deliberately hurt yourself so the other person
will be "sorry"
36. Other Behaviors

_____

_____

_____

During the coming week, review this list once each day,
and note the inappropriate behaviors that have been a problem for you. If you feel the urge to do any of them, take a time
out.

Identify the Effects of Your Anger

One of the roadblocks to change is the tendency to minimize
the consequences of anger. Take a serious inventory of the
price you pay for your current anger patterns. Consider each
of the following items, and rate the effect that your current
way of expressing anger has on it. Use the following scale:

No Effect = 0
Minor Effect = 1
Moderate Effect = 2
Significant Effect = 3
Major Effect = 4

1. _____ My relationship with my spouse or significant other
2. _____ My relationship with a previous spouse(s) or significant other(s)
3. _____ My relationship with my children
4. _____ My relationship with my parents
5. _____ My relationship with in-laws
6. _____ My relationship with other family members
7. _____ My relationship with current friends
8. _____ My relationship with former friends
9. _____ My relationship with neighbors
10. _____ My relationship with teachers, supervisors, or other authority figures
11. _____ My relationship with peers or colleagues at work or school
12. _____ My relationship with subordinates at work
13. _____ Impact on social groups (clubs, religious groups, etc.)
14. _____ Impact on my health from being angry or suppressing anger
15. _____ Impact on my ability to enjoy recreational activities
16. _____ Influence on my use of alcohol or other drugs
17. _____ Influence on mistakes made
18. _____ Influence on accidents I've had
19. _____ Overall effect on my work
20. _____ Overall effect on my relationships

Review your responses once a week for the next four weeks. An awareness of the price you pay for inappropriate anger is one of your most powerful motivators to continue to work through this book.

Take Responsibility for Your Anger

The two roadblocks to change that are described in this chapter are often expressed in statements like the following. Place a check by any you have thought or said to yourself during the past month. If you express either of these two false beliefs in a different way, be sure to write it in the space provided or in your journal.

Common ways in which the false belief "I can't control myself" are expressed

_____ I couldn't stop myself

_____ I lost control.

_____ It was the alcohol, drugs, etc. that made me do it.

_____ She/he made me do it.

_____ That's just the way I am.

_____ I'm too old to change.

_____ Other: _____

Common ways in which the effects of anger are minimized

_____ He/she asked for it.

_____ He/she deserved it.

_____ It's the only way he/she gets the message.

_____ It doesn't really bother him/her.

_____ He/she understands that's just the way I am.

_____ Other: _____

Review your responses once a week for the next four weeks. Whenever you notice yourself saying any of these statements, challenge it with the two statements you are memorizing this week:

- I have the ability to control my behavior.
- Poor anger management has serious negative consequences.

Continue to Record Angry Incidents

Continue to record in your journal times when you become angry, using the guidelines in Chapter 1. In addition, for each incident, be sure to list any of the abusive behaviors described in this Chapter that you exhibited.

3

The Nature of the Beast

W HILE MUCH HAS been written about emotions, a great deal of confusion remains as to what emotions are and why we have them. In this chapter, we will discuss how emotions work, as well as common myths about anger. We will also explore more deeply the dynamics that transform anger into a raging beast. This understanding of emotions is the foundation for your next step toward the goal of effective anger management.

WHAT ARE EMOTIONS?

Emotions are the result of a complex process that has three components:

- Cognitive
- Physical
- Subjective

The word *cognitive* refers to mental processes. Thus, *cognitive psychology* deals with how people think and mentally process information. You think and process information differently when you are angry than you do when you are happy, anxious, or sad. In fact, your conscious and unconscious thoughts are not only shaped by your emotions, but they play a key role in triggering the emotions you experience.

Just as a physical process within the circuits of the television produce the image on a television screen, your emotions are the result of a physical process, which takes place within your body. While a whole book could be written on this aspect of emotions, there are two that I would like to point out here. The first is how anger, as well as other strong emotions, triggers the fight-or-flight response. This response heightens a host of activities in the body that increase your ability to meet a physical challenge while decreasing those that would interfere with that ability. Thus, your heartbeat and respiration rate increase and your muscles become tense while your digestive and other nonessential activities decrease. The result is both an actual increase in your physical strength as well as a physical feeling of increased strength.

A second well-known physical response triggered by emotions is the way they change your facial expression. While we can suppress weak emotions, strong emotions are accompanied by unique facial expressions that are similar in every culture. Indeed, people who have been blind since birth exhibit these same facial expressions. This shows that we are born with this powerful form of nonverbal communication.

In addition to cognitive and physical responses, emotions

produce a subjective response that is impossible to measure reliably. Research, therefore, tends to ignore the subjective side of emotions and focus on the cognitive and physical responses associated with them. However, we all know from experience how anger "feels" and how it differs from feeling sad or excited.

The program outlined in this book is based on a cognitive model of emotions that views the process that generates emotions as follows:

Event ⟶ Interpretation ⟶ Emotion ⟶ Action

An event occurs. Consciously or unconsciously, you interpret this event. This interpretation then triggers your emotion. For example, if you interpret the event as fulfilling a need or desire, you experience the various positive emotions—joy, satisfaction, excitement, and so on. If you interpret the event as threatening the fulfillment of a need or desire, you experience either anger or fear. Which emotion you experience— anger or fear—is determined by the threat and your ability to overcome it. If you interpret the event as representing a loss of some kind, you experience sadness. Common statements such as, "You made me angry" and "That made me sad" are inaccurate. It is not the person or event that made you angry or sad, but your interpretation of it.

Let's look at four examples that show how different interpretations of the same event can be made. Imagine that you won a large sum of money. You might think about all the things you could do with the money. This would probably generate joyful excitement because important needs will be met. Instead of this, you could think about the taxes that you will need to pay and the people who might try to cheat you or ask for a loan. This might generate anger. If you believe you would be overwhelmed by the task of managing the money wisely, you might become anxious. If you thought about how people might view you differently and become distant, you might become sad. Thus, the same event could trigger many different emotions, depending on how you interpret it.

Once an emotion is triggered, it then causes an "urge for action." Indeed, the root of the word *emotion* means, "to move." Sometimes, the action is purely mental. At other times, it involves both thought and physical action. So, the basic function of emotions is to drive us to take action in response to our needs. This aspect of emotions can be diagrammed as follows:

From the above, we arrive at the following definition: *An emotion is a complex response that has cognitive, physical, and subjective components. Emotions are triggered by the perception that the fulfillment of a need has been either satisfied or threatened, or that a loss has occurred.*

In this book, the words anger, fear, and sadness are used in a very broad sense. Anger is being used to represent emotions ranging from irritation to rage. Fear represents emotions ranging from apprehension to panic, and sadness represents emotions ranging from mere disappointment to deep depression.

While most of our emotions are generated through the

cognitive process diagrammed above, there are some important exceptions. Because emotions are generated through a
physical process, many diseases, chemicals, injuries, and genetic defects can, by themselves, generate or distort emotional
responses. Mood-altering drugs can produce a wide range of
inappropriate emotions. Thyroid problems can cause anxiety.
Head trauma can cause excessive emotional outbursts, and
genetic defects can cause bipolar disorder or endogenous depression.

Some emotional responses seem to be "hard wired" into
us, like the excitement felt when seeing an attractive member
of the opposite sex. Many athletes feel a "runner's high" during intense exertion when endorphins are released. Hunger,
fatigue, illness, or stress can all alter your emotional responses by interfering with your mental and physical ability to interpret events accurately. Still other emotions are conditioned
responses (discussed more fully in later chapters).

Three Common Myths About Anger

Now that you have a basic understanding of emotions, let us
challenge three common myths about anger.

Myth 1: It's Healthy to Vent Anger.

Many people believe that venting anger—expressing it either verbally or physically—is healthy, if not necessary. This
myth is often used to justify poor anger management. While
the venting of anger can have value in a limited number of
situations during therapy, it's usually not productive in everyday life. First, taking action while you are angry tends to
increase your anger and lead to inappropriate and self-defeating behaviors. Second, acting out anger (in thought, word, or
action) inhibits your ability to develop an effective plan for

overcoming the threat that first triggered your anger. *Anger is an emotion that needs to be acted on, not acted out.*

As I have described previously, emotions are triggered when our needs and wants are either met or threatened, or when we experience a loss. Venting your emotions takes your focus off the needs and desires that triggered them, and causes you to focus on the emotion. While this could temporarily lessen the tension, it does nothing to address the problem of how you are going to meet your needs and deal with threat or loss effectively.

Myth 2: Responding to Anger with Aggression Is Instinctual and Can't Be Helped.

Several popular books have argued that violent behavior is genetically programmed into human nature and is a natural part of anger. However, the consensus of researchers is that this is not true. While emotions are indeed part of our genetic make-up, the specific emotion that is triggered in a given situation is determined by our interpretation of the event: Whether a need is being met or threatened or a loss has occurred. More important, the behaviors we exhibit in response to our emotions, for the most part, are learned. This can be seen in how Sharon, David, Carmen, and Alex each respond to a threat. While Sharon and David tend to become angry and aggressive, Alex and Carmen tend to become passive and experience anxiety or depression.

Myth 3: It's Normal to Become Angry when Frustrated, Helpless, or Confused.

Frustration results from a situation where a need or desire is not being met. Putting money into a vending machine and receiving nothing, for example, is a situation where a desire for a candy bar is being frustrated. Helplessness is the inability to do something necessary to meet a need or desire. If someone you love is suffering and you do not have the ability to help, you are helpless in regard to their situation. Confusion results from not understanding something. If you are trying to complete a tax form, but cannot understand it, you are confused.

Each of these situations could trigger anger, fear, sadness—or no response. The particular emotion we experience is determined by our interpretation of the event. It's not always anger. For example, you might respond to a confusing tax form with anger or anxiety. Either of these responses would be normal since a failure to pay taxes can result in a real and well-defined threat. In contrast, a riddle or joke that causes confusion at first might cause you to laugh once it's understood. This response is also normal since this type of confusion is a form of play. At the same time, the confusing plot of a mystery novel might provoke only a heightened interest. Since the confusion of a mystery novel is expected and a form of recreation, little emotion other than interest is expected. Thus, confusion can trigger a variety of responses depending upon whether our needs are being met (as with the joke or mystery novel) or threatened (as with the tax form).

Even in the event of a traffic jam, with its accompanying frustration and helplessness, anger is not necessarily the normal response. While many people do become angry in this situation, many others do not. Again, it is your interpretation of the event that determines what emotion is triggered. If you think, "I can't stand this. Why does this always happen to me?" you will probably become angry. If instead you think, "Here's another one of our famous traffic jams, so I guess I might as well relax and enjoy some music on the radio," you'll probably remain calm.

How Anger Is Expressed

The energy and motivation produced by anger can be focused in any one, or combination of, the following four ways:

Suppressed: You do nothing and try to ignore your anger. You ignore the threat as well.

Turned inward: You ignore the original threat that triggered your anger and direct your anger at a real or imagined personal weakness or inadequacy.

Displaced externally: You ignore the original threat and direct your anger at someone or something unrelated to it.

Directed at the source of the threat: You direct your anger at the threat (real or imaginary) that triggered it. This can be done in an ineffective and overly aggressive way that damages relationships or in a way that address needs, threats, and losses in an appropriate way that minimizes the threat with the least amount of harm to yourself and others.

Here are examples of each of the above.

Suppressed: Carmen was asked to work overtime. This caused her to be late for a special family gathering. Instead of speaking up and explaining to her supervisor that she had a special event planned, she swallowed her anger and smiled, as she said, "No problem." She honestly thought that everything was fine. Later, however, she developed a headache, and when she eventually did arrive at the event, she found it difficult to enjoy herself.

Turned inward: Alex's girlfriend canceled a date he had planned. As he became angry, he began to think, "I guess I'm not really that important. I've been stupid to think that someone like her could really care for me."

Displaced: Due to an error by his supervisor, David lost an account he had worked hard to secure. Upon hearing what had happened, he criticized his secretary about an unrelated, trivial matter.

Directed at the source of the threat: Sharon's co-worker was habitually late in getting a weekly report to her. This caused Sharon to be late in completing her assignments. To resolve this, Sharon took the co-worker aside in private and explained how important the report was and how not getting it on time was affecting her ability to do her job. She restated when the report was needed for her to complete her work.

Learn to Recognize the Different Forms of Anger

People who have trouble managing their anger often are aware of their anger only when it's at a high level. When your level of anger is low, you are most able to use all of your reasoning ability and choose appropriate actions. Therefore, you need to be able recognize the early signs of anger. This section describes three different ways to identify these early warning signs.

When you first notice low-level anger, you might not always know what has provoked it. This is both common and normal. At this stage of work, it's more important to know when you are angry than why. As you work through the following chapters, you learn how to identify the source of anger at this early stage.

Identify Body Sensations That Indicate Anger

Because anger and fear are designed to help us deal with threats, both of them trigger what is commonly known as the fight-or-flight response. This response, when triggered, suspends all nonessential activity in the body and increases activity in any system necessary to either fight or flee from an external physical threat. It involves many complex physiological reactions, of which the primary ones are:

Increased muscle tension: This prepares the muscles for action. Different people feel it in different parts of their body, but most commonly in the chest, arms, legs, forehead, face, back of the neck, or stomach.

Accelerated heartbeat: The increased flow of blood helps to prepare the muscles for action.

Deeper and more rapid breathing: This insures a large supply of oxygen and is the basis of the "pant" of anger, fear, or excitement.

Suspension of digestive activity: This provides additional blood for the motor muscles and is the reason that food doesn't settle well when you are angry or anxious. It can also result in loss of appetite, or, in some cases, an increase in appetite.

Dry mouth due to decreased flow of saliva: This accompanies the decreased flow of gastric juices in the stomach, as digestive activity is suspended.

Tendency to void bladder and bowels: This frees the

body for strenuous activity and is often expressed as frequent urination—a need to urinate even though the bladder is not very full—or diarrhea.

"Cold sweat": This occurs in preparation for the warm sweat of actual muscular activity.

Constriction of peripheral blood vessels near the surface of the body: This raises blood pressure and is the basis of "blanching with fear." It's sometimes felt as a tingling sensation in the skin.

When people are faced with real physical threats, the fight-or-flight response is essential for their survival. Fortunately, the most common threats we face today do not require an immediate physical response, yet our bodies are still programmed to respond to any threat as if such a response were required. The stronger the sense of threat, regardless of the type, the stronger the response. Thus, noticing these physical symptoms is one way to become aware of times when we are getting angry.

Identify Behavioral Cues

A second way to identify low-level anger is to identify behavioral cues. Earlier we discussed the four different ways in which anger can be expressed. By recalling times in the past when you were angry and how you behaved, you can develop a list of behaviors that you display when you are angry. Once you have identified how you feel and act, especially when your anger is at a low level, you can use these behaviors to identify times when you are beginning to become angry.

Increase the Number of Words You Use to Describe Anger

A person who knows how to play a musical instrument hears subtleties in music that untrained people tend to miss. Likewise, a person who has a richer vocabulary for anger usually can identify the different levels of anger more easily than someone who uses the same words for a wide range of emotions. Here is a list of common words used to describe the various levels of anger. Since you have been using a scale ranging from 1 to 10 to rate your anger, the words are grouped according to that scale.

Low-Level Anger (1-3)

Annoyed	Displeased	Troubled
Bothered	Disturbed	Upset
Bugged	Irritated	

Medium-Level Anger (4-6)

Aggravated	Exasperated	Mad
Agitated	Incensed	Ticked Off
Angry	Indignant	

High-Level Anger (7-10)

Enraged	Furious	Livid
Exploding	Indignant	Outraged
Fuming	Irate	

As you build your vocabulary of words that describe anger, you will find that you begin to notice anger at its earlier stages.

Summary of Key Ideas

1. An emotion is a complex process with mental, physical, and subjective "feeling" components. Emotions are triggered by the perception that a need has been satisfied or threatened, or that a loss has occurred. Once triggered, emotions push us to take action.

2. In everyday life, venting anger is usually not productive. Venting tends to increase the intensity of your anger and takes your focus off the threatened need that is generating the anger.

3. Destructive and self-defeating behaviors are not instinctual responses over which we have no control. While our emotional response to threat and loss are "hard-wired" into us, we can learn how to manage emotions and choose appropriate behaviors.

4. Anger is not the only normal response to frustration, helplessness, or confusion. It's only one of several possible responses. Likewise, in a given situation, many possible behaviors are available from which we can choose.

5. The force of the energy and motivation generated by anger can be suppressed, turned inward, directed at someone or something unrelated to the threat, or directed at the source of the threat.

6. Healthy anger management requires you to become aware of the early stages of anger while it's at a low level. There are three ways to do this: (1) learn to identify your body sensations that indicate anger, (2) identify your behavioral cues, and (3) increase the number of words you use to describe anger.

RECOMMENDED ACTIVITIES

Identify the Early Signs of Anger

In your journal, make a list of how you feel and what you do when you are angry. Here are the lists that Sharon, David, Carmen, and Alex made describing, how they experienced anger physically along with what they did when they were angry.

Sharon
Things I Feel When Angry

    Tightness all over my body

    Loss of appetite

Things I Do When Becoming Angry

    I begin to see many faults in others and point them out.

    I become bad-tempered.

    I don't enjoy things.

    I'm more emotional.

David
Things I Feel When Angry

    Difficulty in focusing on detailed work

    I lose my appetite.

Things I Do When Becoming Angry

    I become bossy.

    I become "klutzy."

    I tease in a cruel way.

    I withdraw and isolate myself from people.

    I begin to use profanity.

    I don't enjoy or want sex.

Carmen
Things I Feel When Angry

My stomach feels tied up in knots.

Sometimes a headache

I feel sad.

Things I Do When Becoming Angry

I do things that waste time and are unproductive.

I don't want to be around anyone.

I begin to think about how unfair my life seems.

I sit and stare into space.

Alex
Things I Feel When Angry

I don't sleep well.

I clench my teeth so hard my jaw hurts.

I eat more.

I don't feel close to those I care about.

Things I Do When Becoming Angry

I don't want to do anything.

I nitpick.

I'm more demanding and expect more from others, but I don't say anything.

I find fault and blame.

Once you have completed your list, review it twice each week for the next four weeks. As you learn additional tools for managing anger, these physical and behavioral cues will alert you to when you are becoming angry and need to use your anger management skills.

Increase Your Anger Vocabulary
As you record incidents of anger in your journal, begin to use words from the list in this chapter that you normally don't

use to describe the level of anger that you were feeling. In addition, whenever you notice that you are in the early stages of anger, identify what you are feeling by using one of these new words for that level.

Continue to Record Angry Incidents

By now, you should be recording descriptions of times when you became angry in your anger journal. If not, begin to do so this week. Be sure to follow the guidelines given in Chapter 1—you will be using this information in the next chapter.

Continue Using Time-Outs

In Chapter 2, you were introduced to time-outs. If you have not started using them, do so this week. If you have already done so, review the guidelines given in Chapter 2 to make sure you are using them effectively. One of the suggestions made was to take practice time-outs. If you have a problem with explosive anger, I recommend that you take at least three practice time-outs so you can rehearse the steps.

I want to stress once again the importance of saying, "I'm beginning to feel angry and I need a time-out." Not only should you use this neutral statement to initiate time-outs, it's essential that your loved ones understand the concept and agree not to talk to you, and to leave you alone while you are taking your time-out. Again, taking at least three practice time-outs is a good way for both you and your loved ones to learn how to do this.

4

Thoughts That Awaken the Beast

SIX COMMON TYPES of distorted thinking can awaken the beast and cause it to run wild. Learning to gain control over such thinking helps you manage your anger so it stays at an appropriate level. It also helps you to choose behaviors that satisfy your needs more effectively and strengthen your relationships.

SIX COMMON TYPES OF DISTORTED THINKING

One of the marvels of the mind is that once we learn to do complex tasks, they can become automatic and unconscious. For example, when you first learn to drive a car, learning to steer, brake, and judge various driving situations requires all of your attention. Eventually, however, driving becomes so automatic that you need pay little conscious attention to the many tasks involved. Your mind, at an unconscious level, is making many decisions every minute that you are unaware of. Instead, you listen to the radio or talk to the passengers, giving driving only a casual thought. You only give full attention to your driving if something unusual happens such as a car swerving into your lane.

Similarly, while growing up, we need to learn which activities are safe and dangerous, what our role is in society, how to achieve the things we want, and how to interact with others. By the time we are adults, most of this learning has become unconscious habit patterns. As we saw in Chapter 3, most of our emotions are triggered by our interpretations of events. The thinking processes that produce these interpretations—as well as the actions we take—are mostly automatic and unconscious, like those involved in driving.

Since these automatic thinking patterns are developed in childhood, some of the reasoning behind them is faulty. However, because they become automatic, we are mostly unaware of them as we enter adulthood. Thus, everyone uses some faulty reasoning from time to time. Whenever you use a faulty pattern, you misinterpret, and hence, distort the events you are experiencing. Distorted thinking, then, can be defined as *any reasoning process that distorts reality*. Distorted thinking is also a common source of inappropriate anger. Learning to reduce the amount of distorted thinking that you use is therefore a good way to reduce the amount of inappropriate anger you experience.

The first step in reducing your distorted thinking is to become aware of when you are using it. Most of our conscious thoughts take the form of silent conversations in the mind called self-talk. Thus, you can identify the various forms of distorted thinking you use by noticing specific words or phrases that are present in your thoughts or speech.

While different types of distorted thinking sometimes overlap, memorizing specific labels for each form is very useful. The reason this approach is effective is due to what I call the "new car" principle: When you first buy a new car, you suddenly notice cars of the same make as yours wherever you go. It's as if hundreds of them are everywhere, when prior to your purchase there were none. Actually, they were always there—you simply didn't notice them. Because you put so much time, thought and effort into selecting this particular car, your mind has identified it as important. So, now it tends to notice this type of car wherever you go. A similar phenomenon happens when you identify different forms of distorted thinking. Taking time to memorize their labels and definitions helps you become aware of when you are using them, which in turn allows you to challenge them and replace them with more rational and realistic thoughts. As you become skilled at doing this, you will find it a powerful tool for reducing this common source of inappropriate anger.

Overgeneralizing

A generalization is a statement or an idea that has a general application. Generalizations are a necessary and important part of everyday life. If we had to evaluate every situation we encountered in detail, we would be overwhelmed. So, we learn to generalize about the world we live in. These generalizations become the rules that guide our lives.

Like many other aspects of our thinking processes and beliefs, most of our generalizations developed as we grew up. Many were taught to us directly by the adults around us. Others were taught to us indirectly, as we watched how others behaved or absorbed the messages contained in movies, television programs, and advertising. Some are the result of our interpretations of our childhood experiences. Here are a few simple examples of common generalizations that most would agree are useful:

- It's good to be polite.
- Being punctual helps you to be successful.
- Resolving conflicts with others can be difficult and uncomfortable.

The main problem with generalizations is that they often become transformed into absolute rules and become overgeneralizations. For example, the above three generalizations could become:

- I must *always* be polite.
- I can *never* be late.
- Conflict is awful and should *always* be avoided.

Transforming useful guidelines for living into rigid rules is a common form of overgeneralization. Another common form is to use words like *never, always, every, everything,* or *every time* to turn a single negative event into a never-ending or all-consuming pattern of defeat or misfortune. Here are some common examples of such overgeneralizations:

- Why does this *always* happen to me?
- Things *never* seem to work out the way I want them to!
- *Every time* I try to be nice, I get burned!

When you notice yourself using either of these types of overgeneralization, challenge the extreme nature of your statement by asking yourself the following two questions:

- Is this really true?
- Does this always/never mean . . .?

Often it helps, as part of your answer, to recall one or more incidents that directly contradict the negative overgeneralization. Using these two questions, positive experiences, and/or logical arguments to correct distorted thinking is called rational self-talk. A specific logical argument used to correct distorted thinking is called a rational challenge.

Carmen recounted an incident where she had been preparing dinner and forgot to include one of the ingredients. Her first thought was, "Why do I always forget things? I never seem to be able to get things right." Since we had just discussed overgeneralizations, she realized what she was doing, stopped herself, and asked and then answered the two questions: "Is it really true that I always forget things? No! I usually do very well with dinner. In fact, I rarely make mistakes like this. Is it also true that I never get things right? No. Again, I usually do things fairly well. In fact, many people consider me a very good cook. While I like adding this ingredient, I'm probably the only one who will notice that it's missing."

This simple experience was powerful for Carmen. Typically, she would become very angry over small matters like this one. However, once she spoke to herself in this new way, her anger seemed to evaporate. The reason is simple: She reinterpreted the event, so the threat she formerly saw was now no longer present.

Should/Must Thinking

Should/must thinking is a very common type of overgeneralization where preferences have become rigid rules. This usually takes the form of thoughts or statements characterized by words like *should*, *must*, and *have to*. Should/must thinking can also take the form of negative statements using the word *can't*. For example, "I must always be polite" might be expressed as, "I can't hurt others." "I can't be late" is simply the negative expression of "I must be on time."

The key to challenging should/must thinking is to realize there is nothing you *have* to do. Life is a series of choices that we make based on what we think will help us gain the things we want and avoid the things we don't want. Whenever you notice yourself thinking about or stating your wants or preferences with words like *should, must, have to* or *can't*, practice substituting phrases such as *I like, I want,* or *I prefer*. Here are some examples:

> *If you say or think:*
>   "I must be polite."
> *Restate or rethink it as one of these:*
>   "I like to be polite."
>   "I want to be polite."
>   "I prefer to be polite."
> *If you say or think:*
>   "I can't be late."
> *Restate or rethink it as one of these:*
>   "I like to be on time."
>   "I want to be on time."
>   "I prefer to be on time."

Such statements are not only more realistic, but they also help you to remember that your rules are based on your choices and preferences. They are not universal absolutes.

Circular "Why" Questioning

Circular "why" questioning is actually a disguised form of should/must thinking. It takes the form of repeated questions that usually begin with *why* or *how could*. The answers are usually fairly simple, but they violate a belief about how events "should" have occurred and therefore, cannot be accepted. Common examples include "Why is this happening?" "Why am I like this?" "Why did I do that?" "How could this happen?" and "How could they do that?"

The most powerful challenge for a circular "why" question is to stop and answer it. Then shift your thinking to your response. Sometimes this is difficult because it means looking at some aspect of reality that you don't want to acknowledge or deal with.

David's friend Steve was supposed to stop by at a certain time to lend him a special tool for a project David was working on. Steve did not show up when he said he would. David then began to think, "Where is he? I don't understand why people are so inconsiderate. How can he do this to me?" Having just learned about circular "why" questions, however, he realized what he was doing and responded to his questions: "I do understand why people are inconsiderate. Sometimes, it's because they're just self-centered, but I know that's not the case with Steve. I'll bet he just forgot or something came up that sidetracked him. That happens to me sometimes. As for 'doing this to me,' he has only inconvenienced me. There are other things I can do. I really don't 'have to' have that tool right now." Even though David was still somewhat upset because he was unable to complete his project, he became much calmer than he would ordinarily have been.

All-or-Nothing Thinking

All-or-nothing thinking—sometimes called dichotomous thinking—is the evaluation of personal qualities and events in terms of black-and-white categories. The words most frequently associated with this type of thinking are *right, wrong, good*, and *bad*. All-or-nothing thinking is always based on rigid should/must rules that force you to interpret events in absolute "good" and "bad" categories even though everyday events are usually not completely "good" or "bad."

All-or-nothing thinking is usually associated with should/must rules. The most effective way to challenge an all-or-nothing thought is, therefore, to challenge the absolute nature of the should/must rule that underpins it. Simply ask yourself, "Is this event really so 'wrong' or 'bad'?" In addition, find examples from your own experience that contradict the black-and-white categories you have created. You might even be able to find some positive aspects to the event. Finally, it's also a good idea to challenge the specific should/must rule being violated.

In his incident with Steve, David also thought, "It just isn't right for Steve not to be here when he said he would. People should respect other people's time." Then David challenged the thought with, "While Steve's behavior is impolite, it's definitely not a major crime. It's good to respect other people's time, although a lot of people don't do that. Steve is usually pretty good at doing what he says he's going to do. I need to quit being so hard on him and acknowledge that he's human and makes mistakes just like I or anyone else does."

Magnification and Minimization

Magnification—sometimes called catastrophic thinking or catastrophizing—refers to the exaggeration of a minor flaw or problem into a serious one. It's characterized by phrases such as, "how awful," "this is terrible," "I can't take it," and "I can't stand it when that happens." The best way to challenge a magnification is to question the seriousness of the specific situation or problem. For example, when I hear someone say, "I can't stand it when that happens," I usually respond by noting that they are, in fact "standing" it quite well. They are not becoming comatose or losing their mind. They could be very upset, but they are still able to think and choose appropriate actions. Similarly, when someone says, "This is terrible," I have them compare it to a truly terrible situation such as losing a loved one or a painful fatal disease. A comparison like this makes most problems seem much less serious.

Minimization—also called discounting—is the opposite of magnification. It occurs when you reduce or completely disregard the importance of something. For example, Sharon often minimized her ability to perform her assignments at work. At the same time, she tended to magnify the abilities of her coworkers. The result was that while her supervisor regarded her as one of the company's best employees, she felt that everyone else in the office was more competent than she was.

There are two ways to challenge minimization. If, like Sharon, you tend to discount your own accomplishments or abilities, it's useful to develop a mental list of positive evaluations. It's even better if you mentally list positive comments made by others who you regard as objective. If such minimization is an ongoing problem for you, you might want to set aside a page of your journal for this list. In Sharon's case, she reviewed old performance evaluations that rated her as an excellent worker with superior skills. She also listed in her journal several recollections of times when coworkers had praised her work.

A second way to challenge minimization is to imagine the situation you are in but replace a key person in the situation with someone else. Do you still view the situation the same way? During one therapy session, for example, David recalled incidents where his father was raging and throwing things in the house. I asked him how his father's behavior affected him. David replied, "I don't think it really affected me at all. It was just Dad." I then asked him to imagine a teacher or neighbor acting the same way around his young children. David quickly became very animated. He said how wrong this would be and that it would probably frighten them very much. He quickly made the connection with his own experience and became aware of how fearful he had been as a child about saying or doing anything that would upset his father.

Labeling

Labeling is an overgeneralization in which you use simplistic, negative labels such as *stupid* or *dumb* to describe yourself or others. Labeling is usually the result of internalizing a label that your parents or other adults, siblings, or other children used to describe you when you were young. As you matured, you adopted this label and it became a habitual, automatic response that now occurs when you notice a flaw in yourself or make a mistake. Labeling can also be a form of magnification. For example, calling another driver "a self-centered idiot" is not only an overgeneralization, it tends to magnify the threat the person poses.

When you notice yourself using an extreme label, ask yourself, "Is this all-inclusive label really accurate?" For example, when Alex made a mistake at work, he would usually call himself "stupid" or tell himself that he was "incompetent." This in turn would generate lots of anger toward himself. Alex decided to target this behavior. Whenever he noticed that he was labeling himself and his behavior with these overgeneralizations, he would say, "Am I really stupid and incompetent? Of course not. These are just things I heard a lot when I was young. I'm an intelligent and competent worker who just happened to make a mistake."

A THREE-STEP APPROACH TO REDUCING DISTORTED THINKING

The following three-step approach is an effective way to reduce the amount of distorted thinking you use.

- Whenever you are becoming upset, stop what you are doing and examine your thoughts.
- Identify any forms of distorted thinking you are using.
- Challenge these distorted thoughts with rational self-talk.

These steps are easy to learn, but because you have used your current patterns and reinforced them over many years, it might take several weeks of practice before you are able to apply the steps in an effective and consistent way. Fortunately, with practice, this new way of thinking can become the primary way you interpret and react to situations.

You can strengthen your ability to use rational self-talk in three ways. First, take time during the next two weeks to listen carefully to what people say in their everyday speech and identify the distorted thinking they are using. This exercise helps you gain skill in identifying common forms of distorted thinking and shows you that distorted thinking is common. As you begin to notice your own distorted thinking, remember that everyone uses it from time to time. It does not mean you are crazy or abnormal. In fact, it's often simply a sign that you are sick, hungry, tired, or experiencing excessive stress. While you can greatly reduce the amount of distorted thinking you use, you never eliminate it entirely. Distorted thinking is a normal aspect of being human.

The second way to develop rational self-talk skills is to re-view the incidents you have recorded in your anger journal and identify the forms of distorted thinking that are present in them. Then develop phrases you can use as rational challenges.

Using coping self-statements is the third way to strength-en your rational self-talk skills. A coping self-statement is a phrase you say to yourself to cope with a difficult situation. Since anger is triggered by your perception that a threat exists, coping self-statements help you reduce the amount of threat you perceive, which in turn reduces the amount of anger you experience. Here are some coping self-statements that can be used to challenge distorted thinking.

Overgeneralizations
There are few things in life that always happen.
Never say never or always.
Never and always rarely exist in everyday events.

Should/Must Thinking
Life is a series of choices. There is nothing that I "have" to do.
I always have choices.
Things simply happen as they happen. While I would like them to turn out a certain way, there is no reason that they "should" or "must" turn out that way.
Flexibility is the key to success in life.
When I use should and must, I'm simply stating my personal beliefs and how I would like things to be. What is real in this situation? What are my choices?
The only constant in life is change.
The world does not operate according to my 'shoulds'

Stop focusing on how I wish things were and focus on what I choose to do in response to events.

Circular "Why" Questioning

I'm asking this circular question again. Answer the question.

Is there a should/must rule that has been violated?

Stop asking questions for which I already know the answer. Accept reality and decide what you are going to do about it.

I know the answer. It's just hard to accept. Focus on how you are going to respond.

All-or-Nothing Thinking

When I say "right," "wrong," "good," and "bad," it's usually not a universal truth, just my personal preference.

This situation isn't really so bad. It's only inconvenient.

This is not a moral dilemma. This is just a problem to be solved.

Stop condemning and blaming. Focus on facts and solutions.

Magnification and Minimization

Few things in life are truly "awful" and "terrible." Most are only minor inconveniences.

Let the facts speak for themselves.

Focus on accuracy, not exaggeration.

In life, pain is inevitable. Suffering is optional. Stop magnifying.

Disappointment is a normal part of life. Most disappointments are trivial and don't matter in the long run.

How bad is this compared with a real tragedy like losing a loved one?

Children throw tantrums when they are disappointed. Adults accept inconveniences and decide how to minimize their effects.

Labeling

Stop labeling. Be specific and accurate.

Stop using labels from my past that make things seem worse than they really are.

Be specific and avoid overgeneralizing.

Stop name-calling and focus on solving the problem.

These examples are just a small sample of possible coping self-statements. Change them to suit your personality, or develop your own. What is important is to find phrases that help you successfully challenge your specific types of distorted thinking.

SUMMARY OF KEY IDEAS

1. By the time we become adults, most of the thought processes associated with satisfying our needs have become automatic habit patterns.

2. Distorted thinking is any reasoning process that distorts reality.

3. The use of questions, positive experiences, or logical arguments to correct distorted thinking is called rational self-talk. A logical argument that is used to correct distorted thinking is called a rational challenge.

4. Six common types of distorted thinking are overgeneralization, should/must thinking, circular why questioning, all-or-nothing thinking, magnification and minimization, and labeling.

5. You can reduce the amount of distorted thinking you use with the following three-step approach: (1) whenever you are becoming upset, stop what you are doing and examine your thoughts; (2) identify any forms of distorted thinking you are using; (3) challenge these distorted thoughts with rational self-talk.

6. Everyone uses distorted thinking from time to time.

Recommended Activities

Identify Distorted Thinking in Conversations Around You

During the next two weeks, identify the different forms of distorted thinking that you hear in conversations around you. Do not tell people what you are doing. Instead, do this exercise in your mind. The conversations of characters on television, especially in situation comedies, make excellent practice. Your goal is to be able to identify the various forms of distorted thinking easily when you hear them.

Identify Distorted Thinking and Develop Rational Challenges

Review the incidents of anger that you have already recorded in your journal, and identify the various forms of distorted thinking contained in the thoughts you recorded. Then, following the examples given in this chapter, develop a rational challenge for each one.

If you have not yet begun to keep an anger journal, it is essential that you do so this week. This is the only way to apply all the skills in this book effectively. It is also essential that you record as much of your self-talk as you can recall. If you cannot remember what you were thinking, ask yourself, "Why was that situation so upsetting?" Continue to ask yourself this question until you have written down several responses.

From this week on, after you have written down the self-talk associated with the angry incident, add a new section titled "Rational Challenges." Review the self-talk that you have recorded, and see if any distorted thinking is present. Then compose a rational challenge for each instance of distorted thinking you identify. Use the examples in this chapter as models. When David was first learning the skills in this chapter, he wrote this example in his anger journal.

David

Tuesday, June 15

Incident: I was driving to meet a friend for lunch and was caught in a traffic jam. When I realized that I would be late, I became very angry.

Arousal — 5, Aggression — 3

Thoughts: "This is awful. I'm going to be late. I can't stand it when this happens. The traffic in this town drives me crazy. Why do things like this always happen when I'm in a hurry?"

Actions: I drove recklessly, and when I finally arrived to meet my friend, I was in a bad mood.

Rational Challenges:

"This is awful." Magnification. Being in a traffic jam can be aggravating and very inconvenient, but it's not awful. Having an accident like my friend Joe had is awful. My being late had no serious consequences, other than making myself very angry and almost spoiling my time with my friend.

"I'm going to be late." This is actually just a statement of fact. Behind it is the should/must rule that I have to be on time. While I like to be on time, I'm not always going to be able to arrive everywhere on time. Usually the reason for being late is something I have no control over, like the accident that caused the traffic jam.

"I can't stand it when this happens." Magnification. I actually can

tolerate the inconvenience of a traffic jam. I don't really lose anything important. This was just a small insignificant incident.

"The traffic in this town drives me crazy." Magnification. This is a real stretch. I don't like to be caught in heavy traffic, but I don't go insane. If I really hate it that much, I could move to the country. I don't really want to do that. Traffic jams are just a reality of living in this city that I need to accept if I'm going to continue to enjoy the benefits of being here.

"Why do things like this always happen when I'm in a hurry?" Overgeneralization and circular "why" questioning. First of all, this does not always happen when I'm late. Most of the time, I get where I want to go with no problems. The circular questioning is really saying, "Things like this shouldn't happen." In the real world, there are times when things go wrong, and I have no control over them. The only productive response is to accept them and do what I can to make the best of them.

When David first learned to use rational self-talk, he had difficulty remembering to use it at the time when he was angry. This is true for most when they are first introduced to these skills. However, after recording several incidents like this one in his journal and developing rational challenges to his angry thoughts, he eventually did find himself becoming aware of his distorted thinking during episodes of anger. This awareness then caused him to remember the challenges that he had developed in his journal.

As he began to use these challenges during episodes of anger, he was excited to find how effective this approach was in reducing inappropriate anger. This is also true for most of the people I work with and underscores the importance of working with your journal. The more time you practice writing challenges to irrational thinking, the quicker it becomes something you do in everyday life until eventually it becomes second nature.

When Sharon was first learning these skills, she recorded this example in her journal. She placed a number after each sentence and, in the "Rational Challenges" section, used this number as a reference rather than rewriting each sentence. Most people I work with find this a convenient shortcut. However, I continue to rewrite the entire sentence in the following chapters for the sake of clarity. If you prefer the shortcut approach, feel free to use it.

Sharon

Thursday, June 5

Incident: I came home after a hard day and found the house trashed. I yelled at and belittled the kids.

Arousal — 7, Aggression — 6

Thoughts: "What lazy bums.1 I work hard and they don't lift a finger to help.2 It's just too much.3 I don't know what I'm going to do with them.4 Why can't they just look around and see what needs to be done and be a little considerate?"5

Actions: After raging for several minutes, I caught myself and decided I needed a time-out. I told the kids to go to their rooms and left to prepare dinner. After dinner, we discussed a new set of rules for keeping the house orderly.

Rational Challenges

1. *Overgeneralization and magnification, in the form of labeling.* My kids are not lazy bums. They are just typical children. While they can be very helpful, children need to learn discipline. They are in the process of learning it.

2. *Should/must rule.* I'm actually saying that they should help. This is true, but I need to train them to be responsible. Raging is not a good way to do it. I need to develop rules and use logical consequences.

3. *Magnification.* I was feeling tired and overwhelmed, but I was

actually able to manage my household and develop plans for meeting my needs.

4. *Magnification and should/must rule.* This is really just more of my expression of feeling overwhelmed after a hard day. In essence, I'm saying that I should know exactly what I should do at all times and in all situations. The truth is that I do a pretty good job of managing my kids. Sometimes, I just need a little time to get my act together.

5. *Should/must rule.* This is just another way of saying that they should help. In fact, my expectation is that they should be responsible, miniature adults, but they're just typical kids. They can be responsible, if I do my part and train them.

Read through David's and Sharon's examples again. Notice how, in David's example, distorted thinking is often mixed in with simple statements of fact or, as in Sharon's example, is triggered by a real-life problem. Sharon was very tired at the end of that day and was not yet very effective in training her children to help with chores. Whenever you find that your distorted thinking is a response to a real-life problem, use your journal to develop a practical plan for responding to the problem.

Create a "Coping Self-statements" Section in Your Journal

This chapter gave several examples of coping self-statements that could be used as rational challenges to distorted thinking. Set aside several pages of your journal to record coping self-statements that you find useful. During this week, create at least three coping self-statements that you could use for each of the five forms of distorted thinking described in this chapter. Review your statements once each day during the next week. As you work through the following chapters, add additional statements that you find useful to this section. When you are having difficulty developing a rational challenge, you will find this section to be a useful resource.

Make a List of Your Should/Must Rules

Set aside several pages of your journal to list any unrealistic should/must rules that you identify as causing inappropriate anger. Each time you identify a new should/must rule, create a short challenge for it. Here are a few of the should/must rules that Sharon, David, Carmen and Alex identified.

Sharon
I should always be strong.
I must not make mistakes.
People should be reasonable.

David
If you're going to do something, you should do it right (which means perfectly).
I should be able to figure things out and have good solutions for problems I encounter.
People should be reasonable

Carmen
I should always be polite.
I must never become angry.
I should always be a lady.

Alex
I must never look stupid or foolish.
I should always be in control.
I (and others) should be on time.

Each time you identify a new should/must rule, take some time to evaluate its advantages and disadvantages. Then decide whether you want to keep, change, or abandon it. Whenever you find that your thoughts or actions are being generated by a rule you want to eliminate, use the various rational self-talk skills to challenge it. For those you wish to keep, practice using the positive phrases "I like," "I want," and "I prefer" to express them. Here are examples of rules that Sharon, David, Carmen, and Alex decided to keep along with ways that they could be expressed in a more realistic manner.

Sharon and David

Rigid Should/Must Rule:
    I must not make mistakes.
Ways it can be restated:
    I like to do things well, but I will sometimes make mistakes.
    I want to do things well, but I will sometimes make mistakes

Carmen

Rigid Should/Must Rule
    I should always be polite.
Ways it can be restated:
    I like to be polite, but sometimes I need to be assertive.
    I prefer to be polite, but sometimes I need to be assertive.

Alex

Rigid Should/Must Rule:
    I (and others) should be on time.
Ways it can be restated:
    I like to be on time, but this is not always possible.
    I prefer to be on time, but this is not always possible.

5

Stress and the Beast

Y OU WILL NEVER fully tame your beast if you are unable to manage stress effectively. This chapter explores the relationship between stress and anger and examines ways to manage times of excessive stress.

WHAT IS STRESS?

Chapter 3 described how the fight-or-flight response reduces all unnecessary bodily activities while increasing those necessary for intense activity. Stress is a term that refers to a *condition in which the body's normal functioning has been disrupted by the triggering of the fight-or-flight response.* Anything that triggers this response is called a stressor. Stressors can be internal (such as worry about a future event) or external (such as a deadline at work).

Stress can take either of two forms. The first is physical stress that has been caused by a purely physical stressor such as hard work, noise, an accident, disease, or a toxin. The second is psychological stress that is generated by one's mental interpretation of or reaction to events. This chapter focuses on psychological stress, as it's the one you have the most control over. Psychological stress has five basic forms:

- *Pressure:* You are faced with an internal or external demand to complete a task or activity within a limited time frame or in a specific way.
- *Frustration:* You are unable to do or obtain something you need or want.
- *Conflict:* You must make a choice between two or more competing alternatives.
- *Threat:* You perceive a present or impending danger.
- *Loss:* You are faced with the loss of something that was important to you.

A given situation often triggers several forms of psychological stress at once. When faced with a deadline at work, for example, you could face not only pressure, but the threat of possibly not meeting the deadline. You may also be confronted with conflict and experience frustration because events are interfering with your ability to meet your deadline.

Psychological stress usually accompanies physical stress. For example, if you are sick, you are unable to do things you normally can do, causing frustration. Likewise, prolonged psychological stress can cause chronic muscle tension, which can lead to headaches or other physical problems. Prolonged psychological stress can also lower your body's immune response and make you more vulnerable to disease.

Your Body Is a Machine with a Limited Amount of Energy

Your brain is a physical organ. When you are sick, hungry, tired, or stressed, it cannot function as well as it does under normal circumstances. Your reasoning ability is also reduced, causing an increase in distorted thinking, which then causes an increase in inappropriate anger. Thus, effective stress management can reduce the amount of inappropriate anger you experience.

Sharon had an experience that illustrates this well. One night just before starting dinner, she sat down to help her daughter with math homework. This was probably the worst time to help her daughter, as Sharon was hungry and tired from a hard day at work. Her daughter was restless and finding it difficult to concentrate because she too was tired and hungry. The result was predictable. Instead of recognizing her daughter's restlessness as a normal response, Sharon distorted the situation and became angry. Then, after dinner, when they were both relaxed and were in a better mood, she re-engaged her daughter and things went more smoothly.

The first rule of stress management is to *consider your body as a machine with a limited amount of energy.* Like any complex machine, it can do only so much before it needs to be repaired and resupplied with fuel. One way in which David applied this principle was to make a rule that after work neither he nor his wife would talk about anything likely to cause conflict before they ate dinner. Prior to establishing this rule, he would come home tired and hungry and begin discussing a topic such as family finances with his wife. Because she was usually also tired and hungry, this became a time of frequent arguments. Choosing to discuss matters like these only when they were feeling relaxed greatly reduced the amount of inappropriate anger David experienced.

DECOMPRESSION ROUTINES

A diver coming up from a deep dive has to stop periodically and wait for the pressure inside his body to match the pressure of the water around him. Otherwise, bubbles form in the bloodstream and do serious harm. The process of taking time to relieve this internal pressure is called decompression. By extension, in our anger work, a decompression routine is any activity that helps you to relieve the internal stress created by a stressful event or day.

David found decompression routines to be a very helpful technique in reducing his inappropriate anger. He and his wife used it as a second way to avoid arguments before dinner. He developed a decompression routine to do when he came home. Instead of rushing into an activity right away, he would spend fifteen or twenty minutes doing something relaxing. After this short decompression period, he would then do something that was not too stressful, such as performing a simple chore around the house or playing with his children. Problem solving and other activities that could trigger his anger were put off until after dinner.

David also found decompression routines helpful at work. In the past, he would overwork, skipping his breaks and even eating lunch on the run. He justified this intensity by thinking that regardless of how tired he was, he could always function at 100% if he forced himself. While it's true that, when tired, the fight or flight response can enable you to function well for short periods, there is a limit to how far you can push yourself. Nonetheless, its curious how many people believe, like David, that they should be able to function at peak efficiency regardless of the condition of their body. For David, the result was predictable: Because he was often overly tired and stressed out, he frequently exploded over little things.

Once David began to think of his body as a machine with a limited amount of energy, he began to take his breaks. During lunch time, he made a point to do something relaxing and unrelated to work. He also took minibreaks after stressful phone calls or meetings. In the past he had just pushed ahead immediately to the next item on his agenda—and experienced high levels of inappropriate anger over trivial matters. The difference resulting from this new approach both surprised and pleased David. It not only reduced the amount of anger he experienced, but it made him more productive.

MANAGING TIMES OF EXCESSIVE STRESS

Unavoidable periods of excessive stress are one of the realities of life. We all experience the death of a loved one, a serious illness in oneself or a family member, periodic deadlines at work, problems with children, and financial difficulties. At these times of excessive stress, inappropriate anger can be especially troublesome. The following three guidelines can help you manage these times more effectively.

Develop an Early Warning System

One of the biggest problems for many is simply recognizing when the effects of stress are interfering with your ability to think clearly and perform routine tasks. Take a moment now to recall times when you have experienced high levels of stress. As you think about these times, go through the following list of stress symptoms. Check any symptoms you experienced during these times of high stress that you don't normally experience.

Common Symptoms Associated with Stress

Physical
_____ Colds, flu, or other minor illness
_____ Decreased appetite
_____ Headache
_____ Lack of energy, fatigue
_____ Increased appetite
_____ Increased problems with allergies, asthma, arthritis
        or other chronic physical conditions
_____ Muscle tension, aches
_____ "Nervous" stomach
_____ Rash
_____ Sleeplessness
_____ Teeth grinding
_____ Tingling or cold hands or feet
_____ Weight change: increase or decrease
Other:

_____

_____

_____

Mental
_____ Confusion
_____ Difficulty thinking clearly
_____ Forgetfulness
_____ Inability to concentrate
_____ Lack of creativity
_____ Lethargy
_____ Negative attitude
_____ Poor memory
_____ Racing thoughts
_____ "Weird" or morbid thoughts

_____ Whirling mind
Other:

_____

_____

_____

Emotional
_____ Anger
_____ Anxiety
_____ Depression
_____ Increased emotionalism
_____ Irritability
_____ Mood swings
_____ Short temper
_____ The "blues"
_____ Troubled sleep, nightmares
Other:

_____

_____

_____

Behavioral
_____ Difficulty "getting started" on things that need to be
          done
_____ Increase in activities that waste time
_____ Frequent sighing, yawning
_____ Idleness
_____ Increase in mistakes or accidents
_____ Increased use of alcohol, tobacco, or other drugs
_____ Increased use of profanity, put-downs, or sarcasm
_____ Increase in nervous habits: finger-drumming, foot-
          tapping, etc.
_____ Low productivity

Other:

_____

_____

_____

Relational

_____ Blaming
_____ Clinginess
_____ Decreased or increased sex drive
_____ Distrustful
_____ Fewer contacts with friends
_____ Increased arguments, disagreements
_____ Isolation from loved ones and friends
_____ Intolerance
_____ Lack of intimacy
_____ Lashing out
_____ Less loving and trusting
_____ More demanding
_____ Nagging
_____ Needy
_____ Resentful

Other:

_____

_____

_____

Spiritual

_____ Apathy
_____ Cynicism
_____ Doubt
_____ Discouragement
_____ Emptiness
_____ Inability to forgive

_____ Little joy
_____ Loss of direction
_____ Loss of faith
_____ Loss of meaning
_____ Sense of being a martyr
_____ Need to "prove" self
_____ "No one cares" attitude
_____ Pessimism
_____ Sense of helplessness
_____ Sense of hopelessness
Other:

_____

_____

_____

You probably experienced many of these symptoms during times of high stress. Some, however, are more important indicators than others are. Go back through the list and put a second check by the five symptoms you feel are the most important indicators that stress is beginning to have a negative effect on you. Then create a section in your journal where you can list them and refer to them in the future. Here are the indicators Sharon, David, Carmen, and Alex identified.

Sharon's Early Warning Signs for Stress

Increased anger

Mood swings

Restlessness

Sleeplessness

Increased blaming and criticism of others

David's Early Warning Signs for Stress

Increased use of profanity, put-downs, and sarcasm

Increased mistakes

Difficulty thinking clearly

Poor memory

Increased anger, especially over little things that normally don't bother me

Carmen's Early Warning Signs for Stress

Fewer contacts with friends

Pessimism-sense of "what's the use?"

Little joy

Confusion

"Nervous" stomach

Alex's Early Warning Signs for Stress

Increased mistakes

Blaming, with lots of put-downs and name-calling

Idleness, time-wasting activities

Difficulty "getting started" on things

More intolerant, especially of other's mistakes and shortcomings

Focus Your Activities by Setting Priorities and Delegating

During times of high stress, stressors consume much of your mental and physical energy. Because stress leaves you with fewer resources with which to handle your daily tasks, you need to use the available mental and physical energy wisely. The key is to focus on the most important tasks you are facing and to let go of those that are less important. Unfortunately, this is often difficult to do during times of high stress. The decrease in your ability to reason increases all-or-nothing thinking, which in turn exaggerates the importance of little things. This, in turn, increases the amount of inappropriate anger that often accompanies high stress.

Whenever you notice one or more of the stress indicators that you checked in the previous section, take time to set priorities. If possible, delegate small tasks to others. Ask yourself these three questions:

- What are the most important things that need to be done now?
- What can I put off to some other time?
- Is there anything I can delegate to someone else?

Alex demonstrated well how this could be done. A large corporation had bought the company where he worked. The new owners were conducting a review of the various departments to determine which to keep and which to eliminate. The uncertainty of not knowing whether he would have a job, compounded by the pressure of responding to the review process while maintaining his regular work, was very stressful. As one might predict, Alex, along with his fellow workers, experienced a number of stress-related symptoms. Particularly troublesome for him were impatience and an increased amount of anger.

During this time, Alex's mother was about to turn sixty. He and his brothers and sister had discussed having a special birthday celebration for her. Being the oldest son, Alex had taken the lead in planning the event, but the stress of his work situation made this very difficult and caused him to be resentful of his brothers and sister. As he and I discussed this dilemma, he realized that he really didn't have to do as much for the celebration as he thought he should do. Alex discussed his situation with his sister and two of his brothers. They were sympathetic and more than willing to take over some of the tasks. This took some of the pressure off him, which helped him cope with his work situation more effectively. He also found that he was less resentful toward his family and enjoyed his mother's birthday celebration much more than he would have if he hadn't taken action.

Slow Down the Decision-Making Process

Alex's experience with his mother's birthday celebration also illustrates the importance of slowing down the decision-making process during times of high stress. The decrease in mental energy, with the accompanying increase in distorted thinking, tends to raise the likelihood of poor decisions. The best way to counter this tendency is to take more time with important decisions. When possible, consult with someone you trust who can look at things objectively.

Taking time to list things on a piece of paper is a good way to slow down the decision making process. The simple act of writing things down seems to make them more manageable. It also helps you to look at them more objectively. In Alex's case, taking time to discuss the problem with his brothers and sister proved helpful. They had several good ideas and were able to relieve Alex of more tasks than he thought possible.

SUMMARY OF KEY IDEAS

1. Stress is a condition in which a triggering of the fight-or-flight response disrupts the body's normal functioning.
2. Anything that triggers this response is called a stressor. Stressors can be internal or external. The five basic types of psychological stress are pressure, frustration, conflict, threat, and loss.
3. A basic principle for effective stress management is to view your body as a machine with a limited amount

of energy. Like any complex machine, it can do only so much before it needs to be repaired and restocked with fuel.

4.   A decompression routine is any activity that helps you to relieve the internal stress generated by a stressful event or difficult day.

5.   Three ways to manage situations of excessive stress are (1) develop an early warning system, (2) focus your activities by setting priorities and delegating, and (3) slow down the decision-making process.

RECOMMENDED ACTIVITIES

Review How You Use Your Energy

Reread the section on decompression routines, and then take an honest look at how you manage your time and energy during a typical day. Are there times where you could add a short break or rearrange the order in which you do your activities that might relieve some of the pressure or conflict you experience? Is there a way in which you could apply the concept of the body as a machine with a limited supply of energy? How about a decompression routine that would help you experience less inappropriate anger? Devote a few pages in your anger journal to stress management, and record your conclusions there.

Identify Key Early Warning Signs

If you have not gone through the inventory of common symptoms associated with stress presented in this chapter, do so now. Be sure to follow the guidelines. Once you have identified the five symptoms that you feel are the most important indicators that stress is having a negative effect on you, record them in your anger journal in the section on stress management.

Review How You Manage Stress

At the end of each day this week, take a few minutes to review the previous twenty-four hours. Identify times when stress played a key role in the occurrence of inappropriate anger. Then, identify those ideas in this chapter that could have helped you manage the stress more effectively. Record your findings in the section of your journal devoted to stress management.

Continue to Record Angry Incidents and to Create Challenges to Distorted Thinking

Continue to use the format given in Chapter 4 to record incidents where you became angry. Continue this activity throughout the time you are working on this book. It's one of the most effective and powerful ways to change the automatic thinking that triggers inappropriate anger.

Review Your Use of Time-Outs

Over the past few weeks, you have practiced using time-outs. Take time this week to review how you have been using them. If you have not been using them, or if you have not been able to use them effectively, review the sections on time-outs in Chapter 2, and identify those things that you could do differently to make your time-outs more effective.

6

Additional Thoughts That
Awaken the Beast

I F YOU ARE going to manage anger effectively, then you need to evaluate events accurately and respond to threats in a reasonable and realistic manner. Failing to take responsibility for your thoughts and actions by blaming others for your problems interferes with your ability to make such an accurate evaluation. This chapter explores the tendency to blame others. Then it looks at four common erroneous assumptions that trigger inappropriate anger, along with another form of distorted thinking called mind reading.

WHO IS TO BLAME?

Blaming is the act of assigning all of the responsibility for a troublesome event to someone or something besides yourself. Often, blaming also involves condemning and criticizing whoever or whatever you view as the source of the problem.

Like most of our behaviors, blaming is usually learned during childhood and becomes an unconscious habit. Blamers often grew up in households where their parents unfairly blamed them for events over which they actually had little or no control. As adults, they are now simply following the pattern of their parents. For example, when Sharon was a child, her mother was often late because of poor planning. However, as she became angry over being late, she would blame her children and say things such as "If it weren't for you, I'd be on time. You always take so long to get ready."

Alex experienced a different kind of parental blaming. His father had very unrealistic expectations of his children. When he gave them a chore, he expected them to do it as well as he could have done it. At the same time, he rarely showed them how he wanted it done. Alex would do the best job he could, but his father would always find some fault and criticize him with statements such as "Look at how you've messed this up!"

Usually blaming is accompanied by unrealistic should/must rules and magnification. Here are some examples, accompanied by statements that show how blaming has shifted responsibility, along with the should/must rule that underlies the self-talk.

Sharon, on difficulty in managing her children's high level of normal play activity:

"It's really their own fault. They can be so selfish. They won't let me get any rest."

Statement: I have no role in setting limits.

Should/must rule: My children should be able to see I need rest and let me have it.

David on his wife's reasonable request that he help with a few chores around the house:

"It's no wonder that I get angry. My wife is always nagging at me. She doesn't care at all about what I want."

Statement: I'm not responsible for controlling my actions.

Should/must rule: My wife should understand me and not bother me.

Carmen on her husband's jokes about an issue on which she had strong feelings but about which she has said nothing:

"He can be very insensitive. He should know how much this disturbs me. It just goes to show how little he cares."

Statement: I have no responsibility to tell others what I want.

Should/must rule: One's house should be a peaceful haven from the world where there is no conflict. If he loved me, he should be able to see how jokes affect me.

Alex on his difficulty with the many normal conflicts that arise at work:

"I withdraw because people are always so demanding. Why can't they just leave me alone?"

Statement: I have no role in setting limits.

Should/must rule: Work shouldn't be so hard. People should know when I'm stressed out and leave me alone.

These examples illustrate five basic aspects of blaming. First, the should/must rules that underlie blaming usually involve some aspect of reality that is difficult for the blamer to accept or something the blamer doesn't want to do. Sharon resented being a single mother and was not well prepared to handle the normal immaturity of children. David didn't like doing chores.

Second, blaming takes the focus off the blamer's own responsibility in creating the situation. For example, labeling his wife's reasonable requests as nagging, allowed David to avoid looking at his tendency to want to have everything his way, as well as his reluctance to negotiate with his wife. Alex and Carmen's blaming helped them avoid dealing with the fact that they were not very good at handling conflict.

The third aspect of blaming is that it creates the illusion that the blamer has no responsibility for doing anything about the situation; it transfers all the responsibility to the blamed person. By blaming her children, Sharon did not have to look at her own need to gain more effective parenting skills. Similarly, blaming allowed the others to avoid looking at their own inability to communicate effectively.

A fourth aspect of blaming is that it often assumes that the blamer's needs and wants are more important than those of others are. Blamers often label their own actions as "being fair" or "doing what's right," while seeing the other person as unfair or self-centered. The truth is that in every relationship the needs of one person are different from those of the other. Later chapters discuss an approach for resolving this natural conflict and reaching reasonable compromises. For now, focus on the fact that your desire to satisfy your own needs is no more and no less important than that of anyone else.

The fifth and final aspect of blaming is that it doesn't work. Making others responsible for meeting the blamer's needs guarantees failure. While anger and blaming can sometimes cause others to do what you want, they rarely do so in a way that satisfies you. Worse yet, blaming eventually causes others to become insensitive to your anger and ignore you, retaliate in either direct or indirect ways, distance themselves emotionally, or end the relationship. In each case, you ultimately fail to meet your needs and become ineffective.

The key to eliminating blaming is to memorize this basic rule of life:

You alone are responsible for the quality of your life and for getting your needs met.

How do you know this is true? First, you are the only one who really knows what your needs are. Others can guess and sometimes they might be right, but only you know exactly what you need and want. Keep in mind that your perception of the world is unique. What seems obvious to you is often a mystery to others, including those close to you. Equally important is the fact that as an adult you are responsible for yourself. If someone is stepping on your toes, it's your responsibility to say something. It's *not* the responsibility of others to take care of you.

FOUR COMMON ERRONEOUS ASSUMPTIONS THAT TRIGGER ANGER

One or more of four erroneous assumptions often sustain the habit of blaming. Often, these assumptions are not consciously held beliefs. Rather, they are usually the result of early life experiences involving the behaviors and attitudes of the adults who raised you. In fact, as you identify your erroneous assumptions, you will probably find that they also played an important role in the thinking of one or both of your parents.

Erroneous Assumption 1: Life Should Be Fair

It's amazing how many people actually believe that life should be fair. The reality is that life is often terribly unfair. Accidents happen, and people do things that are unfair. Even when events go well and people try their best, total fairness is impossible to achieve in the real world. Because people and events are complex, you treat each person you meet in a somewhat different way. Likewise, the way you behave in every situation is different, no matter how similar they might seem. Wanting life to be fair magnifies inequalities so that they seem much more important than they really are.

Wanting life to be fair, however, goes deeper than just this surface reality. When people say that something is not fair, it's often simply a disguised way of saying that they did not get what they wanted. It's really no different from a child who wants an ice cream cone but is told no because there is no money for it or the time is inappropriate. Desire thwarted, the child stomps his or her foot and declares, "It's not fair." The actual message is "I didn't get what I want, and I'm mad about it!"

When you notice yourself focusing on how unfair someone or something is, take a moment to ask yourself if you were truly mistreated or if you just didn't get what you wanted. If you're just throwing a tantrum, remind yourself that mature adults can tolerate frustration. Also, remind yourself that while tantrums sometimes work in the short run, in the long run they damage relationships.

Look at the event as objectively as you can. If you decide that events truly were unfair, you can respond in either of two ways. First, remind yourself that injustice and inequality are facts of life. Everyone acts in hurtful and unjust ways from time to time. Sometimes, they do it deliberately. At other times actions done with good intentions turn out to be hurtful or unjust because of a lack of knowledge or understanding, or simply by accident. Next, refocus on needs rather than fairness. If a real need is being frustrated or threatened, concentrate on developing a plan to improve the situation. Try to be as objective as possible. Your goal is to be effective at achieving your goal, not to make things "fair."

Erroneous Assumption 2: Because I Want Something Very Much, I Ought to Have It.

An entitlement is something that you are guaranteed. The erroneous notion that something is your entitlement is based on the assumption that when you desire something strongly, it should be provided to you. Thus, desires come to be seen as entitlements. The stronger the desire, the more you feel entitled. Wanting respect, appreciation, love, or a certain standard of living can cause you to believe you are entitled to them. While each of these might be desirable, none of them are guaranteed in life.

This sense of entitlement comes from a variety of sources. Children whose parents find it difficult to set limits often grow up to be adults with a sense that the world should always meet their needs. Children can also absorb a sense of entitlement from parents who have it themselves. Many simply transfer into their personal lives the idea that help from others is an entitlement.

When you say that you have the right to something simply because you want it very much, you are saying that your needs are more important than the needs of others. Like the first erroneous assumption, this one also reflects the immaturity and self-centeredness characteristic of a child. You cannot have a healthy adult relationship that includes true intimacy and respect if you take a childish stance in life. Therefore, a second basic rule of life that you need to memorize is:

The needs of others are no more and no less important than my own.

Erroneous Assumption 3: It's Possible to Change Someone Else's Behavior

People often spend tremendous amounts of time and energy attempting to change others. Many unhappy marriages result from the assumption that the other person will either spontaneously change or can be made to change. However, lasting change occurs only when it comes from within. Consider times when parents, spouses, or friends have tried to pressure you into making changes. Did it work? Probably not. While they might have caused a temporary change, you made a major change that you were able to maintain only when *you* decided you wanted to change.

Erroneous Assumption 4: When Others Hurt or Mistreat Me, They Deserve to Be Punished

In some cultures, vendettas are a time-honored tradition. A vendetta is a vow to seek vengeance on a person, family, or group that has wronged you in some way. For many people, the belief that others should always be punished for their misbehavior is a very conscious and deliberate part of their belief system. In a less formal way, this belief also plays a role in struggles with inappropriate anger.

In normal human relationships, others for a variety of reasons hurt us. Sometimes, people intend to hurt us, but often the hurt is unintentional and simply a mistake. At other times, it's due to a misunderstanding. Punishing others for every slight or instance of misconduct poisons relationships. While being accountable and making amends are important parts of resolving wrongs, truly loving relationships are impossible among those who are unable to forgive and release others.

This is such an important topic that I want to discuss it more extensively in Chapter 13. For now, take a look at the way you respond when you are disappointed or hurt by others and decide whether you are the kind of person who seeks to punish. Once again, seeking revenge and punishing others is often a family tradition. If one or both of your parents were harsh and punitive, it greatly increases the chances that you act in this way as well.

MIND READING

While we can sometimes make good guesses about what another person is thinking, no one can know for sure. Mind reading, sometimes called assumed intent, is a form of distorted thinking where you believe that you know what someone is thinking, feeling or the intentions underlying his or her behavior, without evidence to support your belief. Carmen, for example, often thought others were thinking critically about her and about what she had done, even though she had no evidence. She was mind reading.

Mind reading associated with blaming usually sees others as intentionally trying to harm you. David was prone to such mind reading. His wife left for work earlier than he did, for example, and got up about a half hour earlier. Sometimes, she would unintentionally wake David as she rose. David usually responded with a thought such as "She's deliberately being inconsiderate. She doesn't care whether I sleep or not." The truth was that his wife genuinely felt bad when she accidentally woke him and tried not to do so.

SUMMARY OF KEY IDEAS

1. Blaming is the act of assigning all of the responsibility for a troublesome event to someone or something other than yourself. It often includes condemning and criticizing whoever or whatever you view as the source of the problem.
2. Blaming (1) is often based on a hidden should/must rule (2) takes the focus off any role the blamer might have had in creating the situation, (3) transfers all responsibility for resolving a problem to others, (4)

assumes the blamer's needs and wants are more important than those of others, and (5) is ineffective in helping the blamer meet his or her needs.

3. Four common erroneous assumptions are (1) life should be fair, (2) because I want something very much, I ought to have it, (3) it's possible to change someone else's behavior, and (4) when others hurt or mistreat me, they deserve to be punished.

4. Two key truths that can be used to challenge blaming are (1) You alone are responsible for the quality of your life and for getting your needs met, and (2) the needs of others are no more and no less important than your own.

5. Mind reading is a form of distorted thinking where you believe that you know what someone is thinking or feeling, or the intentions underlying his or her behavior, even though you have little evidence to support that belief.

6. Mind reading connected with blaming can involve the belief that others are intentionally trying to harm you when there is no evidence that this is true.

RECOMMENDED ACTIVITIES

Memorize Two Key Statements

Last week's recommended activities suggested that you set aside several pages in your journal to record coping self-statements. Add the following two key statements from this week's material.

- I alone am responsible for the quality of my life and for getting my needs met.
- The needs of others are no more and no less important than my own.

If you found any other statements in this week's material you feel would be good coping self-statements, add them as well. Feel free to paraphrase or make up your own or draw from other sources, as David has done in the following example. Again, the goal is to develop phrases you can say to yourself that are powerful and effective. Here are some additional statements that Sharon, David, Carmen, and Alex found useful.

Sharon

Others do what is rewarding for them, not necessarily, what I want them to do.

Punishing others doesn't get me what I want. It only drives them away.

Others are not obligated to meet my expectations.

My children are not miniature adults. They are children. When they are being childish, I need to act like an adult.

More encouragement and positive reinforcement and less punishment will make me more effective with my children.

David

Anger and blaming don't work as a long-term strategy. In the long run, it causes me to lose the things most important to me.

The strategies I'm using to meet my needs drives people away. If I want better relationships, I need to think and act differently.

When I was a child, I talked like a child, I thought like a child, and I reasoned like a child. Now that I'm a man, I need to put childish ways behind me.

Carmen

When others disappoint me, it doesn't mean they don't care.

People change only when they want to change.

People make the best choices they can, given their history and beliefs.

I am responsible for getting my needs met. I need to speak up if
  I want something.

Alex

Life isn't fair, but life doesn't have to be fair for me to satisfy my
  needs and be happy.
My desire for something doesn't obligate others to fulfill that desire
  for me.
I can want whatever I want. This doesn't mean I'll get it.
I sometimes disappoint people I care about. They will sometimes do
  the same to me.
No mind reading. Check it out for accuracy.

Continue to review your coping self-statements once each
day. Your goal is to review these ideas regularly so they become the new assumptions shaping your thoughts and actions.

Take a Walk in Their Shoes

This week, for each incident of anger directed at another individual you record, add a journal section that answers the
following four questions:

- What exactly did this person do that triggered my
  anger?
- What needs or wants caused this person to act in this
  way?
- What beliefs or aspects of this person's past (hurts,
  losses, successes, fears, lack of skills, etc.) influenced
  this behavior?
- Considering the above, how could I have responded
  in a different and more effective manner?

The purpose of these questions is to help you to explain the other person's behavior from their perspective as best as you can. The following examples show how David, Sharon, Alex, and Carmen incorporated these questions into their journals. Use them as models for your own journal.

David

Saturday, August 2

Incident: I got up before my wife and decided to do some work outside while it was still cool. I began mowing the back lawn. When I went in, my wife was having breakfast. She said, "How's Mr. Considerate this morning?" in a sarcastic voice.

Arousal — 4, Aggression — 3

Thoughts: "What a selfish bitch. I get up and do something nice, and this is the thanks I get. I don't even know why I bother. I think I'd fall over dead if I ever heard a thank you or a compliment."

Actions: I got angry and told her how rude her comment was. She went into the bedroom, closed the door, and read a book for an hour.

Four Questions:

1. *What exactly did this person do that triggered my anger?*
   She didn't thank me for doing something she had asked me to do, and she made a sarcastic remark.

2. *What needs or wants caused this person to act in this way?*
   She was probably angry because I woke her up. She gets up early during the week and likes to sleep in on Saturday mornings.

3. *What beliefs or aspects of this person's past (hurts, losses, successes, fears, lack of skills, etc.) influenced this behavior?*
   She probably thought I was being inconsiderate. I have a pretty long history of not thinking when I do things. I also know that she is working on some of her own issues from her family.

4. *Considering the above, how could I have responded in a different and more effective manner?* I could have done something that was less noisy and cut the lawn after she got up or in the late afternoon. Instead of going ballistic, I could have kept my mouth shut and walked away when she made her cutting remark. If I wanted to say something, I would have been much more effective if I had waited until I calmed down and she had time to wake up.

Rational Challenges

"What a selfish bitch." I'm labeling her with an overgeneralization that is simply not true. She actually thinks of me a lot and does many nice things for me. For example, she does try to be considerate when she wakes up early during the week.

"I get up and do something nice, and this is the thanks I get." Underneath this statement is the should/must rule: "Others should thank me when I do something nice." This is actually not a bad idea. It's reasonable to expect a thank you when you do something nice. I thought I was doing something nice and was expecting a compliment when I got slammed. I didn't stop to think that sleeping in on Saturday is a small luxury she really enjoys. I also tend to punish people when they don't do what I want them to do. I can still go back and apologize for waking her, tell her that my intention was to help, and that I'll wait until she is up on Saturdays before I begin noisy chores. While it's scary, I could also tell her how hurt I was by her sarcasm and say that I'd like us both to be less abrasive with each other.

"I don't even know why I bother." This is just another way of saying I shouldn't bother. This isn't true and simply an expression of my disappointment that she didn't see that I was trying to be responsible and do my share of the work around the house.

"I think I'd fall over dead if I ever heard a thank you or a compliment." Again, the rule "I should be thanked when I do something nice" is being expressed as an overgeneralization. My feeling of re-

jection is also an overreaction. Actually, she is usually pretty good at saying thank you. She also shows affection in many different ways.

Sharon
Wednesday, July 30

Incident: I was helping my oldest child with her math homework. I was trying to figure out how to do a problem, and she was being whiney and uncooperative.

Arousal — 6, Aggression — 5

Thoughts: "Why can't she just sit still while I try to figure this out? Does she want my help or not? I can't stand her uppity attitude. Why does everything have to be so hard? If she doesn't want my help, she can just do it herself or flunk. What do I care?"

Actions: I finally said, "Just forget it," and stormed off. Later I apologized, and we sat down and finally figured out how to do it.

Four Questions:

1. *What exactly did this person do that triggered my anger?* She was being uncooperative.

2. *What needs or wants caused this person to act in this way?* We were trying to do the homework just before starting dinner, so we were both tired and hungry. She was just showing the natural impatience of a tired, hungry child doing something difficult that she didn't want to do.

3. *What beliefs or aspects of this person's past (hurts, losses, successes, fears, lack of skills, etc.) influenced this behavior?* Math is difficult for her. She also tends to be very hard on herself and doesn't think she's very good at it.

4. *Considering the above, how could I have responded in a different and more effective manner?* First of all, I could have waited until after dinner. I could also have told her to do something else while I tried to figure it out on my own.

Rational Challenges

"Why can't she just sit still while I try to figure this out?" This reflects the should/must rule, "She should sit quietly while I figure out problems I'm having difficulty with." While this would be great, this is the behavior of a mature adult. She is just a child and can be very fidgety. I'm expecting her to be more mature than she is. I need to keep this in mind and either let her fidget, have her do some other type of homework, or have her go play while I figure things like this out.

"Does she want my help or not?" This is just another expression of the should/must rule that she should behave like a mature adult when I'm helping her. If she didn't want my help, she wouldn't have asked.

"I can't stand her uppity attitude." I was magnifying her behavior. It was actually just normal tired kid behavior.

"Why does everything have to be so hard?" Here's one of those combination magnification, should/must rules: "Things should go smoothly." Things don't always go smoothly. That's why there's Murphy's law, which states, "Whatever can go wrong will go wrong." Actually, this particular situation wasn't all that hard. It was mainly my unrealistic expectations that made it so difficult.

"If she doesn't want my help she can just do it herself or flunk." This is one of those erroneous assumptions. I'm actually saying that she should be punished for what I saw as bad behavior. I don't really want her to flunk, and I also really do want to help when I'm needed.

"What do I care?" This is just another variation of that punishing attitude I take when I'm frustrated and angry. I really do love my children and care what happens to them.

Alex

Thursday, August 13

Incident: I was at dinner with my girlfriend and we were discussing what to do on the weekend. I told her about a band I wanted to go see that was playing at the local fair only on Saturday. She said she wanted to go shopping with her girlfriend and wanted to go to the fair on Sunday.

Arousal — 5, Aggression — 2

Thoughts: "If she really cared about me, she'd see how important this is and come with me. Who's more important, me or her girlfriend? I guess this relationship isn't going anywhere after all."

Actions: I became quiet and stewed for the rest of dinner. Finally, she agreed to go with me to the fair on Saturday.

Four Questions:

1. *What exactly did this person do that triggered my anger?*
   She wouldn't do what I wanted her to do.

2. *What needs or wants caused this person to act in this way?*
   I know that she is very close to her girlfriend and that spending time with her is important to her. I also know that doing things away from me can be healthy even though I don't like it.

3. *What beliefs or aspects of this person's past (hurts, losses, successes, fears, lack of skills, etc.) influenced this behavior?*
   Her last relationship wasn't very good, and she wants to take things slowly. Spending time with her girlfriends away from me is one of the ways she does this.

4. *Considering the above, how could I have responded in a different and more effective manner?* I could have compromised and suggested that instead of spending the whole day at the fair, we could just spend the afternoon and evening together when the band was playing. That way she could have spent time shopping with her friend and I could have had a much more enjoyable time with her.

Rational Challenge

"If she really cared about me, she'd see how important this is and come with me." This conditional statement is not true. I'm expecting

her to always agree with me based on the should/must rule that someone who loves you will always meet your needs. This is absurd. I wasn't even thinking about how I could meet her needs. Instead, I was being self-centered just like my father. True love means you work together to find a way that meets both people's needs as best as possible.

"Who's more important, me or her girlfriend?" This all-or-nothing thinking is based on the above should/must rule, "Someone who loves you will always meet your needs." Everything I said above applies here.

"I guess this relationship isn't going anywhere after all." This all-or-nothing thinking is based on my should/must rule that someone who cares for you should always meet your needs. Actually, this relationship is going somewhere. I really like her, and she says she likes me.

Carmen

Thursday, August 13

Incident: My husband and I were visiting my in-laws, when he told a story about something stupid I had done. He went on and on. Everyone laughed, but I felt embarrassed and humiliated. I tried to stop him, but he just kept going and ignored me.

Arousal — 6, Aggression — 0

Thoughts: "How could he do this? Why doesn't he see that I'm dying inside? I can't stand this. Everyone is thinking I'm so stupid. How can I ever face them again?"

Actions: I got very red and finally excused myself. When I came back, I said I wasn't feeling very well and went into the next room to lie down. I was actually okay but just wanted to be left alone. I then told my husband I needed to go home, and we left early. I didn't say anything all the way home, even though he was asking me what was wrong. Later, we talked about it and he apologized. I was crying throughout the conversation.

Four Questions:

1. *What exactly did this person do that triggered my anger?* He embarrassed me in front of his family.

2. *What needs or wants caused this person to act in this way?* He was trying to be funny. He likes to be the center of attention.

3. *What beliefs or aspects of this person's past (hurts, losses, successes, fears, lack of skills, etc.) influenced this behavior?* Nothing I can think of, other than that his family uses teasing as a form of humor.

4. *Considering the above, how could I have responded in a different and more effective manner?* I could remind him not to embarrass me in front of his family before we meet them.

Rational Challenges

"How could he do this?" This is circular "why" questioning based on the should/must rule, "He shouldn't embarrass me." This is actually a good rule, but I know he and his family don't see kidding as embarrassing someone. Even my own family would kid each other. I'm just supersensitive with his folks because of my lack of confidence.

"Why doesn't he see that I'm dying inside?" This is also circular "why" questioning. The should/must rule is "He should be sensitive to my needs and notice when he's doing something that is hurting me." Again, this is actually not a bad rule, but I know that he tends to be unconscious about others. I also tend to be very vague. I need to tell him what I'm feeling in a clearer and more direct manner.

"I can't stand this." This is a magnification. I was very embarrassed, but I get embarrassed very easily. I don't like it, but I can stand it. In fact, I get embarrassed so frequently, I'm an expert at being embarrassed. I'm really just saying that I don't like this.

"Everyone is thinking I'm so stupid." This is mind reading. I don't really know what they were thinking. They probably weren't thinking much of anything, other than how funny my husband was

being. I tend to think that everyone believes I'm stupid. Again, this is just an indication of my lack of confidence.

"How can I ever face them again?" This is circular "why" questioning again for the should/must rule, "I shouldn't have to face people after I've been embarrassed." I don't like to see people after I've been embarrassed. Even though this was a big deal to me, it was probably nothing to them. I get embarrassed all the time and then face the people who saw me embarrassed, and nothing happens other than I feel badly.

7

How the Beast Is Shaped During Childhood

I N THE FIRST six chapters, you learned about the nature of the beast and began to work with the distorted thinking and automatic behavior patterns that generate inappropriate anger. In this chapter, you'll dig even deeper into the heart of anger and identify the forces that drive your distorted thinking and self-defeating behaviors. For many people this is the most difficult part of changing dysfunctional patterns, since it requires them to take an honest look at issues that have probably been buried since they were young. As a child, it was probably essential for you to build strong defense mechanisms to protect yourself from these issues. As an adult, however, you can now identify and work through them. Doing this is the key to making fundamental changes that last a lifetime.

CREATING A RECORD OF YOUR CHILDHOOD

Let's begin by examining the dynamics of your family when you were a child. The best way is to create a genogram, which shows the relationships among the people in your life when you were growing up. Putting these relationships on paper can help you see things that you might otherwise miss. Take a moment and look at Sharon's genogram, showing her family when she was a child. The squares represent males; the circles represent females; the horizontal line represents a marriage. If you look at David's genogram, you'll see a vertical zig-zag line, which represents a divorce. In each of the four genograms, the vertical line drawn to Sharon, David, Alex, and Carmen is a little longer than those drawn to their brothers and sisters. This just makes it easier to distinguish them from their siblings. Notice also that the birth order is shown, with the oldest child on the left and the youngest on the right. Because Sharon was the second of five children, she is the second child from the left in her genogram. Sharon's maternal grandparents (her mother's parents) have been included on her genogram because they played a role in her childhood. Since she never saw her paternal grandparents (her father's parents), they have not been included. Note also that Carmen's genogram includes an uncle and aunt (her father's brother and the brother's wife) who played an active role in her childhood.

Before you create your own genogram, be sure to read the examples given in this chapter. Once you have completed your genogram, write a brief description of each adult you included. Then write three sets of early recollections: one each for grade school, middle school, and high school. An early recollection is a short description of what that period of your life was like.

Sharon

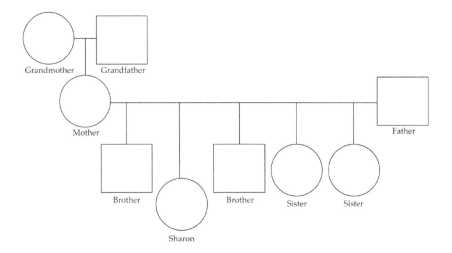

Adults Present During Childhood

Mother: Mother was a homemaker when we were young. Later, she worked part time cleaning houses. She would always be "harassing" us or yelling at Dad. Sometimes she threw things at him when they were fighting. I remember that sometimes she seemed just to get overwhelmed by life. It also seems that whenever I had a problem or wanted to ask her something, she would tell me "not now." When she was in a good mood, she would sing and tell jokes. Mother could be very critical, and it seemed like I never did anything that pleased her.

Father: Father was a mechanic who worked long hours. He never talked much, and when he was angry, he could be very critical to the point of being verbally abusive. He was a binge drinker. Every so often, he would go out drinking with his friends. When he came home, there would always be a loud fight with Mom.

Maternal Grandmother: Grandmother was a critical person who was very proper. She was a private person. Since she only lived about an hour away, we visited her often.

Maternal Grandfather: I don't remember much about Grandfather, as he died when I was still fairly young. I do remember that he was easygoing and always seemed to be in a good mood.

Early Recollections

Grade School: I have lots of good memories of camping during the summers even though there was usually lots of arguing during the trip. This was especially true while setting up camp or preparing meals. Still, there were also many good times while hiking and being in the woods. At home, there was always lots of arguing. At school, I was an average student sort of in the middle of the pack socially.

Middle School: Middle school was similar to grade school. Mother began working part time cleaning homes, so I became responsible for taking care of my two younger sisters in the afternoon when she was gone. The older boys were sort of left on their own. I continued to have a close circle of friends and did okay in school.

High School: Things didn't change much in high school, except that everyone was more on his or her own. Dad continued working long hours and Mother began working outside the home more. When we were together, it seemed like we were always yelling or criticizing one another. Mother seemed more critical than when we were younger. She also seemed to be in a bad mood most of the time when she was home. When we were little, there were some times when she was fun. I don't remember any times like these during high school. I continued to get B's and C's and had a close circle of friends.

David

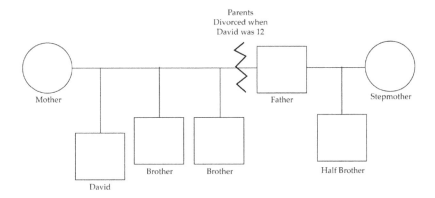

Parents
Divorced when
David was 12

Mother

Father

Stepmother

David

Brother

Brother

Half Brother

Adults Present During Childhood

Mother: Mother wasn't really able to show love. She tended to be stubborn and opinionated. She was very strong-willed in most situations and yet submissive around my father. She was a very smart lady who worked her way through college. She finally was fed up with my father and they divorced when I was twelve.

Father: Father came from a poor immigrant family. His parents died when he was in grade school, and he was placed in an orphanage until he was kicked out at fourteen. He got a job and educated himself. Relatives have commented that he was very handsome as a young man. He became a manager, then owner of a restaurant. He was a strong man in that he didn't let things stop him from doing what he wanted to do. At the same time, he was a very angry man who tended to dominate those around him. After the divorce, I would spend time with him on weekends, but we didn't do very much other than eat together. One area where we did connect was in sports. He would come to my games; and when we did talk, it was usually about the game or some other sport-related topic.

Early Recollections

Grade School: I was fairly rebellious, but very bright, so I got decent grades without really trying. I didn't have many friends. Things were always tense at home, so I often spent a lot of time away from home. Sometimes, I would play with one or two other kids. Just as often, I would just go off by myself.

Middle School: I remember being plagued by small pimples during seventh grade. While I was less of a loner and began to spend time with a small group of guys, I was still somewhat of an outcast. I even prided myself in being different and not accepted by what I thought was the "in" crowd. I enjoyed ruling over my brothers and did some pretty mean things to them. Mom divorced Dad during the summer between seventh and eighth grade. During most of eighth grade, I was left on my own and started to become involved with a wild crowd of kids who were well to do and loved to party.

High School: I did okay in school, mainly because just by sitting in class I could absorb enough to do well on tests. I often didn't bother with homework. If I had been a little more studious, I would have gotten great grades, but I didn't care. I became involved in football when I was a freshman. This was the first time I started to have real friends, and the team became sort of a second family for me. I wasn't a star, but I did well enough to be considered a good player. I think the physical contact helped me release a lot of my energy. If I hadn't been so busy, I'd have probably gotten into more trouble than I did. I really liked the team, so I would back off because I didn't want to get kicked off the team. My teammates also replaced the wild crowd I had been hanging around with in eighth grade. This helped to keep me out of serious trouble.

Carmen

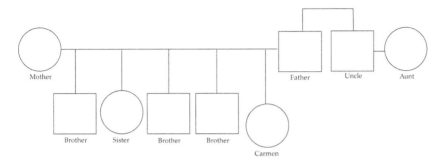

Adults Present During Childhood

Mother: Mother is a wonderful lady. We have always been very close. She has never worked outside the house but had lots to do on the farm we owned. Since her English wasn't very good, she had only a small circle of friends. She was a worrier and was good at putting guilt trips on me.

Father: Father was an immigrant. We owned a farm, and he worked hard. He was shy but very proud of his farm. I wasn't able to talk to him about things and didn't really know him until I was an adult. He was a quiet, hardworking man. I was his princess.

Uncle: My uncle was my father's youngest brother. He had two other brothers who did not immigrate to this country. When I was young, my uncle lived with us. He worked with my father on the farm. Later, he got his own farm nearby, but he and my dad still helped each other a lot. I think my father helped him get his own place or sold him some of his land. I liked my uncle, as he was much easier to talk to than my father was. He was always joking and was a lot of fun.

Aunt: My uncle married when I was in grade school. He and my aunt came over to our house frequently, and we would also visit them at their home regularly. My aunt is a great cook, and I always looked forward to dinner at her home. She has always seemed like a nice lady. She and my uncle didn't have children until I was in high school. She really enjoys children and enjoyed playing with us. She was usually very good-natured when we saw her.

Early Recollections

Grade School: I lived in two cultures, which sometimes made me feel different. We had a very happy home life. Even though father was often busy with the farm, I remember him being a lot of fun when we did spend time together. While living on the farm, I was somewhat isolated. I went to a small school and got good grades. My mother says I was very shy at first, and the teachers said I didn't say much. However, by the end of grade school, I remember being fairly popular.

Middle School: When I started seventh grade I went to a new school. It was much larger than my small grade school. It seemed fairly intimidating at first, but I got used to it. My parents were very strict and old fashioned. I wasn't allowed to go anywhere—no slumber parties, dances, etc. I didn't notice how strict my parents were until middle school. Home life was still basically peaceful and loving.

High School: Starting high school was somewhat scary for me, but I adjusted and continued to be an excellent student. My parents loosened up a little, and I was able to participate in clubs. I developed many friendships and became very well liked. I didn't want to disappoint my parents, so I always tried very hard at whatever I did. My parents had a very strong work ethic. When I went to college, I remember thinking how huge and impersonal it seemed after high school in a small town. At the same time, I enjoyed leaving home, as I had lots of freedom for the first time.

Alex

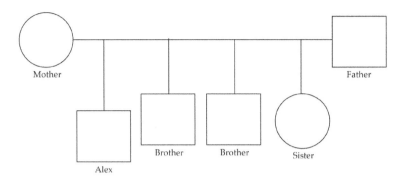

Adults Present During Childhood

Mother: Mother is from a big family. She was always changing things around in the house and buying new stuff. She was very controlling and manipulative but in a quiet, sneaky sort of way. When she was angry about something you did, she made sure you knew it.

Father: Father came from a blue-collar family. He worked hard at two jobs. During the day, he was a full time clerical job. On the weekends, he was a part time custodian in a factory. He was a perfectionist. He also was quiet and he would hold things in. We didn't interact a lot, but when we did, it was usually friendly. Our main interaction occurred when we went on family outings such as picnics, or when we went to sporting events.

Early Recollections

Grade School: Because Father was working two jobs, we didn't see him a lot during the week. However, he would take us to sporting events, such as baseball games and fights. These were usually good times except that sometimes he would drink too much and become explosive. At these times, he would become a different person and talk about Mom in a very negative way. I did well in school and had friends. Home life was okay.

Middle School: Middle school was similar to grade school. Dad was advancing in his clerical position and doing less janitorial work. I continued to do well in school and had friends. I was a people pleaser who didn't like to make waves.

High School: Dad quit doing janitorial work and became a supervisor, so we began to see him around the house more. He was usually busy puttering in the garage or working on a project around the house. Mom went to work at a department store and she was often gone in the afternoon and early evening. At these times, I was put in charge of the house and would make dinner and be responsible for the younger children. Late at night, I remember my parents arguing. I don't think they were really that close, and I believe they stayed together mainly for financial reasons.

THE TIME TUNNEL

The various people we meet and situations we encounter often resemble those from our past in some way. This similarity causes many people to react as if the present person or situation were the same as the past one. I use the term time tunneling to refer to this tendency.

Time tunneling is a common source of inappropriate anger and distorted thinking. Sharon is a good example. Because she had experienced so much negative criticism from her mother, she tended to respond to simple disagreements or helpful suggestions as if they were critical attacks. Even when people disagreed in a very appropriate and friendly ways, she would react to them as she had to her mother, immediately lashing out at them. Her anger was often accompanied by thoughts such as "Who do they think they are?" "Why can't they just leave me alone?" "Why is everyone so critical?" These were all thoughts that she had experienced as a child when her mother criticized her. Even though the situations she encountered as an adult were usually very different, they still "felt" like her mother's criticism, and she continued to respond as if she were still a child being harshly criticized.

CORE BELIEFS

Time tunneling occurs because of a type of learning called conditioned response learning. A conditioned response is an automatic response triggered by some stimulus or cue. I. P. Pavlov coined this term at the turn of the century as a result of his experiments with dogs. He would ring a bell, then immediately place meat powder on the dog's tongue, causing it to salivate. After repeating this many times, he could stimulate salivation simply by ringing the bell.

We all have hundreds of conditioned responses that have developed over the course of our lifetime. Conditioned responses play an important role in many daily tasks and help us to function with little conscious thought. Unfortunately, some of our conditioned responses, like Sharon's reaction to disagreements, interfere with our ability to function effectively. Once we identify them, we can, over time, decondition ourselves. After working through the exercises in this and the following chapter, Sharon found herself reacting to disagreements and helpful suggestions more appropriately.

When a collection of related conditioned responses is interfering with your life, it's useful to give them a descriptive label in order to identify them when they occur. I call these labels core beliefs. A core belief is a descriptive label used to identify a related set of conditioned responses. To understand the concept more fully, let's take another look at Sharon's inappropriate response to simple disagreements.

When Sharon was young, her mother was overly critical. Sharon even comments that it "seemed like I never did anything that pleased her." In addition, her mother was often distant and so overwhelmed by life that she had little emotional energy left over for her children. As Sharon and I looked at this, she realized that her mother had not been very good at showing love and affection. One way that Sharon had tried to connect with her was by doing things to please her. Unfortunately, because her mother was a perfectionist who did not adjust her expectations to the reality of children, she only rarely seemed satisfied with what Sharon did. As a result, Sharon began to believe she could do nothing correctly. Of course, if you had asked Sharon if she actually believed this, she would have said no. When she made mistakes, she would experience tremendous anger and berate herself with such self-talk as, "Why can't I do anything right?"

Because these conditioned responses are mostly unconscious, you have probably never thought much about them. Fortunately, there is an easy way to identify them, based on the old adage "If it looks like a duck, talks like a duck, and walks like a duck, it's probably a duck." Applying this adage to the concept of unconscious core beliefs, we can say, "If you act like you believe something, speak like you believe something, and think like you believe something, you believe it." Again, such beliefs are probably not conscious. Instead, they are a collection of conditioned response patterns. Sharon truly believed that she was skilled at many things, but whenever she made a mistake or was criticized, she acted and thought as if she believed "I can't do anything right."

As you review your genogram, descriptions, and early recollections, ask yourself, "What kinds of beliefs would a child growing up in this situation develop about him or herself, others, and the world?" How did you respond to various people and events as you were growing up? Keep in mind the idea that "if you act, speak, or think like you believe something," that belief is probably playing an important role in your behavior, whether you consciously agree with it or not. What beliefs does your behavior reflect?

As you identify your core beliefs, you will find that they can be grouped into three general categories: beliefs about yourself, beliefs about others, and beliefs about the world around you. Here are the negative core beliefs that Sharon, David, Carmen, and Alex identified while doing the work outlined in this chapter.

Sharon

I can't do anything right.

Something is wrong with me, I don't measure up.

Intimacy is painful.

People aren't reliable, they'll always let you down.

The only one you can depend on is yourself.

Only the strong survive, I must never show weakness.

David

A man should be strong and never let others take advantage of him.

It's a dog eat dog world. I must always be on guard and fight to make sure no one takes what is mine.

I can handle anything.

Never show any sign of weakness.

Winning is everything, losing is for losers.

Carmen

Keep the peace. Don't make others angry or upset with you.

It's wrong and selfish to refuse the requests of others.

Never do anything that hurts others.
I'm not as capable as others.
The world is dangerous.

Alex

Anger is dangerous and causes you to lose control (therefore, you
   must suppress it).
If you're going to do something, do it right (which means perfectly).
My main task in life is to take care of my responsibilities.
Mistakes are unacceptable.
I must avoid asking questions or making statements that might
   make me look stupid or ignorant.
Emotions are dangerous—keep them under control or something bad
   might happen.

The main goal of this chapter is to help you identify the
negative core beliefs that are interfering with your life. Because our focus is on negative core beliefs, it's easy to over-
look the fact that you also developed positive ones that have
helped you. For example, Carmen's close-knit family gave
her the positive core beliefs that "I am loved and lovable,"
and "There are people who are trustworthy." These beliefs
gave her a great sense of security with her husband and made
it easy for her to experience intimacy and trust him. Likewise,
Alex's core belief that "I can succeed if I work hard" and "I'm
a good worker" helped him succeed at work.

SUMMARY OF KEY IDEAS

1. Constructing a genogram, creating descriptions of the
   adults in your life when you were young, and com-
   posing early recollections can help you identify issues
   from childhood that play a role in your current inappropriate responses.

2. Time tunneling is the tendency to react to a present-day situation or person as if it were an event or person from the past.
3. A conditioned response is an automatic response triggered by some stimulus or cue. Time tunneling is caused by conditioned responses.
4. A core belief is a descriptive label used to identify a related set of conditioned responses.
5. We all have at least some negative core beliefs about ourselves, others, and the world that generate inappropriate responses.

RECOMMENDED ACTIVITIES

Continue Journaling and Using Time-Outs

One point I would like to stress is the unconscious nature of conditioned response learning. Many self-help books are insight oriented, which means that they focus on explaining why things occur. The assumption is that once you understand why undesirable behaviors occur, they automatically cease. However, insight by itself does little to change deeply entrenched conditioned responses. Still, insight is valuable. Understanding why you are reacting the way you do is an important first step to change. Insight helps you identify more precisely what needs to be changed along with the steps you have to take. Still, once you have gained insight into the conditioned responses connected with inappropriate anger—once you understand what is happening and what you need to do—the only way actually to change the behavior is to slowly and deliberately practice substituting new behaviors for the old ones.

This is why journaling is so important. Journaling helps you to become consciously aware of patterns that were formerly automatic. It also allows you to practice the new forms of thinking that you want to replace the old ones. Therefore, it's essential that you continue to record incidents where you become upset. As you do so, be sure to identify the distorted thinking and develop rational challenges, as described in previous chapters. Journaling in this manner is one of your most powerful tools for changing the automatic thoughts connected with inappropriate anger.

In addition to working with your thoughts, continue to use time-outs to control your behavior when you're experiencing high levels of anger.

Create Your Genogram and Compose Descriptions of Your Parents and Early Childhood Recollections

Following the examples presented in this chapter, construct a genogram of your family when you were young. Be sure to include grandparents, uncles, aunts, and anyone else who played a significant role during your developmental years. Use a full sheet of eight-and-a-half-by-eleven-inch paper so you can include descriptions of your parents and early recollections on the same sheet. Use more than one sheet if you need to.

After you have completed your genogram, write descriptions of the adults who played a significant role in raising you. Include a few words about their personalities. Were they easygoing, shy, critical, or outgoing? Also, include a few words about your relationship with them. Was it warm or cold? Were they easy to talk to or distant? Some people find it helpful to pretend that they are writing a character description for an actor who is to play the role of a particular parent in a movie.

Finally, write brief descriptions of what your life was like during your grade school years (earliest memories through the fifth grade), your middle school years (sixth through eighth), and your high school years (ninth through twelfth). Do not focus only on what is positive or negative. Instead, list your most common recollections. The goal is to paint a general portrait of what life was like for you during each of these periods.

If you're now in a close relationship with someone—whether a spouse, boyfriend, or girlfriend—ask this person to do this exercise and create a genogram of his or her significant relationships, along with descriptions of the adults and their early recollections. When you have both completed your genograms, take about an hour to share them with each other and discuss what you have learned about yourselves. This will give each of you many valuable insights into why the other reacts the way he or she does. If your partner is unwilling to do this exercise, create a genogram of his or her family on your own as best you can from what you have been told. While this is not as effective as having the person create his or her own genogram, you still will probably discover some important new facts about your partner that can help you respond to him or her more effectively and lovingly.

Identify at Least Four Negative Core Beliefs
Here are several common examples of negative core beliefs that can generate inappropriate emotional and behavioral reactions.

Examples of Negative Core Beliefs About Oneself
- I'm inferior to others. (Common variations: Something's wrong with me, I don't measure up, or I'm not as intelligent or capable as others.)
- I'm worthless.
- I'm unlovable.

- No one sees me or likes me. I'm not interesting or desirable.
- I'm dirty.
- I'm ugly.
- My needs are unimportant
- My needs are bad.
- I'm a bad person.
- I can't succeed.
- I can't do anything right. (Common variations: I always make a mess of things, I'm incompetent.)
- I'm crazy.
- I have no power. There's nothing I can do to make a difference in how events turn out.
- Anger is dangerous and causes me to lose control. (Therefore, I must suppress it.)
- Emotions are dangerous—I must keep them under control, or something bad might happen.

Examples of Negative Core Beliefs About Relationships
- Intimacy is painful (or dangerous), therefore I must not get close to anyone.
- If I get close to someone, I will be hurt.
- Conflict is dangerous.
- People in authority are dangerous.
- People aren't reliable—they'll always let me down
- I can't trust anyone.
- Others are in control of my life.
- Sooner or later people will abandon me.
- The only one I can depend on is myself.
- In many ways, others are my adversaries. I must always be on guard and fight to make sure no one takes what is mine.
- No one can understand me.

- I can lose those I love at any minute.
- I must avoid asking questions or making statements that might make me look foolish or ignorant.
- The opposite sex is inferior/superior.
- I'm responsible for how others feel.
- If people see how I don't measure up, they will not like me.
- If I act "foolishly," people won't like me.
- Never talk about unpleasant things. It might offend others.
- If I offend others or upset them, they'll abandon me.
- I am responsible for others' well-being.
- My only worth comes from caring for others.
- I must keep the peace, and not make others angry or upset. (They might abandon me.)
- I must never do anything that hurts others.
- It's wrong and selfish to refuse the requests of others.
- My only worth comes from performing.
- I am entitled to have and do what I want, no matter what.
- I don't need anyone or anything. I can take care of myself.

Examples of Negative Core Beliefs about the World
- I'm not safe.
- I can be violated at any moment.
- I don't have the right to protect myself.
- I can't trust my own feelings or perceptions.
- There is no safe place in the world.
- The world is fearful and dangerous.
- The dangers of the world are too much for me to handle.
- When bad things happen to me, it's my fault.

- I have no power or control.
- Life is hard. To live is to suffer.
- Life is meaningless.
- Only the strong survive. I must never show weakness.
- If I allow anyone else to be in charge or have power, I will be harmed.
- Illness and death are awful. I must keep a close watch on my body because it's weak and fragile and something terrible can go wrong at any time.
- Winning is everything, losing is for losers.
- Happiness comes from having things. (Common variations: Happiness comes from having power, money, position, etc.)

Review your genogram and the descriptions of the adults who raised you and your early recollections. Now identify those negative core beliefs that apply to you. Keep in mind that I'm using the term belief differently from its normal meaning—it's here simply as a label for complex sets of conditioned response patterns. Labeling these patterns gives you a powerful tool to begin eliminating them. Ask yourself, "What kinds of core beliefs would a child growing up in this situation develop about him or herself, others, and the world?" Keep in mind the idea that "if you act, speak, or think like you believe something," that belief or association is probably playing an important role in your behavior, whether you consciously agree with it or not.

If you find it difficult to identify your core beliefs, discuss this issue with someone you trust and who knows you well. Others often can see us more clearly than we can. If you don't have someone like this in your life, you might find it helpful to work with a trained therapist.

8

When the Beast Is a
Ghost from the Past

N OW THAT YOU have identified how your family shaped some of your core beliefs, we will explore the cultural forces that played a role in shaping your worldview. We will also examine four traits common among people who were raised in dysfunctional families. Then you'll learn a simple but powerful technique to use when time tunneling causes your past to poison your present.

CULTURAL STEREOTYPES

As you grew up, you were bombarded with millions of messages about what men and women should be. You saw the images on television and in the movies you watched and you heard them in the music you listened to. Here are some common messages:

A man should be

A good provider	In charge
A good lover	Intelligent
Able to solve his	Knowledgeable
partner's problems	Smarter and stronger
Athletic	than a woman
Brave	Unaffected by sadness
Handsome	

A woman should be

Alluring	Polite
Beautiful	Selfless
Faithful	Sensitive
Not as smart as a man	Sexy
Not as powerful as a man	Skilled at domestic chores
Nurturing	Thin

Even today, in a more liberated age, these stereotypes are reinforced on playgrounds, in malls, and wherever boys and girls interact. Take a look at a sampling of the derogatory names boys and girls hurl at each other.

Negative Labels Boys Hear

Baby	Girl	Pussy
Chicken	Klutz	Sissy
Coward	Mama's boy	Weakling
Crybaby	Nerd	Wimp
Freak	Punk	Wuss

Negative Labels Girls Hear

Baby	Nag	Tomboy
Bitch	Overly sensitive	Touchy
Crybaby	Shrew	Whore
Daddy's girl	Slut	Wimp
Frigid	Tease	Witch

Names like these send powerful messages that you had better live up to the traditional images of men and women. Unfortunately, since it's impossible to live up to these unrealistic images, they are a common source of inappropriate anger.

Of course, not all of the labels and messages you heard during your childhood were gender related. Negative messages abound, especially when children, siblings, and even parents are teasing or angry. Labels like the following can be hurtful and, if heard repeatedly, can lead to a negative self-image.

Clumsy	Irresponsible	Slob
Disappointment	Klutz	Slow
Dumb	Loser	Stupid
Failure	Misfit	Stupid
Immature	Problem child	Underachiever

This week, take some time to identify negative labels from your past that are still shaping the way you look at yourself and the way you approach life. Once you have identified those that are causing problems, try substituting more accurate and positive words to describe yourself or your actions. For example, Sharon often called herself stupid when she made a mistake—a label her mother often used. In her anger work, she spent several weeks reminding herself to label her mistakes accurately. At first, she would make a mistake and call herself stupid, but it didn't take long before she began catching herself. She would then challenge the negative label with thoughts such as "I am not stupid. I'm actually very good at what I do. I just made a mistake. That is normal and expected." Sharon was surprised that a simple activity like this could make such a big difference. After several week, she found herself experiencing very little inappropriate anger when she made a mistake. The reason this technique worked is twofold. First, negative labels magnify the importance of events. Second, negative labels that have roots in your past tend to reactivate pain from childhood that is associated with them. Using accurate and positive labels helps you interpret events more realistically and stops you from time tunneling.

THE LEGACY OF A DYSFUNCTIONAL FAMILY

A family can be dysfunctional in many different ways. The most obvious is the presence of one or more of the abusive behaviors discussed in Chapter 2: emotional abuse, physical abuse, sexual abuse, cruel and unusual punishment, emotional neglect, and physical neglect. However, subtler forms of dysfunction are very common. For example, Alex's mother was manipulative and controlling, which made it unsafe for Alex to express his opinions or act in any way that would upset her.

The Traits of Healthy Families

One of the best ways to understand these subtler forms of dysfunction is to look at the traits of a healthy family. Traits common to healthy families are listed below. A family doesn't have to have every one of these traits to be healthy, but it will have most of them. Take a moment to use the following scale to rate the family you grew up in.

Never = 0
Rarely = 1
Sometimes = 2
Often = 3
Always = 4

1. _____ *Acceptance of independence:* You were allowed to have ideas and opinions that differed from your adult caregivers without being criticized or condemned.

2. _____ *Acceptance of weaknesses:* Your adult caregivers understood your weaknesses, but treated you with respect and acceptance without being judgmental or punishing.

3. _____ *Availability:* Your adult caregivers made you a priority and would take time to be with you when you needed them.

4. _____ *Care:* Your adult caregivers displayed a genuine concern about your welfare, pleasure, and pain.

5. _____ *Closeness:* You had a sense that a strong bond exists between you and your adult caregivers.

6. _____ *Companionship:* You enjoyed spending time together.

7. _____ *Constructive problem solving:* Your adult caregivers were able to resolve problems in a positive way between themselves and with you.

8. _____ *Cooperation:* You had a sense that you and your adult caregivers were "on the same side" rather than competing against one another.

9. _____ *Empathy:* Your adult caregivers had the ability to tune in to your feelings—to experience, to some degree, your pain or pleasure, suffering or joy.

10. _____ *Encouragement:* You heard frequent encouragement.

11. _____ *Expressions of affection:* You experienced frequent affectionate gestures, such as a parent putting his or her arm around you and speaking words of love.

12. _____ *Feelings of warmth:* Your home had a warm, welcome feeling.

13. _____ *Friendliness:* Your adult caregivers took a genuine interest in you.

14. _____ *Intimacy:* Your adult caregivers shared their thoughts and feelings that were age appropriate with you, and you felt safe sharing yours with them.

15. _____ *Kindness:* Your adult caregivers were considerate and thoughtful in their dealings with you.

16. _____ *Open and free communication:* You felt free to talk about any subject and explore different ideas.

17. _____ *Pleasing feelings:* Your adult caregivers did things that were pleasurable and satisfying.

18. _____ *Reasonable limits:* Limits placed on you were reasonable, related, and respectful.

19. _____ *Safety:* You felt safe.

20. _____ *Sensitivity:* Your adult caregivers displayed an awareness of and respect for your concerns and vulnerable spots.

21. _____ *Spirituality:* Your adult caregivers shared their view of spirituality in a positive way.

22. _____ *Support:* You had a sense that your adult caregivers were dependable and that you could lean on them during difficult times.

23. _____ *Unconditional love:* Love was expressed freely and was not dependent on "good behavior."

24. _____ *Understanding:* Your adult caregivers were able to see events through your eyes.

Items that you scored with a 2 or lower indicate weak areas in your family. These areas are where you are most likely to time tunnel when present situations resemble them in any way.

The Traits of Adults Raised in Dysfunctional Families

Adults raised in dysfunctional families often display one or more of the following four traits. Those raised in grossly dysfunctional families often show all four, but the range varies. Depending on the type and severity of family dysfunction, some traits might affect all aspects of a person's life, or more commonly, they could only affect specific types of situations such as friendships, intimate relationships, or work.

A Tendency to Be Triggered by Specific Events

This is "time tunneling" (see Chapter 7). Everyone does some time tunneling, especially as a young adult. Fortunately, as we age, we tend to time tunnel less frequently, especially if we mature in a healthy environment. The more dysfunctional your family background, the greater the likelihood that time tunneling plays a major role in triggering inappropriate emotional responses.

Difficulty Modulating Emotions

A person who had difficulty modulating emotions tends to feel only emotional extremes: either very little emotion or very strong emotions. Once a person like this is angered or frightened, it's usually difficult for him or her to calm down. This tendency is more common in people who grew up in an environment that was not safe either physically or emotionally. To some degree, each of the four people described in this book had this problem. For David and Sharon, both parents were not safe. For Alex, it was primarily his mother. Carmen experienced safety while at home, but the world outside her home seemed somewhat unsafe because of her sensitive nature, relative isolation from neighbors, and the fact that she lived in two different cultures—one at home and one at school.

As children, David, Sharon, and Alex learned to be careful

about what they said, so they would not provoke their parents' anger. This suppression of their emotions became automatic, with the result that as adults, they really experienced emotions only when they reached a high level of intensity. The next chapter discusses this issue in greater detail, along with ways to develop a "middle range" of emotional experience.

A Tendency to View Oneself and the World Negatively

Being raised in a dysfunctional family tends to create a negative worldview in five different areas. The first three are difficulty in trusting others, difficulty feeling safe, and difficulty believing that it's possible to bring about desired outcomes. All three of these were especially true for David and Sharon. Because Alex enjoyed success at school and had friends, he was able to see himself as competent. His main difficulty was trusting others. Because his parents were not trustworthy in an emotional sense, he found intimacy difficult. With Carmen, the only real problem area in her self-image was doubt about whether she was as capable as others were.

The other two areas are the feeling that one is abnormal or deficient in some respect, and the belief that one is not lovable. Carmen's warm, loving family gave her a strong sense that she was lovable. However, Sharon, David, and Alex each had some problems with both of these areas, as reflected in many of their core beliefs (see Chapter 7).

A Diminished Ability to Understand Events:

People with any one or any combination of the three previous tendencies sometimes go into a daze or become confused or angry when they are stressed, dealing with conflict, or emotionally upset. They use a great deal of emotional energy to protect themselves from painful emotions and negative perceptions, which leaves them with little mental and emotional energy to deal with their present circumstances.

The more you have of each of these four traits, the more vulnerable you are to both inappropriate anger and time tunneling. This is especially true in situations that mirror negative experiences from childhood. Fortunately, a simple technique exists that, over time, can help you escape the time tunnel and slowly reduce these traits.

THE "WHAT'S HAPPENING? WHAT'S REAL?" TECHNIQUE

In the discussion on time tunneling in Chapter 7, we saw that Sharon responded to simple disagreements or helpful suggestions as if they were attacks, because they resembled criticisms from her mother. Weekly office meetings were especially troublesome for her. During these meetings, the staff would discuss problems that had occurred in the office and they would suggest ways for improving performance in the future. Even when the meetings were friendly, Sharon often felt herself becoming anxious and angry, even though she knew it was inappropriate. While a meeting was under way, she was usually able to contain her anger and keep a fairly calm exterior. Then afterward, her pent-up anger would surface and interfere with her ability to work and make it difficult for her to interact with her coworkers. A simple two-step technique helped Sharon pull herself out of the time tunnel. I call it "What's happening? What's real?" To use this technique, you simply:

- State what is happening.
- State what is real.

When Sharon felt her anger rise during meetings at work,

she learned to identify what was happening by telling herself, "I'm reacting to these suggestions as if I were being criticized by my mother." She would then remind herself of what was real with statements such as "This is a simple business meeting. My mother is not here. I am an adult now. The people here conduct themselves in a professional manner. While comments might be made about problems, they are not personal attacks. Everyone here respects my ability. If someone makes a suggestion, they do so with good intentions." Sharon found it helpful to tell herself these things before the meeting in order to prepare herself and reduce the intensity of the old response. After several weeks of practice, she found that the meetings no longer triggered the time tunnel response. Her conditioned response had been extinguished.

Similarly, Alex would become very angry whenever anyone made a comment such as "That was a stupid thing to do." As he went through the lists of negative names at the beginning of this chapter, he realized that his mother had frequently questioned his intelligence with phrases such as "What's wrong with you? Are you stupid or what?" As an adult, whenever anyone made a comment like this, he time tunneled and felt as he had when he was a small child being criticized by his mother.

David found this technique especially useful when he became angry while working on a difficult project. While he could usually contain himself, occasionally he would explode in rage, baffling everyone around him as well as himself. To change this pattern, David began doing two things. First, he began taking informal time-outs whenever he noticed himself becoming angry. After excusing himself, he would use the "What's happening? What's real?" technique to calm himself. Often he found that if he used this technique when he first became agitated, he did not need a time-out.

Here's an example of the self-talk David used: "I'm getting angry. What's happening is that I don't understand how to do this. The old message that 'I should be able to figure things out and solve any problem' makes it difficult for me to acknowledge that sometimes I am unable to do things the way I would like to do them. Calm down. What's real is that I'm not a genius and I can't do everything. I have limitations. This is true for everyone. It's okay not to be able to do this. I need help. This is something I have trouble asking for. Again, it's the old should/must rule that I should be able to figure things out on my own. That's a lie. The truth is that right now I don't understand how to do this. My old man used to ream me out when I couldn't do something 'right,' but he's not here. Now let's figure out how I can get the help I need and solve this problem in a constructive manner."

SUMMARY OF KEY IDEAS

1. The images you saw on television and in movies and the messages you heard in music, played a powerful role in shaping your view of what it means to be a man or woman. The labels used by others and the experiences you had also contributed to your views about what men and women should be like.
2. Trying to live up to unrealistic images and beliefs about being a man or a woman are a common source of inappropriate anger.
3. Four tendencies common in adults who come from dysfunctional families are (1) the tendency for specific events to trigger anger or anxiety, (2) difficulty modulating emotions, (3) a tendency to view oneself and the world negatively, and (4) a reduced ability to understand events.

4. The "What's happening? What's real?" technique is a simple yet highly effective method for combating time tunneling.

Recommended Activities

What Does it Mean to Be a Man or a Woman?

Set aside an hour for this exercise. Have handy your genogram, your descriptions of the adults present while you were growing up, and the early recollections you created while working through Chapter 7.

Begin by reviewing the lists at the beginning of this chapter of common images about what men and women should be like. Then consider the following list of common experiences that boys and girls have. As you go through the list, put a check by any you experienced.

Common Experiences for Boys
- You exercised to make yourself stronger.
- You worried that you were not tough enough.
- You were teased or humiliated by others when you showed weakness or "acted like a girl."
- You stopped a hobby or activity you enjoyed because it was too "feminine."
- You deliberately did less at school, so you would not appear too smart or "nerdy."
- You were hit by someone older.
- You were forced to fight.
- You fought someone to prove you were a "man."
- You were deliberately injured by another.
- You took risks or met a dare to show you weren't afraid.
- You were sexually abused or touched in a way you didn't like.

- You stopped yourself from showing emotion, hugging, or touching someone because of how it might make you look.

Others:

_____

_____

_____

Common Experiences for Girls
- You worried you were not pretty enough.
- You worried about your clothes, hair, and appearance.
- You dieted to lose weight or to prevent yourself from gaining "too much."
- You were teased or humiliated by others when you "acted like a boy."
- You teased or humiliated other girls when they "acted like a boy."
- You stopped doing a hobby or activity you enjoyed because it was too "masculine."
- You stopped yourself from asserting yourself or acting too strong because of how it might make you look.
- You deliberately did less at school, so you would not appear too smart.
- You had sexual remarks made about you.
- You used your sexuality to get something you wanted.
- You were sexually abused or touched in ways you didn't like.

Others:

_____

_____

_____

After you have thought about these lists, review your genogram, the description of the adults in your life while growing up, and the early recollections. Then answer the following questions.

While growing up
- What qualities did you think that men and women should have?
- What caused you to think this way?
- What qualities do you currently think men and women should have?
- Why is this still important to you?
- Are there any times when these beliefs about what men or women should be cause you to become angry?

After you have completed this writing assignment, make a list of the kinds of situations that trigger your anger. If these situations involve unrealistic expectations, write a short sentence or phrase that you can use as a coping self-statement during these situations. For example, Sharon developed the belief during childhood that she should never make a mistake. To counter this unrealistic belief, she now added the following to her list of coping self-statements: "Mistakes are a normal part of life," "It's okay to make mistakes," "In the long run, most mistakes are unimportant."

Identify Negative Labels That Trigger Inappropriate Anger

Before you begin, review the lists (at the beginning of this chapter) of common negative labels given to boys and girls, along with the list of negative labels used for both boys and girls. Then write the answers to the following questions in your journal.

- While you were growing up, what negative labels did you hear from your parents, brothers, sisters, friends, classmates, and other adults in your life?
- What feelings or thoughts did you have as you wrote down these negative labels?
- Which labels are the most painful to recall?
- Are there any labels that you currently use with others?
- Are there any that you currently use with yourself?
- Are there any that still trigger anger when someone uses them on you?

After you have done this, review the list of core beliefs that you identified in the last chapter. Add to your list any new ones that you identified in this exercise.

During the next two weeks, as you record in your journal incidents where you become angry, refer back to your list of negative labels and see if any of them are playing a role in your reaction. If they are, be sure to write a "What's happening? What's real?" statement that follows the examples given in this chapter to reduce their influence.

Identifying Positive Role Models

In order to accomplish any task, you need to have a clear goal in mind. To accomplish the task of increasing your ability to manage anger effectively, you need to have a clear and realistic picture of the skills used to manage anger. Identifying people who are good at managing their anger can give you this picture by providing you with concrete examples of how to deal with specific situations.

List in your journal the names of three people who have the following qualities:

- They can become angry without becoming abusive or violent.
- They can express a broad range of feelings, including anger.
- They can communicate their wants and needs effectively in nonthreatening ways.

During the next two weeks, as you record incidents of anger in your journal, think about these three positive role models. How do you think they would have responded to the situation that triggered your anger?

Use the "What's Happening? What's Real?" Technique Against Time- Tunneling

Identify at least one situation in the past month that triggered a response in you as if it were the past. Use the examples given in this chapter to develop a "What's happening? What's real?" response that you could use in a similar situation in the future.

Add a New Question to Your Journal About Angry Incidents

Continue to write in your journal about times when you become angry. In your analysis of each incident, be sure to answer the four questions from Chapter 6. When considering the fourth question ("How could I have responded in a different and more effective manner?") ask yourself, "How would a positive role model have behaved?" After you have answered the four questions, answer the following additional question.

Were any negative labels, family role models, or incidents from the past affecting this situation?

Here is the format for this week's journaling:

Date
Incident:
Level of Arousal ___ , *Level of Aggression* ___
Thoughts:
Actions:
Five Questions (four from Chapter 6 plus the one from this chapter):

1. *What exactly did this person do that triggered my anger?*
2. *What needs or wants caused this person to act in this way?*
3. *What beliefs or aspects of this person's past (hurts, losses, successes, fears, lack of skills, etc.) influenced this behavior?*
4. *Considering the above, how could I have responded in a different and more effective manner? How would a positive role model have behaved?*
5. *Were any negative labels, family role models, or incidents from the past affecting this situation?*

Rational Challenges

These two examples show how David and Carmen incorporated these questions into their journal writing.

David

Thursday, September 11

Incident: I went to the store to pick up some snack items for a game I wanted to watch. I was in a hurry because the game was going to start soon and the store was fairly crowded. I got in the quick checkout line for people with ten items or less and cash only. The bozo in front of me had twelve items and paid with a check.

Arousal — 7, Aggression — 5

Thoughts: "What a selfish jerk. There's always some bozo like this who can't follow the rules and screws everything up for everyone else."

Actions: I got really hot, pointed to the sign, and said, "Hey, bozo, can't you read, or are you retarded or something?" I also made comments about what a jerk I thought he was, loud enough for him to hear.

Five Questions (from Chapter 6 & 8):

1. *What exactly did this person do that triggered my anger?*
   He didn't follow the rules.

2. *What needs or wants caused this person to act in this way?*
   I have a strong belief that everyone should follow the rules and play fair.

3. *What beliefs or aspects of this person's past (hurts, losses, successes, fears, lack of skills, etc.) influenced this behavior?*
   I don't know since he was a stranger. Obviously, he feels he is entitled to break rules when it's convenient.

4. *Considering the above, how could I have responded in a different and more effective manner? How would a positive role model have behaved?*
   I should have kept control of myself and not been so aggressive. When I think of how Bob might have handled this situation, he would have said something but like, "Excuse me, I believe this line is for ten items and cash only." He also has a way of saying things with humor that often makes them work more effectively.

5. *Were any negative labels, family role models, or incidents from the past affecting this situation?*
   My father was always quick to explode in situations like this. I'm just doing what he did, even though I hated that. I also know that I didn't plan things very well. This was probably triggering some of my anger, since I grew up with the belief that men should always be in control.

Rational Challenges

"What a selfish jerk." This person was being selfish. It was also appropriate to say something. However, the way I said it and the degree of anger I experienced were not appropriate.

"There's always some bozo like this who can't follow the rules and screws everything up for everyone else." This is an overgeneralization. There is not always someone like this guy. Most of the time things go the way they're supposed to. Still, there are times when I encounter people like him. I'm not going to change a person like him by getting all bent out of shape. It's okay to say something, but I need to say it in a more appropriate way. One of the things that triggered me in this situation was my self-talk about how I never get to see a game all the way through. I was pretty hot before I even got in line. Much of my self-talk about the game was magnification and overgeneralization. There were also a lot of 'should' statements. I was also angry at myself for not planning things better. I'm going to make lots of mistakes like this. They're not important. I also need to begin telling myself that in the long run these kinds of delays and frustrations are not that important. I was able to see my game and have a good time, even though I missed a few minutes. I've seen thousands of games from beginning to end. Missing a few minutes at the beginning of one game is nothing.

Carmen
Wednesday, September 17

Incident: I was in a department store with my children. I was trying to find a new dress for work, and they were restless and
whiney and making it very difficult.

Arousal — 6, Aggression — 4

Thoughts: "Why can't these kids behave? Don't they know how important this is? I can't stand it when they act like this."

Actions: I kept telling them to "behave." I tried bribing them with the
promise of ice cream if they were good. After I got my dress,
I went home and told them to go to their rooms.

Five Questions (from Chapter 6 & 8):

1. *What exactly did this person do that triggered my anger?*

   They were misbehaving and causing a scene in public.

2. *What needs or wants caused this person to act in this way?*

   They were responding like normal children who were hungry and tired.

3. *What beliefs or aspects of this person's past (hurts, losses, successes, fears, lack of skills, etc.) influenced this behavior?*

   None; this is a normal response for hungry and tired children.

4. *Considering the above, how could I have responded in a different and more effective manner? How would a positive role model have behaved?*

   I remember being out with Karen a couple of weeks ago when something similar was happening. She just said, "Let's go have lunch," and stopped shopping even though she had some other items to pick up. We got them after we had lunch and allowed the children to spend some time playing. Things seemed to go fairly smoothly.

5. *Were any negative labels, family role models, or incidents from the past affecting this situation?*

   My mother used to remind me often how important it was to think of others. I was told that I was being "impolite" or "unladylike" when I acted rude. At the store, I was behaving the same way she would in a similar situation. It's important to teach my children to be thoughtful and polite, but this was not the time or place or the best way to do this. My children were hungry and tired and had actually been very patient most of the morning.

Rational Challenges

"Why can't these children behave?" This is the should/must rule, "Children should behave," expressed as a question. First, my children do behave pretty well most of the time. On this particular

day, I was trying to do too much. We had already run several errands, and it was past their lunchtime. Things would probably have gone more smoothly if I had put some of my errands off to another time.

"Don't they know how important this is?" This is the should/must rule, "My children should understand my needs," stated as a question. This is ridiculous. Children don't understand things as adults do. Besides, they were tired and hungry. It was my expectations that were unrealistic.

"I can't stand it when they act like this." This is a magnification. While I don't like it, I can stand it when they misbehave. In fact, other than being angry, I was just fine.

9

The Beast as Defender

A NGER IS OUR strongest weapon for coping with threats but it's also one of our greatest weaknesses, especially when we use it to escape from emotions that seem unacceptable, or from pain. In this chapter, you'll learn about the qualities of anger that cause it to be used as a defense mechanism. You'll also learn about the price you pay when you use it this way and how it interferes with your ability to form meaningful relationships and function in daily life.

THE MOTIVATIONAL SIDE OF ANGER

As we have seen, the role of anger is to generate energy and motivation to respond to a threat. Anger produces energy through the fight-or-flight response. Unfortunately, since the workings of the mind are still mostly a mystery, no one is sure exactly how anger generates motivation. However, we can describe four aspects of this motivation.

- *An increased focus on your needs or wants.* As you become angry, your needs and the desire to eliminate the threat that you believe stands in the way of meeting them becomes your primary focus. The needs of others become less important.
- *A greater sense of confidence.* The angrier you are, the more fearless you become in doing whatever is necessary to eliminate the perceived threat or to meet your needs.
- *A sense of righteousness.* Anger produces the belief that what you are doing is morally justified.
- *A reduced awareness of all other emotions.* In the overwhelming psychological and physical sense of strength generated by anger, all other emotions are swallowed up.

When we are faced with a real physical challenge, these four aspects of the motivational side of anger can be very useful. Take, for example, a football coach giving a pregame pep talk to his team. As he fires up the team members and pits them against their opponents, their anger sets off the fight-or-flight response, providing them with extra strength and stamina. Anger also focuses their minds on the game. Thoughts of grades and girlfriends, doubts and fears all fade into the background. The players thereby gain a greater sense of confidence in their ability to crush their opposition. The sense of righteousness generated by the anger makes the goal of winning the game seem like a holy war.

Now contrast this anger with anger that is driven by distorted thinking and an imaginary threat. David stops by a store on his way home to pick up some aspirin for a mild headache. Because it's a busy time of the day, there's a long line. As he waits, he thinks, "Why does everyone in the world have to choose now to come into this store? Look at that clerk—I can't believe how slow he is. People should be more efficient. No one cares about how they work anymore." This distorted thinking leads to the thought, "I'm going to be here forever and never get home." The minor but real inconvenience of waiting in line, along with the imagined threat of being mistreated by the store clerk, fuels his increasing anger.

As David's anger builds, it leads to more distorted thinking and focuses his mind on his immediate need: "I need to be served *now* so I can go home!" He is no longer aware of his headache and thoughts of his wife and children are forgotten as he gains a confident sense of righteousness about the injustice he is enduring. He begins to make loud comments about how slow the line is moving, and about the incompetence of the clerk. He doesn't care whether his actions are appropriate. He only knows he must get what he wants immediately. It's only later, while writing about this incident in his anger journal, that he realizes how inappropriate both his thoughts and his actions were.

Because anger causes us to forget about thoughts and emotions unrelated to the identified threat and because it generates a strong sense of confidence, we often use anger as a defense mechanism.

ANGER AS A PSYCHOLOGICAL DEFENSE MECHANISM

A psychological defense mechanism is a habitual and often unconscious mental process that reduces our awareness of internal or external stress, pain, or danger. The development of defense mechanisms is usually the result of an unconscious process that took place when we were young. Typically, a child who is experiencing a painful situation does something, such as become angry, that reduces awareness of the pain. Eventually, after many repetitions of this experience, the behavior that reduced awareness of the pain becomes an automatic conditioned response. The more the response is repeated, the stronger and more automatic it becomes. This process of stumbling upon a behavior that has a reward, and thus repeating it, is how you, as a child, learned many things, both useful and self-defeating.

Anger causes us to become less aware of weakness and other emotions we are experiencing so we often use it to block overwhelming or unacceptable emotions or experiences or to gain a feeling of being strong when we are weak and vulnerable.

Defending Against Overwhelming Childhood Emotions and Experiences

If you have learned to escape from painful emotions by becoming angry, you will tend to experience inappropriate anger whenever you are time tunneling, because at these times you re-experience painful emotions from the past. Sharon is a good example. Like all children, she had a natural desire to please and to be close to her parents, but she found it impossible to please her mother. No matter what chore she was given, something was always wrong with how she did it. This criticism was especially painful because her mother was emotionally distant and only rarely responded to Sharon in a warm and nurturing manner. As the overwhelming pain of her mother's disapproval and distance became associated with making mistakes, a conditioned response developed in Sharon. Making a mistake as an adult caused her to time tunnel and re-experience this painful sense of inadequacy from the past. Becoming angry allowed her to cover up these feelings and gave her a feeling of strength and control. Using anger as a defense had become a powerful and automatic response. Unfortunately, however, it usually resulted in inappropriate and self-defeating behaviors.

David also used anger to defend against painful emotions from the past. As a child, he grew up in a family where both of his parents, like Sharon's, were fairly distant and unable to nurture their children. When he tried to get emotionally close to his parents, he tended to be ignored. As a result, tremendous hurt and pain became associated with intimacy. One way in which David was able to experience emotional intensity with his parents was to fight with them. This is one of the reasons he was so rebellious. Acting out his pain was what rewarded him with connection. While the attention he got was negative, it was better than nothing. It wasn't until he became involved with sports that he experienced positive relationships. Since this experience was usually connected with his ability to perform, it exaggerated the importance of performing well.

As an adult, David wanted to be close with his wife, but whenever they got too close emotionally, the old association of intimacy with pain would set off loud unconscious alarms that caused him to create distance. Without realizing it, he was time tunneling and reacting to her as if she would treat him like his parents if he tried to get close. Of course, becoming angry is not the only way to escape uncomfortable feelings. Sometimes David created distance by saying or doing something that made his wife angry. Other times he would simply become busy with a chore.

His association between intimacy and pain also made it difficult for David when someone else was experiencing strong negative emotions. Whenever he was watching a movie or television program where the characters were portraying tenderness and acceptance of one another, David would begin to feel uneasy. He would make a joke, discuss something unrelated to the story, or find a reason to leave. Because images like these triggered the pain associated with intimacy, he immediately took action to protect himself. Of course, if you were to ask him why he was uncomfortable with such programs, he would say something such as "I'm feeling fine. This program is boring."

Using Anger to Feel Strong

In Chapter 3, we saw that frustration, helplessness, inadequacy, and confusion are often described as emotions, but are really descriptions of a particular situation or condition. Frustration means you are unable to obtain something you want. Helplessness and inadequacy mean you are unable to do something you want to do. Confusion means you don't understand something. These situations can trigger a wide range of emotions, such as anger, anxiety, sadness, or boredom. For people with a need to always be strong and in control, anger is a common response.

Alex is such a person. He learned while growing up that men should be strong and in control. Frustration and helplessness were unacceptable in his home. As a result, when he was frustrated or didn't understand something, he would become angry. Anger made him feel strong, which allowed him to block these "unacceptable" experiences from his awareness. While the need to be strong and in control is very common among men, and is often seen as a masculine trait, many women, like Sharon, also learn this while growing up.

When Alex's girlfriend decided to break off their relationship, he experienced a tremendous sense of loss. However, because it was not "manly" to grieve, he suppressed these feelings and covered them up with anger. He dwelled on how unfair she had been to him, recalling almost obsessively things she had done that had hurt him. The recurring thoughts about this relationship generated episodes of inappropriate anger that began to interfere with his work and friendships.

During one therapy session, Alex finally admitted how hurt and sad he felt, and he became tearful with sadness. Because of the childhood message that men don't cry or show sadness, he was embarrassed by his show of emotion, but with some reassurance that it's normal and healthy to experience sadness, he talked about his feelings of loss and loneliness. During the next two weeks, when he began to think angry thoughts about his ex-girlfriend, he would recall our session and that he really felt sad and lonely. Usually his anger would disappear and be replaced with sadness. While sadness is not a comfortable feeling, it was appropriate for his situation. What surprised Alex was that, even though he was sad, he was now able to think much more clearly. He was also making better decisions at work and in his personal life. After several weeks, he had become interested in a new relationship and felt much better. In the past, he would have brooded for months after the breakup of a relationship. He was surprised at how quickly he recovered from this loss.

THE PRICE OF USING ANGER AS A DEFENSE

Sharon, David, and Alex all behaved as they did in these incidents, because as children, anger offered them an escape from painful situations. For each, a childhood means of coping with a difficult situation became a problem in adult life. Using anger to feel strong or to avoid painful emotions usually results in one or more of the following six negative consequences.

Anger prevents you from dealing with the source of the problem.

Alex's experience with the breakup with his girlfriend is a good example of anger used this way. The problem he faced was twofold: the hurt associated with the loss of someone he cared for, and the loneliness and sadness of being alone. As long as he kept himself angry, he did not have to address either of these problems. Only when he allowed himself to grieve the loss was he was able to move on and find a new relationship. Similarly, becoming angry so you can feel strong and in control—when in fact, you are helpless, frustrated, or confused—does nothing to solve the problem facing you. It offers only a temporary escape and can often make things worse.

Anger keeps you from correcting distortions in your thinking.

As we have seen, anger interferes with our ability to reason. Ironically, this often occurs when the need to think clearly is most important. In addition, black and white thinking—coupled with the sense of righteousness generated by anger—makes it difficult to identify and challenge distorted thinking.

Anger keeps you helpless by postponing problem solving.

The interruption of your ability to think clearly coupled with an increase in distorted thinking and sense of self-righteousness, make it difficult to engage in meaningful problem solving. Instead, you focus on crushing whomever or whatever is causing the perceived threat. The idea of agreeing to a reasonable compromise feels like defeat, even though it's usually not.

Anger keeps you from processing and releasing painful emotions.

As we saw earlier with Alex, anger interferes with the natural grieving process. When we experience a loss, grieving enables us to let go of the loss and move on. At first, our thoughts connected with the loss trigger painful feelings of sadness, anger, and possibly loneliness. We don't know how it happens, but thinking and talking about a loss and feeling the accompanying pain helps to lessen these uncomfortable emotions. Eventually the event becomes simply information about something that happened in the past and no longer triggers painful emotions. When you do not allow yourself to go through this grieving process, the suppressed emotion tends to smolder in the unconscious. Because you are using much of your mental and emotional energy to block your awareness of it, you have less energy available to deal with the events going on around you. The stronger your emotions, the more this is true.

Anger poisons relationships.

Explosive anger drives people away and causes them to erect emotional walls to protect themselves from the angry person. Anger that is nursed can lead to resentment. Suppressed anger often incites passive-aggressive actions and can trigger anxiety and depression. All of these reactions tend to poison relationships and prevent you from enjoying life.

Anger increases the overall amount of pain you experience.

When you use anger to avoid experiencing painful emotions, you decrease the intensity of the pain, but you greatly increase the overall amount of pain you experience. The two diagrams show how this works.

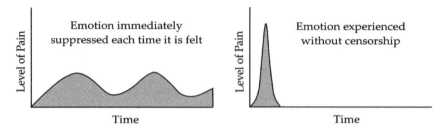

The diagram on the left shows what happens when a feared or unacceptable emotion is suppressed. Notice that the level of pain felt remains low but continues for a long time. The diagram on the right represents what happens when you fully experience an emotion. The level of intensity is much higher, but you feel the emotion for a much shorter time. The total amount of pain experienced can be expressed as the shaded area under each line. Notice that the total amount of pain experienced when suppressing an emotion is much greater than the amount experienced when an emotion is not suppressed. When you experience all of your emotions, you are not only more effective, but you experience less overall pain.

Learning to Experience All of Your Emotions

Your emotions, as a child, flowed freely through you. You were happy one moment, angry the next, then sad, then happy again. One of the tasks of parenting is to teach children to manage their emotions in healthy ways and behave appropriately. Unfortunately, many children are left on their own to figure out how to deal with their emotions. Many others have parents who are unhealthy role models. Sometimes a child's strong-willed or oppositional nature leads him or her to make poor choices when confronted with the problems of growing up. It's no wonder that so many people learn to avoid painful emotions.

When they block awareness of their emotions with anger, anxiety, depression, work, drugs, or anything else, they also block awareness of the need that is not being met. When you were young this might have been the only escape available to you, but as an adult, you now have choices and abilities you didn't have as a child.

Your adult ability to reason, along with the experience and knowledge you have gained, also allow you to experience safely the emotions and unmet needs that were overwhelming to you as a child. You will not go crazy or fall apart. While grief, sadness, embarrassment, and other painful emotions can be intense at times, the period of intensity is usually fairly short. Allowing yourself to experience them causes them to dissipate and enables you to use all of your emotional and mental energy to address events in the present.

One of the themes of this book is that negative emotions are simply a message indicating that a need or desire is not being met. When you fail to listen to the message of your emotions—that a need exists—the unmet need doesn't just go away. If you don't take action and address it, it sends stronger and stronger signals to you via intense emotions, until you do become aware of it. Unfortunately, if you become aware of your needs only when your emotions are intense, you tend to react inappropriately. This often leads to ineffective and self-defeating behavior.

The solution to this self-defeating cycle is to "reconnect" with your emotions in such a way that you can identify both what you're feeling and the need that is generating the emotion while the emotion is still at a low level. It's important for you to be able to determine whether the need is something you desire, a threat, or a loss so that you can develop a course of action that is appropriate for meeting the need. You can reconnect with your emotions and experience them at a low level in three ways:

Develop a more extensive vocabulary for describing your emotions.

Just as a musician enjoys subtleties in music that untrained people miss, people with rich emotional vocabularies are aware of differences between emotions and can detect them at lower levels than those who only use a few words to describe emotions. Developing a list of words that describes various emotions is a good way to develop a wider vocabulary.

Identify physical sensations and behaviors that represent specific emotions.

Four groups of negative emotions are frequently covered by anger. The first is anxiety and fear. In Chapter 2, you learned that these are the flip side of anger in that they also are a response to a threat. Since anxiety and fear are a response to a threat that you might not be able to meet, they are often unacceptable for a person who always needs to be strong and in control. The second group, embarrassment and shame, are triggered by the interpretation that you have done something wrong or that something unacceptable has happened to you. Someone who always needs to be right and make no mistakes usually finds these emotions difficult to experience. The third group, disappointment and sadness, is triggered by the interpretation that you have lost or are unable to obtain something you want. These emotions are especially difficult for people who need to be able to solve all of life's problems—as a way to be in control. The fourth group is loneliness and hurt which are triggered either by a lack of a relationship or by the disruption of a relationship.

As you identify the behaviors and sensations associated with these emotions, make a note of them in your journal. Whenever you notice yourself doing one of these behaviors or experiencing one of the sensations you have listed, ask yourself if you are currently experiencing the emotion that has been associated with it in the past. When you are, you will probably immediately become aware of the painful emotion. You might also become aware of the event that has triggered it. When this happens, do not run away from the experience. Instead, allow yourself to feel the emotion, keeping in mind that as an adult you can control emotions that once seemed overwhelming. You might also find it useful to write about emotional events in your journal.

David realized that whenever he was sad or disappointed, he spent long periods of time doing simple tasks such as weeding, playing computer games, or mindlessly watching television programs. On one occasion, he noticed that he had spent his entire Saturday playing a repetitive game on the computer. At first, he wasn't sure why. Then he remembered that the previous day he had lost a potential customer whom he had worked very hard to gain. At the time, he remarked, "That's just life," shrugged it off, and continued with his work. As he recalled this event, however, he became aware of how disappointed he was. He spent ten minutes writing about his efforts and disappointment. The next day, he was again feeling good and engaged in his normal activities. In the past, after a disappointment like this, he would have wasted several days doing meaningless activities. By taking time to consciously process his emotions, he was able grieve his loss and move on much more quickly. Of course, a major loss such as the loss of a valued job or the death of someone close to you would take longer to process.

Identify recurring situations where you act inappropriately.

If you repeatedly act inappropriately in a given type of situation, this situation is probably triggering emotions you wish to avoid. For example, whenever Sharon was fearful that something bad might happen to her children, such as being hit by a car or falling from a slide, she noticed that she immediately became angry and would give them a safety lecture. She realized that her anger toward her children was actually a mask for her concerns about their safety.

When you identify such recurring situations, remember that emotions are just messages that you have business to take care of. If you are experiencing emotions because something has caused you to time tunnel, allowing yourself to experience the emotion and using the "What's happening? What's real?" technique (described in Chapter 8) will probably be sufficient to identify the events from the past that are causing it. If you are experiencing a loss, your work is to grieve that loss no matter how small or large. If there is a real threat, you need to decide how to address it.

Sharon applied these ideas to her tendency to become angry whenever she was concerned about her children's safety. When she noticed herself becoming angry and beginning to lecture her children about safety, she would take a short time-out. During this time, she would ask herself, "Am I covering up my fear with anger?" Usually, she would become aware of either of a childhood fear or a real concern in the present. She also often became aware of how her mother had reacted when she was little and realized that she was just following her mother's poor example. After reminding herself that she was an adult and could choose different ways of responding, Sharon would then consider the danger that had triggered the reaction. If it was not important, she would dismiss it. If it was a valid concern, she would wait until she cooled down, and then talk to her children about it. The big difference was that she now was able to speak calmly and express her concern, so they experienced it as teaching rather than as punishment. This, in turn, allowed them to be more responsive to Sharon's words.

BEHAVIOR AS CODED MESSAGES

Misinterpreting the behavior of our loved ones is a common cause of inappropriate anger toward them. Often, we misinterpret their behavior due to the fact that we view it as coded messages. Most of the time, we are not consciously aware of the fact that we are interpreting their behavior in this way. However, this phenomenon plays an important part in all human interactions. The coded messages that are especially important are our 'language of love.' As we grow, we learn to identify specific behaviors as indicators that others care for us. We then tend to show caring to our loved ones by behaving similarly. We also look for these behaviors to determine whether others care for us. If a given behavior tells you that a person doesn't care, it can cause you to become angry in order to defend yourself against the pain of rejection. Unfortunately, behaviors that mean caring to one person can often mean something quite different to another person.

Carmen's case provides a good example. Carmen's mother expressed her love through hugs, touching, and reaffirming how precious Carmen was. Carmen's husband was raised in a home where there was little touching and people rarely complimented each other. Instead, his parents showed love by doing things for others. They were hard workers and very responsible. They would attend all of their children's school and sports activities, and they always took care of their children's needs, from helping with homework to buying a new pair of shoes. Of course, Carmen's parents also did these things for Carmen, but it was a secondary way of showing love. For her husband's parents, it was primary.

Carmen, following the pattern in her family, often told her husband that she loved him and freely displayed affection through hugs and touching. While he enjoyed this, he rarely initiated this type of intimate contact. Like his parents, however, he was a hard worker and always tried to take care of Carmen's material needs. His focus on being responsible and solving problems was how he showed his love. Unfortunately, because Carmen was looking for him to demonstrate love for her in the same way that she was expressing it, she often felt unloved. While she appreciated her husband's sense of responsibility, it did not communicate his love in a way that she could relate to. In turn, this caused her to time tunnel and to re-experience the isolation of her parent's farm. Sometimes, she would even react by pouting, like a child. Other times when she experienced sadness or anger, she quickly covered it up by becoming busy.

One of the challenges in marriage is to learn your partner's "language of love," so you can express your love in a meaningful way. Carmen needed to learn ways to communicate her needs more effectively while also understanding that verbal expression and touching were like a foreign language to her husband. While he could learn it, it was not his native way of communicating love. When he failed to show love in a way that was meaningful, Carmen needed to learn how to stay in the adult present and ask for what she wanted.

Identifying Coded Messages
Here are two ways to identify behaviors that serve as coded messages for you.

Identify how you show caring.

The second way to identify coded messages is to answer the question, "How do I show my partner that I love him or her?" The things you do to show others that you care usually are the same behaviors that you look for to see if others care for you. When I asked Carmen how she showed her husband that she cared, she said, "I tell him I love him. I give him lots of hugs and try to be affectionate. I also do little things I know he enjoys, like making him food that he likes." These are the same behaviors whose absence in him caused her to feel hurt. Carmen discussed with her husband how important these ways of expressing love were to her. Like most couples, he hadn't realized how his partner was feeling. Carmen then asked him what made him feel loved. Some of the things he mentioned, such as helping him put a work report together when he was running late, were equally surprising to her. As each learned more how to show the other how much they cared, both found their love for one another deepening. This does not mean that they did not slip into old patterns from time to time—they did. However, they now had a way of discussing this aspect of their relationship and meeting more fully their need to feel loved.

Identify recurring situations where you over-react that are due to coded messages.

This is actually similar to the third approach for experiencing all of your emotions (see previous section). The only difference is that, in recurring situations where you overreact, you ask yourself, "Am I overreacting because the situation contains the coded message that this person does not care for me?" Occasionally, David was late getting out of the house and found that he had misplaced his keys, business papers, or some other item he needed. If his wife and children did not get up and help him, he would become very angry. The fact that his anger was out of proportion to the situation was an indication that for him, others not helping meant they didn't care about him. I asked him what he usually did when his wife or children were having difficulty with something or couldn't find something they needed. He said he usually would stop what he was doing and try to help. The main way David's father showed love was through solving problems and being helpful. David was now following his father's example and expecting others to respond in the same way. When they didn't, it was a loud message that he didn't matter. Most of us tend to show and look for love in ways that are similar to those used by our parents.

Summary of Key Ideas

1. The motivation generated by anger has four different aspects: an increased focus on our needs or wants, a greater sense of confidence, a sense of righteousness, and a reduced awareness of all other emotions.
2. A psychological defense mechanism is a mental process that prevents us from being aware of an internal or external stress, pain, or danger.
3. Anger is frequently used to block emotions or experiences that were overwhelming as a child or that are considered unacceptable.
4. Anger that is used to feel strong or to avoid painful emotions or difficult realities can (1) prevent you from dealing with the source of the problem, (2) stop you from correcting distortions in your thinking, (3) keep

you helpless by stopping problem solving (4) prevent you from processing and releasing painful emotions, (5) poison your relationships, and (6) increase the overall pain you experience

5. There are three ways in which you can reconnect with your emotions and experience them while they are at a low level: (1) develop a more extensive vocabulary for describing your emotions, (2) identify physical sensations and behaviors that represent specific emotions, and (3) identify recurring situations where you act inappropriately.

6. We often view the behavior of others, especially our loved ones, as coded messages. This can cause us to misinterpret their behavior and trigger anger, in order to defend ourselves against the pain of rejection.

7. Two ways to identify your language of love are: (1) identify how you show caring, and (2) identify recurring situations where you overreact because the situation represents a negative coded message.

RECOMMENDED ACTIVITIES

Use a More Extensive Vocabulary for Describing Your Emotions

Here are common words used to describe positive and negative emotions.

Words that Describe Positive Emotions

At Ease	Excited	Passionate
Calm	Exhilarated	Pleased
Comfortable	Glad	Proud
Content	Happy	Relaxed
Delighted	Joyous	Relieved

Elated	Loving	Satisfied

Words That Describe Negative Emotions

Afraid	Discontent	Irritated
Angry	Embarrassed	Jealous
Anxious	Envious	Miserable
Ashamed	Frightened	Repulsed
Bored	Guilty	Resentful
Depressed	Hateful	Sad
Disappointed	Hurt	

The following three activities use these lists of words to help you increase your emotional vocabulary.

- Copy the list of emotion words onto a card that you can carry with you. Over the course of the next week, stop several times during the day and identify which of the emotions on the card you have experienced over the past few hours.
- After you have written about an angry incident in your journal, review the lists and identify those words that apply to your situation. Make a note of them in your analysis.
- When others are describing events that had a strong emotional impact on them, pay special attention. Listen to the words they use and the way they describe their emotions. As you listen, identify emotional reactions this person had that resemble ones you have had. If any of the words they use to describe their emotions are not on your list, add them.

Identify Physical and Behavioral Cues
That Indicate Specific Emotions

In this chapter, you learned about four groups of emotions that frequently trigger anger. Recall several times when you experienced anxiety or fear due to some uncertainty or danger. Describe in your journal how you acted during these times. After you have finished, do the same for times when you experienced shame and embarrassment. Then write about times when you were disappointed or sad because of a loss. Finally, write about times when you were lonely or hurt. As you write about these times, keep in mind that anger is only one way in which people avoid these emotions. Other common defenses against them are becoming involved with activities that keep you busy, depression, seeking excitement, or doing something that offers pleasure such as eating a treat. Here are David and Carmen's lists:

David

Anxiety/Fear: I have lots of energy and tend to pace, tap my fingers, or work at some trivial task. I might have long talks in my head about the event. These usually take the form of thinking about how I'll get even if such-and-such happens. As I'm thinking about something like this, I tend to get angry. Getting angry with those around me for little insignificant things can make it hard to live with me.

Embarrassment/Shame: I try to make a joke, become quiet, or get angry at something, unrelated to whatever is going on.

Disappointment/sadness Due to a Loss: If the disappointment does not involve another person, such as when a game I want to watch is canceled, I'll get angry and do lots of negative self-talk. If the disappointment is due to the actions of another person, I'll get angry and think lots of negative things about that person like how incompetent or unfair they are. Often I'll use the phrase

"They don't care about anything." If I'm really disappointed, I'll mope around the house and not do much. I'll watch a lot of TV or fiddle with the computer. I'll get angry at people for little reasons and stop talking. Sometimes I become mean and do hurtful things.

Loneliness/Hurt: Sometimes, I pick a fight with my wife or whoever is around me. Other times I'll react as I do when I'm sad or disappointed. I'll isolate myself from others and do nonproductive activities. When I was younger, I would sometimes take unnecessary risks such as driving too fast.

Carmen

Anxiety/Fear: I do lots of catastrophizing, thinking of the worst possible outcomes. I also do lots of negative self-talk of how awful it will be if the things I'm fortune-telling were to come true. I look to those around me for reassurance, much as a child would go to her mother.

Embarrassment/Shame: This depends on how embarrassed or ashamed I am. If it's something small, like when I told the joke all wrong to my friends at work, I'll turn red and be quiet for a while. Then I'm okay. If it's something big, such as the time I spilled my drink on the supervisor in front of everyone at the awards banquet, I'll spend days thinking about how embarrassed I was and put myself down. I also have a lot of "How can I face others?" types of thoughts.

Disappointment/Sadness Due to a Loss: When I've lost something small, I become upset and think about how terrible or awful it is. When it's something big, I might cry. I'll also think about how I can never get what I want or how unfair life is. When something happens at work, I'll think about it a lot afterward. My thoughts tend to take the form of "Why did this happen?" or "Why did that person do that?" When my husband or kids do something unkind or disappointing, I'll withdraw and think a lot about how hurt I am and how they don't care about me. Sometimes, I'll also think about how useless or worthless I am. I might also cry depending on how disappointed I am.

Loneliness/Hurt: I'm pretty direct when I'm lonely. I go to my husband and tell him I'm feeling blue and need a hug, or I might call my mom and chat for a while. I'm less direct when I'm feeling hurt. I often mope around for a while. If the person who hurt me is my husband or someone I know well, I'll eventually say something and we'll make up. If it's someone I don't know well or someone like my supervisor at work, I'll dwell on it and tell myself how awful it's. Often I'll tell my husband or someone in my family about it. This usually makes me feel better.

Begin Identifying Emotions More Accurately

Write the following list of words on a card you can carry with you:

Situation/Condition	*Possible Emotional Reaction*
Frustration	Anxiety/fear
Helplessness	Shame
Inadequacy	Embarrassment
Confusion	Anxiety/Fear
Disappointment	Sadness due to a loss

The words on the left are situations or conditions that can trigger anger. The words on the right are possible emotional reactions to these situations that many people use anger to avoid. During the next two weeks, whenever you experience anger, take out your card and look at the left-hand column. Ask yourself, "Am I experiencing one of these?" If the answer is yes, take a short time-out and go somewhere where you can be alone. If this is not possible, take a few moments to calm yourself down and remind yourself that your anger is just a defense mechanism for this situation.

If you can take a time-out, go to a place where you will not be disturbed and allow yourself to experience the emotion that triggered your anger. If you are frustrated, helpless, inadequate, or confused, identify the emotion other than anger that has been triggered by this situation. Keep in mind that any of these triggers can result in any of the emotions. One person might be disappointed at their inadequacy, another embarrassed, and so on. Learn to identify your triggers.

As you become aware of the emotion underneath your anger, identify one or two similar situations from your childhood where you experienced this same underlying emotion. As you recall them, think about how your parents and others around you responded. If you recall events that evoke strong emotions, use the "What's happening? What's real" technique to remind yourself that these events happened long ago. You are now an adult in a very different world, with many abilities and choices that you did not have when you were young.

Next, think of situations as an adult that are similar to the ones you identified from childhood. Were you also experiencing this unacceptable emotion at these times? If so, did you use anger to escape from it? Did you act inappropriately? If so, what would have been a more appropriate response? Record your discoveries in your journal.

Explore Your "Language of Love"

As we have seen, we often decide whether someone cares for us by interpreting this person's behavior as a coded message. Our interpretation often assumes that others show love in the same way that we do. Misinterpreting behavior because of this false assumption is a common cause of inappropriate anger toward loved ones. Take time this week to make a list of the things you do to show love. Try to be as specific as you can. The ways in which we show love usually are also the things that make us feel loved when others do them. Here are lists from David and Carmen:

David

Taking care of things around the house.

Helping when my wife or children need something such as a ride somewhere.

Saying thank you.

Offering to read the rough drafts of her reports and offer comments.

Making sure the kids and I are quiet when she goes to bed early.

Making coffee Saturday morning while she sleeps in.

Carmen

Hugs.

Affectionate touches, stroking.

Saying I love you.

Making special dishes that my husband or children like.

Asking how he spent the day.

Stopping what I'm doing and looking at him when he talks.

Being together even if we are doing something different.

During the week, ask your partner to make his or her own list. (If he or she is unwilling to do this or you are reluctant to ask, make a list on your own of how you think this person shows caring.) Compare your lists, and note ways in which you are the same as well as how you differ. Keep in mind the principle that the things you do to show you care tend to be the things you look for in others to see if they care.

When working in your journal, take a moment to see if any of the angry incidents you've recorded were due to your interpreting your loved one's behavior as saying "I don't care." When this is the case, remind yourself that behaviors that have a high emotional value to you might not mean the same thing to the other person.

Apply the Concepts from this Chapter to Your Journaling

Continue to write about incidents when you become angry, using the same procedure you used in the last chapter. In addition, add one more section after your description of your actions, titled "Was I feeling any emotion other than anger?" Your goal is to identify such emotions. The format for this week's journaling is as follows:

Date
Incident:
Level of Arousal ___ *, Level of Aggression* ___
Thoughts:
Actions:
Was I feeling any emotion other than anger?
Five Questions:
1. *What exactly did this person do that triggered my anger?*
2. *What needs or wants caused this person to act in this way?*
3. *What beliefs or aspects of this person's past (hurts, losses, successes, fears, lack of skills, etc.) influenced this behavior?*
4. *Considering the above, how could I have responded in a different and more effective manner? How might a positive role model have behaved?*
5. *Were any negative labels, family role models, or incidents from the past affecting this situation?*

Rational Challenges
    Here are two examples from Sharon and Alex's journals.

Sharon

Saturday, October 25

Incident: My girls were playing in the front room on a rainy Saturday afternoon. I walked in and saw one balancing on one foot on a chair, trying to reach something high on a bookshelf.

Arousal — 5, Aggression — 5

Thoughts: "Look at what she's doing, she's going to pull all the books off the shelf, spill them on the floor and ruin them. Then she's going to fall down and break her neck. These children don't have any sense at all. I have to watch them day and night."

Actions: I exploded and scolded her because she might spill books and damage them. I then yelled at them both for making such a mess in the front room.

Was I feeling any emotion other than anger? I was frightened when I first came in and saw what was going on due to the possibility that she might fall. I then covered my fear with anger.

Five Questions:

1. *What exactly did this person do that triggered my anger?*
   She did something stupid that was dangerous and that could damage property.

2. *What needs or wants caused this person to act in this way?*
   She wanted a book from the top shelf.

3. *What beliefs or aspects of this person's past (hurts, losses, successes, fears, lack of skills, etc.) influenced this behavior?*
   She just wanted the book and figured out how to get it as best she could. She's just a child and doesn't know any better.

4. *Considering the above, how could I have responded in a different and more effective manner? How would a positive role model have behaved?*
   I could have simply told her to stop and get down. Then I could have asked her what she wanted and showed her how to get it in a safe way. While doing this, I could have expressed my concerns about danger and calmly explain why what she was doing was not a good idea. This is one of those recurring

patterns where I need to make sure the children are safe then put everything else on hold until I calm down. My friend, Karen, is really good at handling situations like this. I remember how she spoke to her son the other day, when he was hanging from a tree in the park in a dangerous way.

5. *Were any negative labels, family role models, or incidents from the past affecting this situation?*

My reaction was exactly the same as my mother's in situations like this. I used to hate her acting this way. I bet my children respond the same way.

Rational Challenges

"Look at what she's doing, she's going to pull all the books off the shelf, spill them on the floor and ruin them. Then she's going to fall down and break her neck." This is catastrophizing. While she could damage something and hurt herself, she has more ability than I often give her credit for. What really triggered my exaggerated reaction was my fear, because there was a small but real danger in what she was doing.

"These children don't have any sense at all." Actually, both girls are very smart. They're just children and don't know all of the things I sometimes expect them to know. Times like these are an opportunity to teach them how to do things more safely.

"I have to watch them day and night." This is another magnification based on my fears. I don't have to watch them every minute. In fact, I've left them on their own lots of times, and they do well. While the way she was trying to get the book was dangerous, the truth is that she probably would have been fine. I probably wouldn't have even known what she had done if I hadn't walked in at that moment.

Alex

Thursday, November 3

Incident: I was at my parents' house with my brothers helping with yard work and doing some minor repairs. I made a mistake and my brothers made fun of me.

Arousal — 5, Aggression — 5

Thoughts: "I can't stand it when they do this. Why don't they leave me alone? Everyone's always picking on me. They just wait for me to fall on my face so they can stand there and laugh at me. It just isn't fair."

Actions: I became angry but kept calm on the outside. I immediately recalled a very embarrassing time for my brother that made him squirm. My other brother and I started laughing at that. Then we resumed our work.

Was I feeling any emotion other than anger? I was embarrassed at first but really got into my anger as I started to get even.

Five Questions:

1. *What exactly did this person do that triggered my anger?*
   One of my brothers made fun of me. Then both of them started laughing.

2. *What needs or wants caused this person to act in this way?*
   As kids, we were always competing with one another over everything. Because I'm the oldest, I usually won. Actually, I used to be pretty mean to both of them. I was pretty good at teaming up with one against the other, as I did at my mother's house. Both of my brothers have always tried to trip me up whenever they can.

3. *What beliefs or aspects of this person's past (hurts, losses, successes, fears, lack of skills, etc.) influenced this behavior?*
   They both probably felt like they can't win against me. This is usually true. I'm pretty good at turning the tables on them. When I was young, it was easier because I was older and knew more. Now we're just caught in an old childhood pattern.

4. *Considering the above, how could I have responded in a different and more effective manner? How might a positive role model have behaved?*
   First, I could have reminded myself that small mistakes like the one I made are unimportant. Second, I could remind myself that

my brothers are still time tunneling back into the past and replaying our old childhood rivalries. It's time I grew up and quit playing that old game. Next time I'll refrain from getting even. I'll just agree that my mistake was dumb, laugh, and move on. I like the way Tony handles himself in these types of situations at work. He just laughs, changes the subject, and moves on.

5. *Were any negative labels, family role models, or incidents from the past affecting this situation?*

This was a good example of how our family ganged up on whoever was the weakest or most vulnerable. I remember many incidents like this while growing up. My brothers are still very much into being right and first in the pecking order. I don't need to do this anymore. I'm not a weakling or sissy if I make a mistake.

Rational Challenges

"I can't stand it when they do this." This is magnification. I can stand it. In fact, I stood it very well. I just didn't like it. What was happening was I was embarrassed.

"Why don't they leave me alone?" This is one of those disguised should/must rules: "They should leave me alone and not embarrass me." While it would be nice if everyone treated everyone else with kindness and respect, it does not always happen in the real world.

"Everyone's always picking on me. They just wait for me to fall on my face so they can stand there and laugh at me." First of all, this is a magnification. Everyone isn't always picking on me. It's a pattern primarily between me and my brothers. While it's true that our kidding can sometimes be pretty mean, we wouldn't want anything bad to happen to any one of us. In fact, we would be the first to help and defend each other. They are really on my side. This is just a negative pattern from when we were kids.

"It isn't fair." This is a true statement. Life isn't fair. My statement in this case was simply a wish for things to be different. I need to focus on what I'm going to do rather than on how unfair something is.

10

Learning New Ways
to Resolve Conflicts

C ONFLICT IS A normal and healthy part of every human relationship. Your needs and wants are often different from, and in conflict with, those of others. This natural conflict is a frequent and appropriate trigger of anger. Developing healthy conflict management skills allows you to use the energy and motivation generated in situations that trigger anger in a positive way. This enables you to meet your needs more effectively and enjoy closer and more positive relationships. Being more in control of yourself and more effective when dealing with conflict situations also generates a more positive self-image.

THREE STYLES OF CONFLICT MANAGEMENT

There are three basic styles of conflict management: nonassertive, assertive, and aggressive. You respond with a particular style because behavior is goal-oriented. Unfortunately, you are often unaware of the goal behind a particular behavior. As we have seen, the interpretation and decision-making processes that generate your emotions and drive your behavior are mostly unconscious. Here is a brief summary of these three styles, along with their underlying goal.

Nonassertive

The goal of nonassertive behavior is to avoid conflict. Frequent nonassertive behavior usually results in one or more of the following: loss of self-respect, a poor self-image, passive-aggressive behavior (getting back in indirect ways), a tendency to sulk or cry to get one's way, or the "seesaw" effect, in which a person swings back and forth between nonassertive and aggressive behavior. Many people are nonassertive in some areas of their lives but assertive in others. This is called situational nonassertiveness. Alex was usually nonassertive around coworkers, friends, and family, but he could be fairly assertive with customers and strangers. He could also be aggressive toward others, especially when he had been brooding over an issue.

Others are nonassertive in most areas of their lives. Carmen used this general nonassertive style for managing conflict. Such people often blame others for problems and fail to take responsibility for the quality of their lives, or they might do the opposite, which is to blame themselves for all their problems, and take the role of martyr.

There are two major problems with nonassertive behavior. First, though it succeeds in avoiding conflict with others, it almost always results in internal conflict and irritation because a need is not being met. Second, you are less likely to change relationships or people's behavior with nonassertive behavior, as it tends to reinforce the other person's unwanted behavior.

Assertive

The goal of assertive behavior is to satisfy your needs and wants and to resolve conflicts in a way that is satisfying to both you and others. The four main features of an assertive style are (1) the ability to express needs and feelings freely in a way that is self-satisfying as well as socially effective, (2) a focus on reasonable compromise rather than on winning, (3) the ability to negotiate reasonable changes and solutions, and (4) the ability to plan, "sell," and implement agreeable solutions. While some people might not respond well to an assertive style, most healthy adults respond positively.

Aggressive

The goal of aggressive behavior is to dominate and get one's own way. People who rely on an aggressive style, like Sharon and Alex, often feel guilt over their mistreatment of others. Their aggressive style tends to make others hostile and defensive. As with nonassertiveness, aggression can be either a situational or a general style.

These three styles form a continuum that can be summarized as follows.

Nonassertive
Goal: Avoid conflict
Behavior: I ignore my needs if they interfere with yours.

Assertive
> *Goal:* Resolve conflict in a mutually satisfying manner
> *Behavior:* I work for reasonable compromise so that some of both our needs are satisfied

Aggressive
> *Goal:* Win
> *Behavior:* I focus on satisfying my needs and ignore your needs if they interfere with mine.

FIVE GENERAL APPROACHES TO RESOLVING PROBLEMS AND CONFLICTS

Here are five general approaches to conflict management. The first two reflect a nonassertive style, the next two an assertive style and the last an aggressive style. Each has a time and place where it's the most effective one to use.

Conform to the Situation (Nonassertive Style)

With this approach, you do what others want, offering little or no resistance. This nonassertive approach is sometimes your best choice when you are in a "no-win" situation involving a person of higher rank or authority than you, such as an employer, or an inflexible bureaucracy where the benefits of fighting are not worth the trouble. It's also sometimes appropriate in situations where you value another person's friendship and the discomfort you feel is small.

Before David began working on changing his anger patterns, he would often get into heated arguments with his parents over trivial issues. As he began to examine his behavior and thoughts, he realized that his need to be right and have others think like him was the force behind many of these conflicts. Since he wanted to have a less stormy relationship with his parents, he began to tell himself the following before meeting with them: "My parents are rigid black-and-white thinkers. They will not change. I want to have a relationship with them where we aren't fighting and arguing all the time. I can have different beliefs and allow them to think what they want to think." David also learned to respond to comments with which he disagreed simply by saying, "I can see how you might think that." He would then change the subject. If either parent persisted on the topic that he disagreed with, he would find a reason to walk away for a short period of time. As he practiced doing these things, he found that he argued less during these visits and that his visits were becoming more enjoyable.

Withdraw from the Situation (Nonassertive)

This nonassertive approach could be your best choice when other approaches are not working, or when the conflict is becoming a destructive force in your life.

Sharon was working in a high-stress situation, where workers tended to quit or transfer after a short period of time. A high turnover rate is often an important sign that a job is unhealthy. When we first discussed her situation, Sharon believed that she "should" be able to make things work, even though the stress she was experiencing was having a negative effect on her. Her belief that she should always be strong and never show weakness made it difficult for her to consider transferring to another unit. As we talked about it, she began to see that transferring out of this unit would not be a sign of weakness and inadequacy. Instead, it would be a wise decision. In fact, emotionally healthy people are usually the first ones to recognize an unhealthy situation like this and leave.

Change the Situation Through an Assertive Approach (Assertive)

This is the preferred way to cope with most everyday conflicts. Unfortunately, David and Sharon tended to adopt an aggressive approach as their primary method for resolving conflict, while Alex and Carmen tended to use a nonassertive style. Learning to direct the energy and motivation generated by anger into an assertive style was an important goal for all four. You'll learn a simple but highly effective assertive approach later in this chapter.

Substitute a New Goal or Want for One That Is Clearly Impossible (Assertive)

This approach is often your best choice when you're dealing with a nonnegotiator and you are either unwilling or unable to motivate the nonnegotiator. Sharon's decision to transfer to another unit at her company is a good example of this approach. Her transfer allowed her to perform her job effectively and made life much less stressful.

Change the Situation Through an Aggressive Approach (Aggressive)

This approach is sometimes your best choice when life or property is threatened or you are dealing with an irrational person who respects only an aggressive approach. Fortunately, these types of situations are few in everyday life. One of the things that made David successful in his business was his ability to deal forcefully with suppliers when they did not follow through on promises. Unfortunately, his aggressive style also sometimes drove customers away.

While David and Sharon tended to overuse an aggressive style, Alex and Carmen found it very difficult to be firm in situations where an aggressive style was appropriate. Just as

Sharon held the belief that compromise or retreat was a sign of failure, Alex and Carmen held beliefs that viewed aggression as bad.

For Sharon, David, Carmen, and Alex, using inappropriate approaches resulted in the damaged relationships, missed opportunities, and unmet needs. As they learned when a given approach was most appropriate and as they became comfortable with the approaches they had formerly avoided, they found their ability to meet their needs and maintain important relationships increased tremendously.

COMMON ERRONEOUS BELIEFS ABOUT ASSERTIVENESS

In Chapter 6 we explored four common erroneous assumptions such as, "Life should be fair," that tend to trigger inappropriate anger. Similarly, there are several common beliefs that tend to generate aggressive or nonassertive behavior. Like the core beliefs described in Chapter 7, they are often not conscious beliefs but tend to be ideas that describe automatic behaviors. Several common examples are listed below. Notice that each focuses on the "worst possible" outcome of being nonassertive or aggressive. Check any that describe your behavior or how you have felt during conflicts. Remember the rule from Chapter 7: "If you act like you believe something, speak like you believe something, and think like you believe something, you believe it."

Beliefs That Generate Nonassertive Behavior
- If I speak up or assert myself, others could become angry or upset with me.
- If others become angry or upset, I might not be able to handle the situation.
- It's wrong and selfish to refuse the requests of others.

If I allow myself to be selfish in this way, it makes me a "bad" person.
- I must avoid asking questions or making statements that might make me look stupid or ignorant.
- If I speak up, others might not like me.
- I prefer others to be open and straightforward with me, but if I'm straight forward and open with others, I will hurt them.
- I am responsible for how others feel. (Common variation: I should be able to find a way of acting that does not hurt others.)

Beliefs That Generate Aggressive Behavior
- I must always be strong. People who compromise are weak.
- I must always be in control.
- Life is a win-or-lose game. If I don't win, I've lost.
- "Giving in" in any way, means I am weak and the other person has "won." It also means this person has taken advantage of me.
- My solutions and methods are best. If they are not accepted, I am a failure.
- People are always trying to take away what is mine. I must stay on guard and fight to keep what's mine.

Add any of the above items you checked to the list of negative core beliefs in your journal that you began as you worked through Chapter 7.

RIGHTS AND RESPONSIBILITIES

Just as inappropriate anger, aggression, and nonassertiveness are rooted in irrational beliefs, appropriate assertive behavior is rooted in a balanced set of beliefs about your rights and responsibilities. Nine basic rights and responsibilities are listed below. As you read through them, notice that each right has a corresponding responsibility printed in italics. Those who use inappropriate behavior tend to view these pairs in an unbalanced way. For example, those who tend to be aggressive, like Sharon and David, are overly focused on their rights and need to develop a stronger commitment to their responsibilities and respect for the rights of others. Those who tend to be nonassertive, like Carmen and Alex, tend to be overly aware of their responsibilities and need to develop a stronger belief in their personal rights. Take time now to consider each of the following. Place a check by any that are difficult for you.

1. I have the right to be treated with dignity and respect.
   I have the responsibility to treat others with dignity and respect.
2. I have the right to decide what is best for me.
   I have the responsibility to allow others to decide what is best for them.
3. I have the right to have and express my own feelings and opinions.
   I have the responsibility to express those feelings and opinions respectfully without insults or putting others down.
4. I have the right to ask for what I want and need.
   I have the responsibility to allow others to refuse my request even though I might not like being refused.
5. I have the right to say no without feeling guilty.
   I have the responsibility to allow others to say no.
6. I have the right to be listened to and taken seriously.
   I have the responsibility to listen to others and take others seriously.
7. I have the right to make mistakes.

I have the responsibility to accept the consequences of those mistakes.

8. I have the right to all of my human weaknesses and limitations without guilt or shame.
   I have the responsibility to be compassionate toward others' weaknesses without ridiculing or resenting them.
9. I have the right to do what is necessary to protect my physical and mental health even though this some-times requires non-assertive or aggressive behavior and discomfort in others.
   I have the responsibility to do this in a way that causes the least amount of harm to both myself and others.

Individuals who enjoy positive, healthy relationships live by this set of beliefs. Ultimately, these are the type of people you want in your life. When considering how others will re-spond to an assertive approach, remember the phrase: "When you use a truly assertive style, those who matter don't mind, and those who mind seldom matter."

HIT-AND-RUN SITUATIONS

One of the best places to begin developing an assertive style is in a simple situation where someone has clearly violated your rights or treated you disrespectfully. These types of situations are often called hit-and-run situations because they tend to happen quickly and unexpectedly They also violate your boundaries. A boundary is the limit you set on how much you disclose to others, how much others can influence you, and what you allow others to do to you.

Those who are non-assertive, like Alex and Carmen, often have very weak boundaries and find it difficult to set limits and respond to hit-and-run situations with an appropriate assertive reply. They might not even recognize these types of situations as violating their rights. Those who are aggressive, like Sharon and David, tend to have overly rigid boundaries that set limits in disrespectful and overly aggressive ways.

Five common hit-and-run situations are described below, along with suggestions for responding in an assertive rather than an aggressive manner. As you read each example, think of similar situations you have experienced in which you needed to set limits, and recall how you responded. If your response was timid, angry, or hostile, think of how you could have shown the other person firmly but calmly that you do not allow your rights or dignity to be disregarded. Write your responses in your journal.

Having the Wisdom of Your Choices Questioned
   Examples: "Do you really think that shirt suits you?"
      Do you think you should do that?"
   The best response to this type of question is simply to
      state your right and ability to make personal judg-
      ments.
   Assertive Responses: "Yes, I think it suits me just fine."
      "Yes."

Receiving Unwanted Advice
   Examples: "If I were you . . ." "You should . . ."
   While others are entitled to their opinion, you have the
      right to make decisions for yourself. Respond to un-
      wanted advice by stating this right in a tactful way or
      by denying the "if."
   Assertive Responses: "That might be right for you, but I . . ."
      "I can see how you would think that, but I . . ."

Vague Remarks, Criticism, or Insulting Labels

    Examples: "You seem to be defensive lately." "That was a dumb thing to do."

    Often the best response is a simple, polite, but direct refusal to accept the label. State your own opinion in a simple, direct sentence. If you think this person has good intentions, ask for concrete examples.

    Assertive Responses: "I don't think so." "That might be how it appears to you, but I don't agree." "Exactly what have I done that makes you say that?"

Questions That Invade Your Privacy or Are Embarrassing

    Examples: "Are you busy tonight?" "Maybe I shouldn't ask, but . . ."

    You do not need to respond directly to questions like these when they are asked in situations or by people to whom you would rather not respond. Instead, find out why the person is asking such a personal question. If it's being asked out of idle curiosity or with malicious intent, the person will probably back off. Occasionally there's a good reason for the question.

    Assertive Responses: "I really don't care to say." "Why do you ask?" "What did you have in mind?" "Why would you want to know that?"

Negative Predictions Based on Observations of Your Personality

    Example: "You're not skilled enough for the job."

    If you believe the person is insincere or simply a troublemaker, affirm your ability to judge your own strengths and abilities. If you believe the person is offering a sincere opinion, ask for clarification.

    Assertive Responses: "That might be how you see it, but I think I'll do just fine." "What skills do you believe that I lack?"

D.E.R. Scripts

Learning to set limits and to respond firmly but respectfully to hit-and-run situations is an important aspect of an assertive style. However, more complex situations require a different approach. Learning to use D.E.R. scripts is an effective way to address these situations assertively. The three letters represent the different parts of the script:

D = *Describe* the problem.
E = *Express* your thoughts or feelings.
R = *Request* what you want.

One general characteristic of an effective D.E.R. script is the use of "I statements." An "I statement" is a message that tells the listener what you see, think, feel, or want in an objective manner that does not assign blame or put the listener down. The statement you learned in Chapter 2, "I'm beginning to feel angry, and I need a time-out," is a good example of an "I message" A "you message" is a statement that assigns blame or puts the listener down.

Another general characteristic of effective D.E.R. scripts is that they are short. Your goal is to use one or two sentences for each of these three parts. The shorter and more direct your script, the better.

Here are Sharon, David, Carmen, and Alex's first attempts at writing D.E.R. scripts. Notice how they are vague and frequently use "you messages," while the final scripts that follow are clear and use simple "I messages."

Sharon to her daughter:
First Script with "You Messages":

Describe: The dirty dishes from last night have been sitting on the table all day.

Express: I can't stand it when you're so inconsiderate.

Request: What are you waiting for, a written invitation?

Final Script with "I Messages"

Describe: Last night's dishes have not been put into the dishwasher.

Express: I'm concerned that we might have a problem with ants like last week.

Request: I'd like you to load them now.

David to his wife while working on household finances:

First Script with "You Messages"

Describe: Don't you have anything better to do than bother me? You seem to think you're the only one who lives here.

Express: That talk-show host makes me crazy. How do you expect me to do this?

Request: You shouldn't listen to that anyway.

Final Script with "I Messages"

Describe: The radio is making it hard for me to think.

Express: I don't like that talk-show host and find him distracting.

Request: Would you listen to that in the other room?

Carmen to her husband:

First Script with "You Messages"

Describe: You never sit with me.

Express: It really hurts when you're so distant.

Request: Why can't you be nice to me?

Final Script with "I Messages"

Describe: It's been a while since I've sat with you.

Express: I'm feeling a little lonely right now.
Request: Could we sit together for a while?

Alex to his girlfriend:
First Script with "You Messages"
Describe: Why do you always try to annoy me by watching these stupid programs?
Express: It ticks me off that you're so inconsiderate."
Request: I wish you'd think of others instead of just yourself."

Final Script with "I Messages"
Describe: I don't like these types of shows.
Express: They bother me a lot."
Request: Could we watch something else?

Now, let's take a closer look at each of the three parts of a good D.E.R. script. Be sure to compare the above examples with these guidelines.

D: Describe the Problem.

Your goal in the first part of the script is to describe the problem you wish to resolve as clearly and objectively as possible. The more objectively you can describe the problem, the less likely you are to trigger defensiveness in the other person. Often this is difficult for people who come from families that used criticism and put-downs frequently. If this is true for you, pay special attention to avoid negative labels that ridicule or shame the other person, such as dumb, stupid, inconsiderate, or selfish.

Two common mistakes in descriptions are, engaging in mind reading, and attributing negative motives to the other person's behavior. When David said, "You seem to think you're the only one who lives here," and, "Why do you always try to annoy me," he was mind reading. Try to think of yourself as a scientist who is trying to describe what you see objectively, using words that have no emotional connotation. In addition, try to focus on only one well-defined behavior or problem. Avoid words that overgeneralize, such as never, always, and every. Take another look at the descriptions in the previous examples to see how they either violated or observed these guidelines.

E: Express Your Thoughts or Feelings

This part of the script is important when you are dealing with long-term problems or issues that are very important to you. However, for minor conflict situations, you can skip this part. For example, if you are returning a shirt that was not sewn properly to a store, you just need the description and request: "This shirt was not sewn properly. I'd like to exchange it for another."

When dealing with someone you don't know very well, it's often best to focus on your thoughts: "I'm concerned that I might be late." Or "I think that will be too small." When dealing with someone with whom you have a close relationship, expressing your feelings is often more effective: "I get anxious." Or "I was hurt."

When expressing what you think or feel, understatement is often best, as you need to focus on what you want rather than blaming or punishing the other person. This also helps to reduce the tendency to magnify and overgeneralize. As with your description, avoid mind reading or psychoanalyzing where you guess at the other person's, goals, attitudes, or intentions. Note how the examples either violate or use these guidelines for expressing thoughts and feelings.

R: Request What You Want

This is often the most difficult part of a D.E.R. script. It's usually easy for people to identify what they don't want, but all too often difficult to identify what they do want. When I first asked Sharon what she wanted from her daughter in the dishwasher situation, she said, "I want her to be responsible." In fact, she made several statements like this before she identified what she really wanted: "I wanted her to load the dishes right then." The same was true for David, Carmen, and Alex. It took each one several minutes to pinpoint exactly what he or she wanted because they were so focused on what was wrong. Because of this, it's often best to decide what you want before you compose your script.

As you develop your request, keep in mind that you cannot change the other person's personality or beliefs. Statements like "I want you to be more responsible" and "I want you to be nicer" are meaningless. Instead, describe a specific action you want performed or stopped. Do this as directly, clearly, and explicitly as you can.

SUMMARY OF KEY IDEAS

1. Conflict is a normal and healthy part of every human relationship because each person's needs and wants are often different from or in conflict with the needs of others.
2. People respond to conflict with one of three basic styles: nonassertive, assertive, or aggressive.
3. Five general approaches to resolving conflict are (1) conforming to the situation, (2) withdrawing from the situation, (3) changing the situation with an aggressive approach, (4) changing the situation with an assertive approach, and (5) substituting a new goal or

want for one that is impossible to achieve or causing harm.

4. Aggressive and nonassertive behavior is often rooted in irrational beliefs about assertiveness.

5. An assertive style reflects a balanced set of beliefs about one's rights and responsibilities.

6. Use D.E.R. scripts to develop an assertive style. The letters stand for *Describe* the problem, *Express* your thoughts or feelings, and *Request* what you want.

RECOMMENDED ACTIVITIES

Identify Beliefs and Attitudes that Block Assertiveness

Your beliefs and attitudes about conflict and the ways you resolve conflicts developed during your childhood. The following questions are designed to help you identify more clearly the models that influenced you and the behaviors you learned. Record your answers in your journal so you can refer back to them in the future.

1. How did each member of your family handle conflict?

2. How did you react to each person's style for handling conflict?

3. How did the adults in your childhood shape the way you deal with conflict?

   • What were you told about conflict? (*For example:* "Don't rock the boat," "People won't like you if you're nasty," "Ladies should always be polite," "Gentlemen don't fight.")

   • Did your brothers and sisters receive the same training and the same messages you did? If not, how was it different?

4. What are the core beliefs you developed about conflict as a result?

5. How did you get what you wanted?
   - What direct methods did you use to get what you wanted? (*For example:* asking or taking.)
   - What methods did you use to get what you wanted indirectly? (*For example:* hinting, whining, sulking, or having someone else ask for you.)
   - Did you get what you wanted in any other way?
   - Which of these methods do you use today to get what you want?
   - What were the core beliefs (positive or negative) about getting what you want that developed as a result of this?
6. When you were young, what did you say to yourself when you were in conflict with others?
7. What do you say to yourself now when you are in conflict with others?

After you have answered these questions, identify any irrational beliefs about conflict that interfere with your ability to be assertive. Then develop rational responses you can use to challenge them. Add these responses to your list of coping self-statements.

Practice Using "I Messages"

This chapter described the difference between "I messages" and "you messages." Review this description several times this week and practice stating simple requests using "I messages." If "I messages" seem awkward to you, remember that learning to use them is a mechanical process that simply requires repetition. Developing the habit of using them is simply a matter of practice. The rewards of learning this style of non-blaming, direct communication are well worth the effort.

Responding to Hit-and-Run Situations

During the next two weeks, record in your journal any hit-and-run situations where you had difficulty asserting yourself. Then develop an assertive response that uses the suggestions given in the chapter. If this is difficult for you, pay attention to how people with a positive, assertive approach respond to these types of situations. If you have a friend with this ability, ask this person how he or she would respond to situations that are difficult for you. Record any responses you like in your journal. As you do this exercise, remember that a given situation can have many different assertive responses that are appropriate. Your goal is to find one that fits your personality and that effectively sets limits. Keep in mind that more complex conflict situations or problems require a D.E.R. script.

Practice Creating D.E.R. Scripts

Create at least three D.E.R. scripts this week. Write them in your journal. They can be scripts either for past situations that you handled poorly, or as preparation for a conflict that you wish to address. After you create a script, take time to review the guidelines given in the chapter to see if your script follows them.

Continue to Record in Your Journal

While your main focus in this chapter is on developing a more assertive style, continue to spend at least two days each week recording incidents where you became angry. Use the same format, shown below, that you used in Chapter 9.

Date:
Incident:
Level of Arousal ___ , *Level of Aggression* ___

Thoughts:

Actions:

What emotions other than anger was I feeling?

Five Questions:

1. *What exactly did this person do that triggered my anger?*
2. *What needs or wants caused this person to act in this way?*
3. *What beliefs or aspects of this person's past (hurts, losses, successes, fears, lack of skills, etc.) influenced this behavior?*
4. *Considering the above, how could I have responded in a different and more effective manner? How might a positive role model have behaved?*
5. *Were any negative labels, family role models, or incidents from the past affecting this situation?*

Rational Challenges

11

More on Conflict Resolution

W HILE YOU ARE learning to replace an aggressive or passive style of behavior with an assertive one, keep in mind that others often resist your efforts to be assertive whenever your needs conflict with what they want. This is just the nature of conflict. Therefore, in addition to learning to be more assertive in asking for what you want, you also need to learn how to react in an assertive, nonaggressive manner to the natural resistance you encounter from others.

FIVE COMMON FORMS OF RESISTANCE

There are five common ways in which others resist requests. These tactics are listed below, beginning with the ones that are usually easiest to overcome. While people do sometimes choose one or more of these behaviors intentionally, for many it's an automatic behavior learned early in life as a way of self-protection.

When I discussed D.E.R. scripts in Chapter 10, I emphasized the importance of identifying clearly, what you want before you try to resolve a problem. This was used to create the "request" portion of the script. As you read the examples for each of the following tactics, notice that the key to keeping a discussion focused on seeking a solution is to repeat your request. Whenever you find that you are not sure what you want, take time to create a simple D.E.R. script in your mind to clarify this before you begin your discussion.

As you read these tactics, keep in mind that from time to time you probably use some of them to resist the requests of others and to protect yourself. As you read each description, place a check by any you use frequently. During the next few weeks, whenever you notice yourself using one of these tactics, decide whether you could accomplish the same goal more effectively by using a simple "I message" or a D.E.R. script.

Avoiding Discussion of Your Request

The simplest and most direct way to avoid dealing with a request is to simply postpone discussing it. When someone uses this tactic with you, you can usually overcome it either by pushing to discuss your request immediately or by having the other person specify a time and place to discuss it. When pushing to discuss your request immediately, a response called "Yes, but" works well. You have already seen this approach used in the description for hit-and-run situations (see Chapter 10). When you "Yes, but," you agree with the other person, then say, "but" or "however" to refocus on your need or perception. Sometimes it's useful to specify the consequences of not discussing your request.

Person: "I'm too busy to talk now."

You: "I can see that you're busy, but this is important and won't take long."

Person: "I'm too tired to talk now."

You: "When would be a good time for us to talk?"

A less direct method to avoid dealing with a request is to sidetrack the discussion with irrelevant comments or questions. You can respond by ignoring the distracting comment, by dismissing it with a short statement, or by giving a quick answer. Then refocus the discussion on your request by repeating it.

Person: "That reminds me. We need to talk about the car."

You: "You're right. However, let's discuss that after we decide about . . ."

Person: "Don't you have to go and pick up the kids?"

You: "Not yet. As I was saying, I would like . . ."

Challenging Your Description

Another way someone might avoid resolving a problem you raise is to challenge your description of the problem behavior or situation. In fact, this is one of the more common ways of sidetracking a discussion. When others have a different perception of what happened, discussing whose view is correct can become an endless and unproductive debate. The best way to avoid this challenge is to keep your goal—your request—in mind. Accept that others often see things differently and use a "Yes, but" response to acknowledge that your perception is different. Then return to your request.

Person: "That's not how I saw it."

You: "I can see that we view things differently. However, I would still like . . ."

Person: "You've got it all wrong."

You: "I understand that you feel I have it all wrong, but I still want to decide how we can . . ."

Refusing to Accept Responsibility

Another common form of resistance is to refuse to accept responsibility for either the creation or resolution of a problem. Here are four ways in which this is done.

Blaming

A person can blame either you or someone else for the problem behavior or situation. Since blaming is essentially a different description of the behavior or situation you're concerned with, your most effective response is to concentrate on your request and avoid focusing on who or what is to blame.

Person: "I didn't know it was important."

You: "That's not the issue. What I want is . . ."

Person: "John is the one who screwed everything up by not sending his request in on time."

You: "That might be the case. However, I still need you to . . ."

Person: "Nobody told me to do that."

You: "That's true, but, I still need . . ."

"Everybody Does It"

The argument that "everybody does it" avoids responsibility by dismissing your request as trivial. You can respond by acknowledging the other person's perception without endorsing it, then repeating your request ("Yes, but"); or you can redefine the situation in terms of your own needs. The claim that "everybody does it" is usually not true.

Person: "Everybody does it this way."

You: "That could be; however, I need . . ."

Person: "You're the only one in the office who doesn't like how I do things."

You: "That could be; but what I need is . . ."

Reinterpreting

Sometimes a person might respond to your description of a problem by stating that you either have misinterpreted the problem or lack important but relevant information about it. When this happens, a simple exchange of opinions or information might achieve your goal. However, people often reinterpret their behavior by saying it was based on good intentions. They use the argument that no harm was intended in order to avoid responsibility for doing anything about your problem. When this happens, use "Yes, but" to acknowledge the other person's stated good intention, then refocus on your request.

Person: "I didn't really mean it."

You: "That might be the case; however, I feel . . ."

Person: "I was just trying to help."

You: "I appreciate your wanting to help. However, what would really help would be to decide on how we can . . ."

Psychoanalyzing

Another way a person might challenge your description of a problem is to reinterpret the events in terms of a "psychological problem" or "character flaw" that you supposedly possess. Most such psychological explanations are inaccurate and simply a sophisticated form of name-calling. When someone is psychoanalyzed you, it's easy to become sidetracked since the explanation offered might sound logical on the surface or else trigger strong emotions in you. As with any challenge, avoid becoming involved in an argument over differing perceptions and refocus the discussion on your request. Depending on the person and situation, you may also want to affirm your own ability to assess your actions and personality with a simple and direct "I message" before you press on.

> *Person:* "You've really been getting pushy since reading that book on anger."
>
> *You:* "It has been easier for me to ask for what I want directly. Now, as I was saying . . ."
>
> *Person:* "I think you're just trying to control me."
>
> *You:* "I'm sorry you see it that way. What I really want is . . ."

Triggering Guilt or Embarrassment

When someone triggers guilt and embarrassment in you, it can seriously interfere with your ability to assert yourself. This was especially true for Carmen. On the other hand, Sharon, David, and Alex often used blaming that caused guilt or embarrassment in others as a mechanism for getting what they wanted.

Guilt and embarrassment are generated in others in four common ways. While our focus here is learning how to respond to behaviors that trigger blaming and embarrassment, be sure to note any of the following that you might use in your own actions.

Tears

When having a discussion with someone who is uncomfortable with strong emotions, tears can be very manipulative. As you learn to become more comfortable with your emotions, your ability to stay on track in the face of tears increases. However, if "water power" tends to make you feel so guilty or embarrassed that it's hard for you to assert yourself, write your D.E.R. script as a letter, email or text that can be read in your absence.

The best response to tears is simply to ignore them. Commenting on the other person's emotions can open the door to a long discussion of the other person's discomfort or unhappiness. If you believe you need to acknowledge that the other person is upset, do so as simply and gently as possible, then quickly refocus on your request.

> *Person:* (With tears) "You're making me feel like everything I do is wrong."
> *You:* "I'm sorry you choose to feel that way. However, I feel . . ."
> *Person:* (With tears) "You're making me so upset."
> *You:* "I can see that this is difficult for you. However, we need to decide how . . ."

Offended Martyr

A martyr reinterprets events so as to portray you as doing something inappropriate. Playing the offended martyr is sometimes combined with tears. Martyrs usually describe your behavior as being "mean" or "cruel." Refuse to accept this interpretation, and redefine your behavior objectively. Continue to redirect the discussion to your request, and do not become sidetracked by arguments over your motives.

> *Person:* "I've worked hard and done my best to help you and this is how you treat me."
> *You:* "I appreciate your efforts. However, it's important

that we figure out how we can . . ."

Person: "You're being so mean to talk to me like this."

You: "I can see how you might feel that way. The important thing is that we decide how we can . . ."

Excessive Apologies

A person who upon hearing your description of a problem offers excessive apologies can trigger guilt or embarrassment. When this is the case, simply accept the other person's apology and continue with your request.

> *Person:* "I'm so sorry! How could I do that? Please forgive me."
>
> *You:* "I accept your apology; but, we need to discuss how . . ." Or "I'm sorry you feel so badly. However, we need to decide . . ."

Physical Symptoms

This tactic is not very common, but the person uses distressing physical symptoms as a way to trigger sympathy and avoid discussing your request. If you assume responsibility for causing this person's physical symptoms, your guilt could even prevent you from confronting this person in the future. Respond in the same way as you would with someone who is trying to avoid discussing the problem. Either request a specific time when you could discuss the problem, or press to discuss it now in spite of the physical symptoms. If this person continues to use this tactic to avoid discussing the problem, send an email or text with a D.E.R. script that can be read in your absence.

> *Person:* "Let's not talk now. I have this terrible headache."
>
> *You:* "I know you're uncomfortable, but this won't take long" Or "When do you think you'll be feeling better?"

Intimidation

This section describes five common forms of intimidation. When faced with people who use them, people with explosive tempers like Sharon and David, tend to become angry and aggressive. Those who suppress anger, like Carmen and Alex, tend to back away from their assertive goal. In either case, intimidation can cause you to be ineffective and fail to get what you want.

When dealing with intimidating people, it's often helpful to meet them in a public place where other people are present. People usually behave better in public than they do in private.

Take time before meeting with them to recall how you react to this behavior. If this person causes you to time tunnel and triggers emotional responses from the past, use the "What's happening? What's real?" technique (described in Chapter 8) to keep yourself in the present. If their behavior has triggered distorted thinking in your previous encounters with them, take time to develop rational challenges that can help you maintain a realistic perspective and manage your own anger more effectively.

As you develop your rational challenges, review the list of rights and responsibilities in Chapter 10 to see if any of them would be important to include in your self-talk when dealing with this person. Developing a D.E.R. script can also help you stay focused on your goal. Keep in mind that nonnegotiators commonly use the tactics in this section. So, if these suggestions do not work, switch to those described in the next section, on nonnegotiators.

Verbal Abuse/Name-Calling

Verbal abuse takes many forms such as sarcasm, criticism, jokes, ridicule, insults, and swearing. It can be directed at you personally or at your ideas. The most effective response is to ignore the other person's bullying and continue pressing for what you want firmly but respectfully. If this is difficult for you, develop coping self-statements that will help you stay objective in the face of this type of intimidation.

When you choose to redefine insulting labels, do so in a restrained way. Otherwise, you could become involved in a fight that sidetracks you from your goal. One response is to use, "Yes, but." Another would be to label the insulting label for what it's, then quickly refocus on your request.

Becoming angry and punishing someone for his or her inappropriate behavior might make you feel better, but the intimidation has kept you from getting what you want. Learning to stay in control in the face of verbal abuse shows both, you and the other person, that you are not intimidated and that you do not allow others to control you. It also shows both of you that your goal remains important to you.

> *Person:* "Why are you bothering me with stupid things such as this?"
> *You:* (negative label is ignored) "It's important that we resolve the problem of . . ."
> *Person:* "You're just trying to be a kiss-up to the boss, aren't you?"
> *You:* "That may be how you see it, but we need to work out a way to . . ."
> *Person:* "What makes a stupid jerk like you think you can tell me what to do?"
> *You:* "Being insulting is not going to help. I'm not interested in trying to tell you what to do. I only want to solve the problem of . . ."

Hostile or Negative Body Language
People sometimes use facial expressions, body posture,

or tone of voice to let you know indirectly that your request is angering, boring, or hurting them or that they are not interested. The best approach is to simply ignore their nonverbal behavior and continue to press for what you want. If you do decide to comment on the nonverbal message, you might need to switch to listening skills (described later in this chapter) before continuing.

Person: (frowns and looks angry.)

You: (nonverbal message is ignored) "I appreciate your willingness to work this out. Now, what do you suggest we do about . . ."

Person: (the other person appears upset by what you are saying.)

You: "It seems that something is bothering you about this, but we need to discuss . . ."

Person: (the other person yawns while you are talking.)

You: (non-verbal message is ignored.) "What I want is . . ."

Person: (the other person begins to walk away while you're talking.)

You: "Excuse me. I wasn't finished with what I was saying. I feel that . . ."

Interrogation

Occasionally, someone might bombard you with questions that sidetrack you from your request. They could ask why the request is important to you or why you are feeling the way you do. You do not need to justify your emotions. As with other types of challenges, give a quick response or dismiss the question as unimportant. Then return to your request.

Person: "Why is this so important to you?"

You: "It just is. Now, as I was saying . . ."

Person: "Why do you feel so strongly about this?"
You: "I just do. Now, we need to decide . . ."
Person: "Do you really think this is necessary?"
You: "Yes. What I need is . . ."

Debating

A person with strong intellectual abilities, or who is knowledgeable about the issue that concerns you, could try to use his or her superior knowledge or logic to overwhelm you. This often takes the form of trivializing your problem or challenging your description. When this happens, simply state that while you understand that your concerns may seem illogical, it's just the way you feel and that is enough. Then proceed to press for your assertive goal. You do not need to justify or logically explain your emotions.

Person: "Why are you so concerned about this?"
You: "I just am. Now, how are we going to . . ."
Person: "If we're going to discuss this, I need to understand why you feel this way."
You: "I don't think I can explain it to you in a way that will make sense. However, this is something I need to resolve. So, how are we going to . . ."
Person: "You are being totally illogical."
You: "You're right. It is illogical. However, I still feel very strongly that . . ."

Postponing a Decision

A person who appears ready to listen and respond to your request but then postpones making a decision is using a subtle form of nonnegotiation. If you are not sure whether the postponement is sincere or merely a procrastinating tactic, you can grant one postponement, then use one of the two following approaches.

Set a Deadline for Making a Decision

If this person will not agree or continues to postpone making a decision, you are dealing with a nonnegotiator. Use the approaches for nonnegotiators in the next section.

Press for an Immediate Tentative Agreement

Your basic message is "I want a temporary agreement now that will continue to be in effect until we work something else out."

THE NONNEGOTIATOR

When you are trying to resolve conflicts, most of the resistance you encounter can be overcome with the approaches described in the previous sections. At the same time, people who continue to use the previous tactics to avoid resolving a conflict are nonnegotiators. In addition to those tactics, a really tough nonnegotiator might also resort to one or more of the following four tactics.

There Is No Problem

The nonnegotiator could simply refuse to accept that a problem exists. If you have a relationship with this person, you can try emphasizing how important the problem is for you.

> *Person:* "I just don't understand why this is so important."
> *You:* "I understand that this is not important to you. However, it's important to me that we . . ."
> *Person:* "I don't see where there's any problem to discuss."
> *You:* "I understand that you don't see any problem. However, I do feel strongly about this and want to figure out how we can . . ."

All Solutions Are Unacceptable

If the nonnegotiator continues to find every proposed solution unacceptable, try giving him or her the task of developing an acceptable solution. If they claim to be unable to think of anything, try setting a deadline for when a reasonable solution has to be ready for discussion.

> *Person:* "Nothing you've proposed so far will work."
> *You:* "Maybe you have some ideas that could be useful."
> *Person:* "I don't think anything you've suggested is workable."
> *You:* "Why don't we take a break and think about it? See if you can come up with few ideas that we can discuss after lunch."

The "Price" for Change Is Too High

A frequent tactic of nonnegotiators is to make unreasonable demands. Point out the unreasonableness of the demands while emphasizing the importance of resolving the conflict.

> *Person:* "I think that's the best way to resolve this."
> *You:* "It seems to me that you're asking for too much for your cooperation."
> *Person:* "That is what I need from you if you want me to get that done."
> *You:* "I don't think that's reasonable. We need to cooperate if we're going to resolve this."

A Refusal to Negotiate

Some nonnegotiators will refuse even to discuss what you want. When this occurs, point out the refusal to negotiate and press for a commitment to discuss your request.

If, after trying all these tactics, the other person continues to be a nonnegotiator, you have two choices. The first is to specify the negative consequences that you will take if the conflict is not resolved. Do not take this approach unless you are both *willing* and *able* to carry out the negative consequences you specify. If the nonnegotiator continues to refuse to cooperate but you do not do what you said you would do, this person will be even more unwilling to cooperate in future conflicts. If you decide that you are unwilling or unable to carry out negative consequences, your only other choice is to adopt one of the three nonassertive approaches discussed in Chapter 10: conform, withdraw, or substitute a new goal for the one you cannot achieve.

BECOMING AN EFFECTIVE NEGOTIATOR

While we all occasionally have to deal with nonnegotiators, most of the conflicts we encounter involve people who negotiate in good faith. Here are several negotiation skills that can increase your ability to resolve problems and conflicts successfully.

Active Listening

Active listening is a form of listening where you focus on identifying the issues that are important to the other person and communicating that understanding to him or her. One component of active listening that is essential for effective negotiating is paraphrasing—restating what the other person has said in your own words.

If this is difficult for you because you are busy thinking about the problem or rehearsing arguments you will use while the other person is speaking, practice mental paraphrasing. Whenever it's the other person's turn to speak, as you listen, restate in your mind what they are saying. We often do this when someone is giving us directions. Our internal dialogue is similar to this:

> *Speaker:* "Go two blocks south"
> *Listener's internal self-talk:* "Two blocks south."
> *Speaker:* "Take a right"
> *Listener's internal self-talk:* "Two blocks south then take a right."
> *Speaker:* "Go straight for a quarter of a mile and the store is on the left."
> *Listener's internal self-talk:* "Straight for a quarter of a mile and the store is on the left."

To establish that we heard the directions accurately, we then repeat back the directions—we paraphrase them verbally. This process is very different from how most people listen and comment during conflict situations. This conversation between David and his wife is typical of conversations where one person is not really listening to what the other is saying.

> *Wife:* "I wish we could do more things together."
> *David:* "You know I need time for myself. It seems you're always pushing me to do things I don't want to do."
> *Wife:* "I really don't want to make you to do anything you don't want to do. I just want to see us function as a couple more often and go out and do something we both enjoy."
> *David:* "It's important for me to have free time; like on Monday when I watch the game."

David was clearly not listening to his wife. Instead, he was feeling threatened that he might have to do something he didn't want to do. He was thinking about how unfair it was that he would have to give up his free time, and he was developing arguments to resist her request. Because he wasn't really hearing what she said, David became angry and his wife felt more misunderstood than ever. A simple active listening exercise commonly used with couples having this difficulty is to have the listener paraphrase the speaker's words until the speaker believes he or she has been heard accurately. Here's what happened when David and his wife tried this:

Wife: "I wish we could do more things together."

David: "You want me to spend less time on the things I want to do."

Wife: "No. I want you to have free time, but I also want us to have some couple time together."

David: "You want us to go off and do those dancing classes that Steve and Mary go to."

Wife: "No, that's not what I'm saying either. I really don't have any specific thing in mind. What I want is to do something together that we both enjoy, like when we were first married."

David: "You just want to spend some time together."

Wife: "Yes."

Notice how long it took David to hear what his wife was trying to tell him. This lag in comprehension is very common. In fact, it takes some people ten or fifteen minutes of active listening to hear a simple message accurately.

Once the other person believes you have heard them accurately, the next step in the process is for you to respond to what the other person said. The person then paraphrases what you said until he or she does it accurately. Here is how David's conversation with his wife continued:

David: "I would be willing to do something with you. I just don't want to give up my Monday night game or do something where I feel stupid, like those dance classes."

Wife: "You want to have your free time and do something you enjoy."

David: "Yes."

As David and his wife continued with this approach, they eventually worked out an agreement where they would have a couple's night once every two weeks and spend at least half of a Saturday once a month doing something together.

Identifying the Other Person's Needs

The key to effective negotiation is to identify what the other person wants so you can develop a solution that meets your needs as well as those of the other person. After you present your needs with a D.E.R. script, shift gears to active listening so you hear clearly the other person's needs. Since it's often very difficult for people to identify what they really want, be patient, it might take several minutes. Once you have identified what the person wants, be sure to convey your understanding with paraphrasing. *Most people are not willing to work out a compromise until they believe you have heard them accurately.*

What Are You Willing to Do?

In most situations, it is unreasonable to demand that only one person should change or take action. Be willing to make reasonable concessions—it shows respect for the rights of others. For example, if you are requesting that a coworker change his or her schedule to accommodate you, think of something you might do that would make the change easier.

What Might This Person Ask For?

In most conflict situations, you know the person. Think about your interactions with this person in the past. While people can be unpredictable, you often can make a good guess about what the other person might want in this situation. As you identify the possible requests, think of potential solutions that will meet the needs of both of you.

What Negative Consequences Are You Willing and Able to Use?

If you do not think that other person will be willing to negotiate in good faith, identify negative consequences you might be willing and able to use. Fortunately, most everyday conflicts do not require the use of negative consequences.

A Five-Step Approach for Resolving Conflict

The process of resolving a conflict usually involves the following five steps. As you read through them, identify those that you find difficult or tend to avoid.

1. Make Your Request/Identify the Problem

If you are initiating the negotiation session, make your needs and wants known in a way that causes the least amount of resistance. The best way is to use a D.E.R. script. If the other person has initiated the session, use your active listening skills to identify what this person wants. Again, take your time, as people are often not clear about what they want when they begin to talk about a conflict.

2. Identify the Other Person's Perceptions, Needs, and Wants

If you have initiated the negotiation session, listen to identify the other person's perceptions, needs, and wants. Make sure you periodically paraphrase what you are hearing to ensure that you understand accurately what is being said. Periodic paraphrasing also lets the other person know you are hearing and understanding. This reduces emotional tension and greatly aids the negotiation process.

One simple way to stay on track while listening is to use the D.E.R. format as a guideline. Find out:

- What is this person's description of the problem?
- How does this person think or feel about the conflict?
- What is this person's request?

As you listen, keep in mind that you do not need to agree with the other person's view of the conflict. You are just giving this person a chance to express his or her view of the situation and showing that you have understood by paraphrasing. Most people will resist proceeding with negotiations until you do so.

3. Generate Possible Solutions

After the needs and wants of both individuals have been identified, it's time to generate possible solutions. A common way to do this is by brainstorming. Brainstorming is a technique used by government and business professionals, as well as by scientists, to generate a list of possible solutions for a problem. When brainstorming, everyone thinks of as many possible solutions as possible. The key to successful brainstorming is to avoid evaluating ideas until several have been suggested. Analyzing each idea as it's suggested tends to stifle the creative process. Instead, respond to ideas that are suggested with comments such as "That's one idea. Do you have any others?" If the other person begins to evaluate an idea you are suggesting, respond with, "Let's not evaluate our ideas until we can think of several different possibilities." If you are dealing with a difficult conflict, it could be useful to write down your ideas. Seeing your ideas listed helps to stimulate the creative process.

4. Evaluate Possible Alternatives and Agree on the Best Solution

After several possible solutions have been suggested, it's time to evaluate each one for (1) practicality, (2) the degree to which it satisfies everyone's needs, and (3) the degree to which it's agreeable to everyone involved. During this evaluation, be sure to shift between stating your own ideas and listening to the other person. The better you do this, the more successful you will be at negotiating.

As you evaluate each suggestion, keep in mind that the best solution is one that leaves everyone feeling satisfied. As much as possible, avoid solutions that cause people to feel that someone has won and someone has lost. Your goal is to find a solution that everyone believes to be fair. While this is not always possible, the closer you come to finding such a solution, the greater the chances it will work.

The best way to arrive at a solution agreeable to everyone is to think in terms of competing needs rather than competing solutions. Sometimes a person has already decided upon a "correct" or "best" solution before negotiating. This person then uses the negotiation session to try to sell this solution. It usually doesn't work. Usually for a given problem, there are many different solutions that would satisfy everyone's needs and wants. The challenge is to identify them.

If none of the proposed solutions is adequate, do more brainstorming. If everyone is stuck, take a break, and then start again. Taking a break is especially helpful when strong emotions have been generated.

Sometimes, it's necessary to encourage a person to cooperate and negotiate in good faith. Concentrate on conveying the positive consequences that the person will enjoy when the problem is resolved. In a business setting, you might stress the increased savings or productivity that will result. In personal relationships, you might stress increased closeness, additional free time together, or your personal appreciation for the other person's consideration. In some cases, you may even want to offer a reward for the change or action you want. For example, offer to do some of the other person's work in exchange for help with your project. If you offer a reward, select one that is appropriate for the person with whom you are dealing. Avoid offering rewards that only you would find desirable or that you can't deliver. If you decide to try a reward, you may even want to ask what this person would find rewarding.

Resort to negative consequences only when positive ones have failed to win cooperation. Again, if you decide to use negative consequences, be sure they are ones you are both willing and able to carry out. If none is available and the other person remains uncooperative, your only other alternatives are to conform, retreat, or find a substitute goal.

5. Restate the Agreement, and If Appropriate, Formalize it

Once you have reached an agreement, restate it so everyone understands what they have agreed to. Do not let embarrassment or discomfort over an emotionally sensitive problem pressure you into ending your negotiation session too quickly. If you fail to restate your agreement, you and the other person could walk away with a different understanding of its content.

If you think the other person might try to back out of the

agreement later, formalize it in writing. In counseling, this is often done when working with couples or with parents and children. Even when you trust the other person, it's usually best to formalize a business agreement in writing. This can be done through an email, an exchange of letters, or a formal contract.

Whenever you reach a mutually satisfying solution through a negotiation process, thank the other person for agreeing to change or take action. If you have been negotiating with a person who has been difficult to deal with in the past, suggest that future conflicts or problems be handled in a similar manner. Avoid bringing up new problems at this time, as it could jeopardize the gains you have just secured.

SUMMARY OF KEY IDEAS

1. There are five common ways in which people resist requests to which they do not want to respond. Sometimes this is an automatic behavior; other times it's conscious and deliberate.
2. One key to keeping a discussion focused on the conflict you want to resolve is to identify clearly what you want before the discussion. Creating a D.E.R. script before you begin is a good way to do this.
3. From time to time, you probably use some of the tactics described in this chapter to avoid the requests of others and to protect yourself.
4. One general technique that works well with many forms of resistance is "Yes, but." You paraphrase what the other person has said, then say "but" or "however" to emphasize your need or perception.
5. A nonnegotiator will not respond when you attempt to overcome his or her resistance. When dealing with

such a person, you sometimes need to become more aggressive and decide what negative consequence you're willing and able to use if they continue to resist. If you're unwilling to do this, your only alternatives are to conform, retreat, or find a substitute goal.

6. Active listening is a form of listening where you focus on identifying the issues that are important to the other person and paraphrasing them back.

7. Whenever possible, work toward creating a "win-win" solution.

8. An effective negotiation session usually has five steps: (1) identify the problem, (2) identify each person's needs, (3) generate possible solutions, (4) evaluate the possible solutions and choose one, and (5) restate the agreement.

RECOMMENDED ACTIVITIES

Continue to Use D.E.R. Scripts

Create at least three D.E.R. scripts this week. Write them in your journal. After creating one, review the guidelines given in Chapter 10 to see if your script follows them.

Practice "I-Messages" and Paraphrasing

If "I-messages" and paraphrasing are still new to you, or if they are uncomfortable, find at least one situation each day during the week where you can practice both of them. The easiest way to build these skills is to use them in friendly situations: while driving in a car with a friend, chatting with your partner, or discussing something at work. With paraphrasing, remember that you are not trying to repeat everything that has been said, just one or two key points. After you become comfortable using these skills in positive situations, you are ready to use them during negotiation sessions.

Have at Least One Negotiation Session

During the week, identify one conflict situation that you would like to resolve. Develop a simple D.E.R. script, approach the person involved, and practice your negotiation skills. As you follow the five-step problem solving approach described in this chapter, make a deliberate effort to use "I messages" and active listening. Record this experience in your journal. Then review the steps and list any that you either skipped or had difficulty with. List specific things you could do differently that would make you a more effective negotiator. If you are having trouble doing this on your own, find someone that you trust who is skilled at negotiating to help you. If you do not know anyone like this, find a counselor who can help.

Continue to Record and Respond to Hit-and-Run Situations

Chapter 10 described six common hit-and-run situations where others treat you disrespectfully. Continue to record in your journal any such situations in which you are not satisfied with your response. Then develop an assertive response, using the suggestions given in Chapter 10. You might also find it useful to record assertive responses that were effective.

Continue to Record in Your Journal

Your main focus while working on this chapter is to develop a more assertive style. At the same time, it's also important to spend some time on past material. Therefore, record in your journal at least one incident where you became angry. Use the same format as you used in Chapter 9:

Date
Incident:
Level of Arousal ___, *Level of Aggression* ___

Thoughts:

Actions:

What emotions other than anger was I feeling?

Five Questions:

1. *What exactly did this person do that triggered my anger?*
2. *What needs or wants caused this person to act in this way?*
3. *What beliefs or aspects of this person's past (hurts, losses, successes, fears, lack of skills, etc.) influenced this behavior?*
4. *Considering the above, how could I have responded in a different and more effective manner? How might a positive role model have behaved?*
5. *Were any negative labels, family role models, or incidents from the past affecting this situation?*

Rational Challenges

12

Embarrassment and Shame

T HIS CHAPTER EXPLORES how embarrassment and shame can trigger anger. It then shows you how to use a tool called 'summary sheets' to change deeply ingrained beliefs and habit patterns that are causing problems.

EMBARRASSMENT

Embarrassment is the feeling of distress we experience when some aspect of who we are, something we have done, or something that has happened to us might be noticed and cause others to think poorly of us or reject us. Within the simplified model of emotions presented in Chapter 1, embarrassment is based on fear that others might think poorly of us. Here are incidents where Sharon, David, Carmen and Alex each experienced embarrassment.

Sharon was sensitive about the size of her nose. One day, while talking to a group of coworkers about cosmetic surgery, one said, "Have any of you ever thought about having anything done?" Although her nose was not specifically mentioned, Sharon became embarrassed. She covered her embarrassment with anger and told her coworker that she was very rude to ask such a question.

David was telling a joke to a friend about an old man with poor memory when he remembered that his friend's father had Alzheimer's disease. David became embarrassed and responded to his feelings by abruptly saying that he had work to do and leaving.

Carmen was having lunch at work when a coworker teased her in a lighthearted way about trouble Carmen had with a difficult customer earlier in the day. In this workplace, Carmen and her coworkers often used humor to ease the tension that situations like these caused. However, Carmen became embarrassed and blushed, managing only a polite laugh. She then sat quietly while her coworker moved on to other topics. She spent the rest of the afternoon dwelling on how thoughtless this person had been.

Alex was explaining to a coworker how to operate a new copier when it jammed. He became embarrassed that he was unable to fix it. He became angry at the machine and said it was poorly made. For the next hour he quietly stewed thinking, "Why do I have to explain everything to everyone?"

In all of these experiences, the force that triggered the embarrassment was the threat of disapproval. For each person the specific cognitive, emotional, and behavioral response to embarrassment was different. This is to be expected since each person developed different core beliefs and habits as a child. To see how this works, let's take a closer look at each example.

Upon reflection, Sharon realized that the person who had asked about cosmetic surgery had been asking her and her co-workers, not specifically Sharon. Unfortunately, one of Sharon's core beliefs was "Something is wrong with me. I don't measure up." This belief caused her immediately to think about her nose and the embarrassment she had experienced in school when other children teased her. This in turn triggered a brief time tunnel experience, where the feelings of shame and embarrassment she had experienced as a child overtook her. Because Sharon also had the core belief "I must never show weakness," she used anger as a defense mechanism (discussed in Chapter 9) to escape her feelings of fear and shame. While this habitual response did help her avoid experiencing the painful feelings, it also caused her to react inappropriately.

David had the core beliefs "Never show any sign of weakness" and "I can handle anything." These made it difficult for him to admit that he was wrong to joke about the old man and to say he was sorry. When he realized the joke was inappropriate, he experienced confusion as to what he should do, as well as embarrassment. He was afraid he would be seen as uncaring or insensitive, when he had no intention of being that way. Since his confusion and sense of vulnerability were in direct conflict with his beliefs, his only course of action was to suppress his awareness of the event and retreat.

Even though the friendly teasing about the difficult customer that Carmen experienced was common, her overreaction to it was due to her core belief "I'm not as capable as others." Instead of seeing the teasing as the way her coworkers relieved tension, she personalized it and saw it as disapproval, which triggered her embarrassment. Her passive response was due to her core beliefs "Keep the peace," "Don't make others angry or upset with you," and "Never do anything that will hurt others."

Alex's overreaction to the problem with the copier was due to his core beliefs "If you're going to do something, then do it right (which means perfectly)" and "Mistakes are unacceptable." His embarrassment was triggered by his sense that the coworker perceived him as inadequate. Like Sharon, he used anger to feel strong. He continued to stew over the event because of his core belief "I must avoid asking questions or making statements that might make me look stupid or ignorant."

When you have done something foolish, embarrassment is a common reaction. However, embarrassment due to a simple everyday mistake, or embarrassment that is out of proportion to the situation, is clearly inappropriate. Two ways are available to reduce the amount of inappropriate embarrassment you experience. (1) Learn to view your weaknesses and shortcomings as normal and acceptable, and (2) consider mistakes as normal and acceptable. You might find that only one is relevant to you, or you might need to address both.

When discussing the need to view weaknesses and shortcomings as normal and acceptable with clients, I often say that they need to "normalize" themselves. Normalizing yourself is a term I use to describe the process of developing the core belief, "Everyone has weaknesses and issues they struggle with. They are a normal and acceptable part of the human condition."

The negative core beliefs listed in Chapter 6 for Sharon, David, Carmen, and Alex include unrealistic beliefs about both themselves and others. Sharon and David believed that they should always be strong and in control because they live in a hostile world. Carmen believed that she was inferior and responsible for the feelings of others. Alex had the impossible goal of making no mistakes, as well as a general sense of danger. Sharon, David, and Alex all had strong prohibitions against "weak" emotions such as embarrassment and shame, while Carmen often wallowed in them.

Embarrassment was a difficult issue for Sharon, David, and Alex because they were raised in families where little approval and love was shown to them. When approval was given, it was usually connected to some kind of performance, such as when David became active in sports. While children need encouragement when they show skill at various activities, they also need to know they are loved and accepted for who they are, even when they make mistakes or fall short in some task. Since Carmen experienced this kind of love and acceptance, this was not an issue for her.

The second way to reduce embarrassment is to learn to view mistakes as a normal and acceptable part of life. People who experience shame and embarrassment often grew up in families with perfectionistic and critical parents. When parents continually magnify the seriousness of a child's mistakes, it gives the hidden message that the child's value as a person depends upon performing tasks well. Some parents are so perfectionistic that most of the things the child does fail to meet their unrealistic standards. The child is left feeling like a failure and eventually develops the core belief that all mistakes, even minor ones, are terrible and must be avoided at all costs. The next section shows you how to develop a more realistic view of mistakes by using a tool called summary sheets.

SUMMARY SHEETS

Remember that you are in the process of transforming deeply ingrained beliefs and habit patterns. Because they are deeply ingrained, sometimes it's normal for you to forget important insights and new skills you've been learning. Having to relearn these insights and skills several times before they replace the old patterns and become automatic is normal. Summary sheets can speed up this process.

A summary sheet is a page that summarizes the work you have done on a specific issue. The first step in creating one is to identify a specific negative core belief that causes problems for you. Write the negative core belief at the top of the page. Then summarize the work you have done on this issue in four sections like this:

Why This Belief Is an Issue
In a short paragraph, summarize all the factors that contributed to the development of this core belief. Typically, these factors include the personality you were born with, things your parents, teachers or siblings did, and negative experiences such as excessive teasing, illness, abuse, or trauma.

Situations Where This Belief Causes Problems

List at least three specific types of situations where this core belief is the driving force behind your thoughts and behavior. Be as specific as possible.

Ideas That Can Help Change How I Think

Summarize all of the logical arguments you have developed to challenge the core belief. The list of coping self-statements you have been developing can provide you with ideas. Reviewing the sections of the book, which deal with the core belief or issue you've selected can also be helpful.

Things I Can Do

Go back through the second section of this summary sheet, titled, "Situations Where This Belief Causes Problems." Identify at least one positive behavior you can substitute for each inappropriate or self-defeating behavior you listed. If you can think of more than one positive behavior, then so much the better. Be as specific as possible.

Here is a summary sheet that Alex developed in response to his embarrassment and resulting anger when he made mistakes. As he and I discussed such incidents, he identified the main force behind the problem as his fear of making mistakes and the tendency to equate his value as a person with his performance. Because these two issues are usually closely connected, he dealt with them both in one sheet.

Mistakes are Terrible/My Value Depends on My Performance

Why This Belief Is an Issue

Both my father and mother were perfectionists. They always stressed that if you do a job, you should do it well. They were critical and always seemed to find something about what I had done that fell short of their expectations. As a result, I became very focused on doing things correctly and began to see myself as a failure when I failed at even a small task. I now see that this has also caused me to have a poor self-image because I never measure up to my own perfectionist standards.

Situations Where This Belief Causes Problems

1. When someone sees me make a mistake, I become embarrassed and often cover it with anger.

2. When I make a mistake, I tend to berate myself.

3. I tend to be very critical of the performance of others. Sometimes I nitpick at my girlfriend when she is cooking or doing some other household chore.

4. If I make a mistake at a formal dinner or other social occasion, I become very red and embarrassed.

Ideas That Can Help Change How I Think

1. Mistakes are unavoidable. They are a natural part of the learning process. Most mistakes are unimportant in the long run.

2. My value as a person has nothing to do with what I do. My value comes from the fact that I'm a human, and humans are valuable. That's why we care for old people and those who have severe disabilities. They are valuable even though they are limited in what they can do.

3. When I make a mistake, it has no bearing on who I am—I can fail at a task, but it does not make me a failure. I can remind myself, "I am not a mistake. I simply made one."

4. Perfection is impossible to achieve. Nothing that anyone does is perfect. There is always room for improvement. That's the beauty of life. We always have room to grow and improve. So, don't expect things to turn out perfectly. Remember, "Perfection is a direction, not a place."

5. While I like to do things well, most things in life do not require perfection. I am a good worker and usually do things more carefully than others do.

6. When I make a mistake, remind myself that mistakes are simply an opportunity to learn. Focus on the lesson to be learned and look at mistakes as gifts of wisdom.

7. Everyone makes mistakes. The difference between successful people and those who don't do much in life is that successful people focus on learning from their mistakes and don't waste time beating themselves up.

8. In healthy relationships, who I am and my relationship to the other person are far more important than how well I do things. If the other person is reasonable and mature, he or she will accept me as I am even when I fail at a task or make a mistake.

Things I Can Do

1. When I make a mistake, use a three-step problem solving approach.
   - What happened?
   - Can it be corrected? If so, how? If not, move on.
   - What have I learned from this mistake? Is there any way I could avoid making the same mistake in the future? (There are some things that you can't prepare for or prevent.)

2. When I make a mistake, I can admit it without apologizing. It often helps if I say it with humor.

3. I can remind myself to focus on learning something from my mistakes and repeat some of the ideas I've written here.

4. I can be kind and accepting when I see others make mistakes. I can use the ideas I've written here to encourage them instead of laughing at them or criticizing them. This is especially important with my girlfriend.

As you read the various summary sheets presented in this and the following chapters, notice that each one focuses on specific thoughts and behaviors associated with the core belief listed at the top. The more detailed you are when creating summary sheets, the more powerful they will be. Also, remember that everyone is unique and that each example was created for a specific person. The same issue can be addressed in many ways. So, even if the issue in Alex's or another's summary sheet is a problem for you, your summary sheet will probably be different. The key to making an effective summary sheet is to be as specific and detailed as possible and to tailor it to your beliefs and personality.

SHAME

Shame and embarrassment are closely related and are often used as synonyms in common speech, but shame is actually more closely related to loss than to threat, which makes it a type of sadness. Shame is the feeling generated when you believe you have been tainted or "stained" in some way. At the same time, you fear that if others become aware of your "stain," they will reject you.

When Sharon was embarrassed by her coworker's innocent comment about cosmetic surgery, she felt both shame and embarrassment. She was ashamed because she thought her nose made her unacceptable to others. Her shame caused her to feel embarrassment in front of her coworkers because she thought they were viewing her as unacceptable because of her "disfigurement."

Because her nose was only a minor issue for Sharon, her shame and embarrassment were short-lived and quickly eased when the conversation shifted to another topic. Sometimes, however, shame becomes a deep-seated and recurring experience, especially shame due to an event such as a rape, childhood molestation, or the core belief that one is inferior to others in a significant way. Carmen's belief that she was not as capable as others were caused shame related to this to be a frequent experience. Whenever she was around others and thought they noticed her incompetence, her shame would trigger embarrassment. For David and Alex, as well as Sharon, shame was an unacceptable emotion, so they usually either suppressed it or covered it with anger.

If you have done something that was truly thoughtless or hurtful some degree of embarrassment or shame is appropriate. Normal people feel these emotions because of their conscience and sense of right and wrong. Only those who are amoral or lack a conscience can cause unnecessary pain to others without any shame or embarrassment. Shame is inappropriate when it's either out of proportion to the event that triggered it or occurs when there is no objective reason for its existence.

As with embarrassment, the key to reducing inappropriate shame is to normalize yourself and view mistakes as normal and acceptable. Here is a summary sheet that Sharon developed in response to her need to always be strong. Again, notice how detailed and specific she was in each section.

Only the Strong Survive, I Must Never Show Weakness
Why This Belief Is an Issue

The message that one must never show weakness was given to me in many ways. My grandparents were "depression era" people who had tough lives. They were still struggling when my parents were young. As a result, they modeled this belief in their behavior and speech. The constant battling in my family also reinforced this idea. If anyone showed any kind of weakness, everyone else in the family seemed to jump on it at once.

Situations Where This Belief Causes Problems

1. Any time I become aware of a personal flaw, such as my nose, how I speak, or some important skill that I think I lack, I become anxious and often find something to become angry at.

2. When my children have a problem that I don't know how to handle or they do something that I don't think is right, even though it might be age-appropriate, I lecture or scold them.

3. Whenever I make a mistake, I become angry and find someone or something to blame.

4. Whenever something touches me deeply, such as a sad scene in a movie, I immediately need to hide my soft feelings by making a joke or changing the subject.

Ideas That Can Help Change How I Think

1. While being strong is a good quality that has helped me in many situations, there are also times when it's okay to be vulnerable and show weakness.

2. It's normal and healthy sometimes to feel hurt, sad, and lost. It's also normal and healthy to express these feelings in appropriate settings.

3. My father and mother's need to always be strong and never show weakness was one of the things that kept me from developing a closer relationship with them. It caused them to pull away from me and fail to support me, even though they loved me, when I needed them the most. When I choose to follow their example, I distance myself from my children and hurt them.

4. There is nothing weak or demeaning about choosing to express normal, healthy emotions in appropriate ways to people you love and who love you. It's actually a sign of self-acceptance and trust and an important part of true intimacy. It's also necessary for my mental health.

5. When someone I love hurts, it's healthy and loving to comfort them. I do not need to "make them strong."

Things I Can Do

1. Whenever I become aware of a flaw, such as my nose, how I speak, or some skill that I am poor at, I can remain quiet for a short time and not respond in my old way. During this time, I can identify what I'm feeling and choose to experience it rather than run away from it. I can also remind myself of the ideas I wrote here. If the person and situation are appropriate, I might also share what I'm experiencing.

2. When my children have a problem that I don't know how to handle or they do something that I don't think is right, I can stay silent and remind myself of these things. If I take some time to think about it, I usually have a more appropriate response.

3. Whenever I make a mistake, I can remind myself that mistakes are normal and that most of them don't matter. I can also use "I statements" and take responsibility for what happened rather than blame someone or someone else, as I did in the past.

4. Whenever something touches me deeply, such as a movie, I can choose to accurately label what is happening and then experience it fully. If I shed a tear or look sad, I don't need to cover it up. If the situation and person are comfortable, I can share what I'm experiencing in an honest way without making a joke or trying to cover it up.

ADDING A SPIRITUAL/EXISTENTIAL DIMENSION TO YOUR WORK

In the first two chapters, we saw that one of the main functions of emotions is to provide energy and motivation to help us meet our needs. There are many different ways to look at and classify the various needs that people have. A simple system I use is to divide needs into three basic groups:

- *Basic Survival Needs.* These include physical needs, such as food, water, shelter, and safety. I also include the psychological or mental need to understand how the world works so we can satisfy our basic physical needs.
- *Relational Needs.* The need to have meaningful relationships with others and experience intimacy.
- *Spiritual/Existential Needs.* The need to give meaning to our existence. At some point in our lives, we all ask, "Why am I here?" "Is there life after death?" "Is there a God?" and "How can I find true happiness in life?"

Many self-help books do not address the last category, spiritual/existential needs. This is unfortunate because the beliefs you hold in this area can play a major role in either maintaining or changing the core beliefs that generate inappropriate and destructive behavior. The value you place on yourself and others, your ability to work through loss in a constructive way, and your ability to have courage in situations where you have little control are all influenced by your spiritual/existential beliefs.

Unfortunately, the struggle to find meaning in life is intensely personal. Especially in our modern high-tech culture where much of our music and entertainment derides spiritual ideas, it's difficult to give clear guidelines. Yet every culture throughout human experience has devoted tremendous time and energy to answering the spiritual questions "Why am I here?" "Is there life after death?" "Is there a God?" and "How can I find true happiness in life?" This search underscores the importance of our answers to these four fundamental questions. The thinking that flows out of our answers influences how we interpret events and respond to the various difficulties and losses we encounter.

If you have never taken time to consider these four spiritual/existential questions, consider how you might address them. Many people find the religion in which they were raised is a good place to start. If you had no religious training or you have no interest in religion, you can take a more philosophical approach. Go to a bookstore and look at books such as "The Road Less Traveled" and "Man's Search for Meaning." There are many others. Find one or two that suit your personality and beliefs.

Sharon had a general belief in a "higher power" but no specific religious beliefs. She began reading a variety of books that dealt with spirituality and visited several churches until she found one where she felt comfortable. Alex held very negative beliefs against all religions and found philosophical books that were more suited to his nature. You can see this preference in the rational arguments he used in his summary sheet "Mistakes Are Terrible/My Value Depends on My Performance"

In contrast, David had joined a church a few years earlier, and even though neither of his parents had been particularly religious, he had become deeply committed to his faith. Indeed, he originally came to see me because his behavior and emotional responses were so contradictory to his newfound belief. David found it gratifying to incorporate his faith into his efforts to change his behavior. Here is an example of how he used his spiritual beliefs to challenge the idea that his value was determined by his performance. Notice how different David's sheet is from the one Alex made on the same issue. Again, this emphasizes the fact that the summary sheets you create need to match your personality, your background, and how you think.

My Value Is Determined by My Performance
Why This Belief Is an Issue?

Both my mother and father could be very critical. Because they were so distant, I never felt much connection with them. In grade school, I did poorly, and the other kids often teased me because I was such a loner. The only positive part of my childhood was sports. I found friends and acceptance there because I was good at it. Performing well became very important for me.

Situations Where This Belief Causes Problems

1. Whenever I make a social error or mistake in front of someone, I am very uneasy for quite some time afterward. I usually express this discomfort as anger, but underneath it's a sense of embarrassment and shame.

2. I often think of how poor a father I am to my children, especially when I am too harsh or fail to say the right thing.

3. When I don't have enough money to buy something for my kids or wife, I feel very bad.

Sometimes this feeling can last for several days if it's a big item. During this time, I tend to think about what a failure I am.

Ideas That Can Help Change How I Think

1. While I like to do things well and it's good to have skill, this has no bearing on my value as a person. The love I have for others and how I treat them is what really counts. (Matt. 5:3-10, Ephesians 2:8-10, 1 John 3:23-24).

2. My value comes from the fact that I am God's child. Just as I love my children even when they don't succeed at a task, God loves me (John 3:16, 1 John 3:1a).

3. I need to remember that everything I do in this life will eventually disappear. My true home is in another place. Focus on what is eternal rather than on what is temporary (1 Peter 1:22-25, 1 John 2:15-17).

4. True riches are not found in the things of this world (Matt. 6:19-20).

Things I Can Do

1. I can ask God to help me with each of the following regularly during my devotional time. This needs to be a regular activity.

2. I can read the above scriptures periodically to remind myself of what is important and what is not. Regular group Bible study also helps to keep me on track.

3. When I take time-outs, I can use the above self-
talk to change how I'm seeing things. I can also
say a short prayer and ask for help and recon-
ciliation with the person I'm angry with.

4. When I do something stupid or disrespectful,
I can admit it and apologize. This is especially
important with my wife and children.

5. I can join a men's group at church that will
help me be accountable for my actions and provide positive role models.

6. I can practice giving compliments and encouraging others.

7. I can practice the listening skills I've learned
and strive to understand how others feel and
see things.

Carmen's family had strong ties to a traditional church, but
Carmen's own connection with her church had been mostly
one of formality. She now welcomed the idea of reevaluating
her faith and incorporating it into the work of changing her
behavior and emotional responses.

If you have a sacred text you use, incorporate key verses
or ideas into your challenges, as David did. If you're not sure
how to do so, ask a fellow believer who is mature in his or
her faith or a member of your church's clergy to help you. If
you practice any form of daily prayer or meditation, devote a
small portion of this time to wrestling with the erroneous and
irrational beliefs from childhood that are still playing a role in
your distorted thinking.

If, like Alex, religious beliefs and ideas do not appeal to
you, take a more philosophical approach. I would still en-

courage you to think about and clarify your beliefs about the larger issues in life such as "What is it that makes a person happy?" "How do I define success?" and "What is my purpose in life?"

SUMMARY OF KEY IDEAS

1. Embarrassment is the feeling of distress we experience when an aspect of who we are something we have done, or something that has happened to us might be noticed and cause others to be critical or reject us. Within the simplified model of emotions presented in Chapter 1, embarrassment is a form of fear.

2. If you believe that you must always be strong and in control, or that mistakes must always be avoided, you will tend to cover your embarrassment with anger. This will make you feel strong and in control.

3. Normalizing yourself is the process of developing the core belief: "Everyone has weaknesses and issues they struggle with. They are a normal part of the human condition."

4. Inappropriate embarrassment can be reduced by normalizing yourself, developing a realistic view of mistakes, and separating your value as a person from what you do.

5. Summary sheets are a powerful tool that can speed up the process of changing deeply ingrained beliefs and habits.

6. Shame is the feeling generated when you believe you have been tainted or "stained" in some way. At the same time, you fear that if others become aware of your "stain," they will reject you. While shame and

embarrassment are commonly used as synonyms, shame is actually more closely related to loss than threat, making it a type of sadness.

7. Like embarrassment, shame will be covered with anger if you believe you must always be strong and in control.

8. The key to reducing inappropriate shame is to normalize yourself.

9. If you have done something that was truly thoughtless or hurtful some degree of embarrassment or shame is appropriate. Shame and embarrassment are inappropriate when they are either out of proportion to the event that triggered it or occur when there is no objective reason for their existence.

10. Your answers to the four basic spiritual/existential questions— "Why am I here?" "Is there life after death?" "Is there a God?" and "How can I find true happiness in life?" —play an important role in your core beliefs.

Recommended Activities

Create at Least One Summary Sheet

During your work on this chapter, create at least one summary sheet. Set aside a special section of your journal for summary sheets so you can find them easily. Your first summary sheet can be about one of the topics in this chapter, or you can create one that deals with a core belief or problem issue you identified in one of the previous chapters. For your first summary sheet, you will be most successful if you choose an issue that is important to you and one on which you have already done some work. When you create it, be sure to include the four sections described in this chapter:

Why This Belief Is an Issue
Situations Where This Belief Causes Problems
Ideas That Can Help Change How I Think
Things I Can Do

Take time to reread the sample summary sheets several times. Remember, the more specific and detailed you are, the more effective your summary sheet will be. If creating one is difficult for you, find someone you trust—a friend, relative, or maybe even a counselor—to help you. After you have completed your summary sheet, compare it with the examples and guidelines given in this chapter. Once you begin using summary sheets, you will find them a valuable tool for changing behavior.

Practice Identifying Embarrassment and Shame When You Experience Them

In Chapter 9, we discussed the importance of being able to identify accurately the various emotions we are experiencing. This week, as you review your day, identify any times when you experienced the emotions of embarrassment or shame. These will usually occur when you have made a mistake or some weakness has surfaced. As you consider these times, answer the following questions.

- Did you allow yourself to experience the negative emotion?
- If not, how did you run away from it? (Perhaps by covering it with anger or suppressing it?)
- What behavior was triggered by this emotion?
- If your behavior was inappropriate, what could you do differently next time?

Add a Spiritual/Existential Dimension to Your Work

Write in your journal answers to the following four spiritual existential questions. Take time to explore each question as fully as you can and include reasons for your answers.

- Why are we here?
- Is there life after death?
- Is there a God? (If your answer is yes, how does it affect your answers to the other questions?)
- How can you find true happiness in life?

If you do not have personally satisfying answers to these four questions, decide how you can begin to find them. This search might include:

Finding a book that deals with these issues.
Reconnecting with the religious tradition that you were raised in.
Talking to a good friend whom you trust.
Talking to a religious leader in your faith.
Joining a group that has a spiritual focus.

Continue to Create and Use D.E.R. Scripts

Continue to create and use D.E.R. scripts when you are in conflict situations or have a problem that you wish to resolve with others. If this process is difficult for you, take several days to review Chapters 10 and 11.

Continue to Record in Your Journal

Record at least one incident in your journal when you became angry, and analyze it using the same format you used in Chapter 9.

Date:

Incident:

Level of Arousal ___ *Level of Aggression* ___
Thoughts:
Actions:
What emotions other than anger was I feeling?
Five Questions:
1. What exactly did this person do that triggered my anger?
2. What needs or wants caused this person to act in this way?
3. What beliefs or aspects of this person's past (hurts, losses, successes, fears, lack of skills, etc.) influenced this behavior?
4. Considering the above, how could I have responded in a different and more effective manner? How might a positive role model have behaved?
5. Were any negative labels, family role models, or incidents from the past affecting this situation?

Rational Challenges

13

Resentment, Envy, and Jealousy

R ESENTMENT, ENVY, AND jealousy can be seen as different forms of anger that occur in specific types of situations. In this chapter, we'll discuss what those situations are, along with ways to release resentment and avoid becoming envious and jealous.

RESENTMENT

Resentment can be thought of as recurring anger about a past event. You recall the past event over and over and tell yourself things about it that make you angry. Someone who has allowed resentment to dominate his or her life is often said to be bitter. This description is apt since resentment tends to sour everything in life and leads to much heartache and many missed opportunities.

Five approaches for letting go of resentment are described below. Depending upon the nature of the event generating the resentment and your personality, different approaches work best at different times. For a small incident, you might need to use only the first approach. For a major event, you might need to work through all five several times before you are able to release your resentment and live in the present once more.

Ask whether the resentment is worth it.

For simple situations ask yourself, "Is holding on to this resentment worth the price I pay?" Keep in mind that dwelling on the past interferes with your ability to live in the present and enjoy life. In addition, your resentment usually has no effect on the people you're resenting. They are going on with their lives, while you are stuck being angry over something that is now out of your control.

Take a short walk in the other person's shoes.

Understanding why others acted the way they did, even when those actions were inappropriate, often helps you to let go of resentment toward them. Whenever you are resenting someone, ask yourself:

- What needs or wants caused this person to act in this way?
- What beliefs or aspects of this person's past (hurts, losses, successes, fears, lack of skills, etc.) influenced his or her behavior?
- Have I ever felt like this or responded in this way? If so, how would I have liked others to react to me?

Take action on the problem that underlies the resentment.

When resentment is due to an ongoing problem at work or with family or friends, it could be a strong message that you need to deal with the problem. Create a D.E.R. script that clearly identifies what triggers your resentment, why you think and feel the way you do, and what you would like to happen. If there is someone to whom you can deliver your script who is directly involved, do so. If this is a situation involving a nonnegotiator, such as an alcoholic parent or a complex bureaucracy, identify what actions you can take that would make the situation more tolerable, such as setting limits to when you talk to the alcoholic parent or considering a different job. (See Chapter 10 if this is difficult for you.)

Occasionally, resentment is due to something or someone in the past that is impossible to address directly, such as a parent who has died. A common symbolic action that has helped many people let go of such resentments is to visit the person's grave to state your feelings. Another common symbolic action is to write a letter that expresses your anger. You can hold the letter in a safe place as a symbol or burn it as a ritual of releasing your resentment. An unsent letter could also be written for someone you resent who is alive but not available.

Eliminate the distorted thinking that is causing the resentment.

Distorted thinking and unrealistic expectations often play a significant role in resentment. Ask yourself, "How should this event have occurred?" and "How should this person(s) have acted?" Take time to answer these questions and be as specific as possible. For situations that have caused long-term resentment, write down your response. Then evaluate your response in terms of the following questions. For ways to challenge this type of distorted thinking, look at the section of the book mentioned in parentheses.

- Do I have an exaggerated need for things to be "fair?" (Chapter 6)
- Am I assuming that because I want something very much, I ought to have it? (Chapter 6)
- Is my resentment based on the idea that when others hurt or mistreat me, they deserve to be punished? (Chapter 6)
- Is my resentment due to negative core beliefs or should/must rules that are unrealistic? (Chapters 4, 6, and 7)
- Is my resentment due to time tunneling? Does this situation or person remind me of something or someone from my past that was hurtful? (Chapter 8)
- If my resentment is directed toward a loved one, am I interpreting his or her behavior as a coded message that I don't matter or they don't care? (Chapter 9)

Obtain secondary gains in a more positive way.

A secondary gain is an indirect and usually unconscious benefit resulting from an otherwise undesirable behavior. The basic principle for changing a negative behavior that is providing a secondary gain is, identify the secondary gain, and learn to obtain it directly.

In Chapter 8, we saw how David's childhood had produced a conditioned response association between intimacy and pain. When he and his wife started to become close, David would grow anxious, which—because of his need to feel strong and in control—would cause him to become angry about some trivial matter. By staying resentful, he could create distance and calm the anxiety that the intimacy triggered.

Of course, this process was all unconscious. The secondary gain in David's resentment was reduced anxiety when he experienced too much intimacy. As David learned to identify these types of situations and become aware of what he was doing, he slowly became comfortable with intimacy (something we'll discuss in detail in Chapter 15), and his need to use resentment to create distance eventually disappeared.

Alex often felt resentment when he believed that someone had wronged him. His resentment allowed him to feel justified in punishing the other person and avoid looking at his role in the conflict. Sometimes resentment also brought him extra attention from his girlfriend, who would be especially nice in an attempt to get him into a better mood. Therefore, the secondary gain in Alex's resentment was the ability to assert himself and gain attention. Unfortunately, he was usually more aggressive than assertive. In addition, he wasn't able to fully enjoy the extra attention because he was busy nursing his resentment. In order to overcome this pattern Alex needed to do three things: (1) challenge the distorted thinking that fueled his resentment, (2) learn to be more assertive and speak up when he didn't like what someone did, and (3) learn to satisfy his need for attention more directly by telling his girlfriend what he wanted.

Several common types of secondary gains are associated with resentment. In order to see if they play a role in your resentment, recall several times when you were resentful and answer the following questions:

- Did resentment allow you to continue punishing someone for their "bad" behavior?
- Did you receive some special reward, benefit, or attention when you became resentful? (Examples: the other person left you alone or tried to "get on your good side.")

- Did resentment allow you to avoid looking at your own actions and taking responsibility for what happened?
- Did resentment allow you to assume the role of a victim and avoid the reality that you are responsible for getting your needs and wants met?
- Did resentment allow you to feel sorry for yourself and justify poor behavior on your part because others "made" you feel this way?
- Did resentment help you to protect yourself from or stay away from people who were unhealthy for you to be around (such as a parent) without feeling guilty?

If you answered yes to any of the above, decide how you could have obtained the same benefit in a more direct and positive way. The next time you find yourself resenting something, go through this list of questions to see if you're repeating an old secondary gain pattern. If you are, decide what positive action you could take to obtain the secondary gain directly.

Of the four people we have been following, Alex had the greatest problem with resentment. Because it was such a major part of his life, he decided to make a summary sheet on this issue. As he discussed with me times when he experienced intense resentment, he realized that it often came from should/must thinking that reflected the erroneous assumptions discussed in Chapter 6. Here's the summary sheet Alex created.

Resentment Generated by the Erroneous Beliefs: "Life Should Be Fair;" "Because I Want Something Very Much, I Ought to Have it;" and "When Others Hurt or Mistreat Me, They Deserve to Be Punished"

Why This Belief Is an Issue

My mom was a resentful person who held grudges. While my dad was quiet and he would hold things in, he could also hold a grudge for a long time. Being the oldest, I often was put in charge of my younger brothers and sister. As we grew older, they had many privileges I didn't have at their age, and I resented it. I also resented the fact that my parents didn't have much money when I was young, so my brothers and sisters had more than I had. Because I was a people pleaser, I held things in and would just stew over them.

Situations Where This Belief Causes Problems

1. When something happens, like a traffic jam, I think about how people are "idiots" and how screwed up things are.

2. When someone does something they "shouldn't," I think about it with lots of anger for a long time, but I don't say anything.

3. When my girlfriend is late or does something that is hurtful, I tend to keep score and throw it back at her later whenever I'm unhappy with something she's done.

4. When my girlfriend doesn't respond as positively as I would like, I become angry and resentful and say mean things.

Ideas That Can Help Change How I Think

1. Fairness doesn't exist in the real world. When I dwell on the lack of "fairness," I'm usually

just throwing a tantrum because things aren't the way I want them to be. I'm too old to throw tantrums. Grow up, and accept that injustice and inequality are facts of life. Everyone acts in hurtful and unjust ways from time to time. Sometimes they do so deliberately. At other times, actions done with good intentions turn out to be hurtful or unjust because of a lack of knowledge or understanding, or simply by accident.

2. Focus on needs rather than fairness. If something I need or desire is being frustrated or threatened, concentrate on developing a plan to get it. My goal is to be effective at taking care of my needs, not to make things "fair."

3. The needs of others are no more and no less important than my own. Just because I want something doesn't mean that I'm entitled to it. I need to accept that sometimes I won't get what I want. I can have a happy and fulfilling life without getting everything I want.

4. My father believed in punishing others when they did something he thought was against him. This approach to life did not bring him happiness. He had an unhappy marriage and no real friends. I do not choose to follow in his footsteps.

5. In normal human relationships, people regularly do things that are hurtful for a variety of reasons. Often it's unintentional and simply a

mistake. At other times, it's due to a misunderstanding. Punishing others for every thoughtless behavior or misdeed poisons relationships.
While accountability and amends are an important part of resolving true wrongs that have
been committed, I will only experience truly
loving relationships if I am able to forgive and
release others.

Things I Can Do

1. When I am holding onto a resentment, I can
   work through the five-step approach for releasing resentments given in Chapter 13.

2. If I'm using resentment for a secondary gain,
   such as asserting myself or getting attention, I
   can take positive action to obtain these things
   directly.

3. I can read ideas I've written here daily for several weeks, until they are easy for me to recall.

4. I can practice using my assertive skills to speak
   up when people do things I don't like or when
   I want something.

5. When I'm unhappy with someone, I can be
   quiet and cool off. If I need to ask for something or address a problem, I can use the D.E.R.
   approach once I've cooled off.

ENVY

Envy is the feeling of discontent that occurs when you want what someone else has. Because you lack what this person has, you believe that you are somehow diminished or can't be happy or that life is not fair. Often you erroneously assume that what this person has "should" belong to you, and you feel that somehow, in some mysterious way, either it has been stolen from you or you have lost it to them. You might also have an underlying core belief that the number of good things in the world is limited. Every time someone else gets one of them, it means there is one less available for you.

The distorted thinking that you "should" have what this other person has along with your belief that life is unfair because you don't have it, triggers your anger and resentment. Mild envy usually causes you to demean the other person's good fortune. For example, when a coworker received a promotion or special recommendation, Carmen would become envious and find something negative to say about this person. Intense envy can cause people to act, directly or indirectly, to sabotage the other person's good fortune. Sometimes Alex would deliberately fail to give important telephone messages to coworkers he envied.

The distorted thinking that triggers envy is connected with the spiritual/existential question, "How do I find happiness in life?" Movies, television programs, popular music, and advertising constantly bombard us with messages that the way to be happy is to have lots of money, possessions, sex, power, or fame. People who believe that these types of things provide true happiness and make obtaining them their chief goal in life often experience intense envy when they see others with them.

If you experience envy, take time to clarify your beliefs about how one obtains happiness. Often this involves taking a look at your spiritual/existential beliefs. As you do so, develop several coping self-statements that you can use to reinterpret events when you become envious. In addition, develop rational challenges for the erroneous assumption that someone else's good fortune means fewer good things are available for you. Carmen decided that this was a big enough problem for her that she created this summary sheet.

Envy at the Good Fortune of Others

Why This Is an Issue

At school, because I lived in two different cultures and was overprotected by my parents, I often had the feeling of being on the outside looking in. My parents were content with what they had and we always had the things we needed even though they were very careful with their money. We rarely indulged in new clothes and often made do with old things. When I got to high school, I remember feeling like everything I owned was old-fashioned and out of date. I longed to have the latest fads like the other kids and dreamed that someday I would be the envy of everyone.

Situations Where This Belief Causes Problems

1. At work, when someone receives a promotion or commendation, I usually find something bad to say about them or about the reward or promotion they have received.

2. When I see people on TV, in the movies, or in magazines who are rich or famous, I often make derogatory remarks.

3. Sometimes when I see people on the street who seem trendy or well to do, I make negative comments.

4. When I want something that I cannot afford, I often feel intense disappointment or sadness.

Ideas That Can Help Change How I Think

1. Having money and nice things does not make you happy. Things that bring true happiness include having a strong spiritual center, being comfortable with who you are, having loving relationships, and having something meaningful to do.

2. While my family was fairly humble financially, we were and still are very close to one another. We also genuinely enjoy each other's company and look out for one another. In fact, we probably share much more love than many of the people whom I envy. In this sense, I'm richer than most of the people I know.

3. When I get new things or achieve some commendation, the happiness that comes with them is only temporary. When I fix my eyes on these things, it's like I'm on an endless treadmill, seeking more and more but never truly satisfied. True happiness doesn't come from things but from relationships.

4. It's okay to want things and recognition, but while they are enjoyable, they do not bring the deep contentment I truly want. Watching my

children and being with my loved ones is when I'm truly happy.

5. There are plenty of good things to go around for everyone. Just because someone else has something nice, it doesn't mean I've lost it. My needs are different from those of others.

6. I'm not a little girl trying to fit into a world she doesn't fully understand. I'm a woman who has "made it." I have a great job and am respected. I have many blessings I can count and be thankful for.

Things I Can Do

1. I can memorize the above statements and practice saying them to myself when I'm envious of what others have or their talents.

2. When I pray, I can practice being more thankful and ask God to help me rejoice more when others enjoy good fortune.

3. I can remind myself of the true and lasting riches I have, and that the things of the world all become dust with time.

4. I can practice encouraging and building others up.

JEALOUSY

In common usage, jealousy is sometimes a synonym for envy. However, envy and jealousy are actually two different emotions. While envy is based on the belief that someone else has what you want, jealousy is based on the belief that you have what you want but might lose it to someone else. This belief is generated by insecurity and a sense that others can't be trusted. It often comes from being raised in a family where the adults were not trustworthy or who themselves were suspicious of others.

Because jealousy is based on a belief that others are a threat, it triggers anger that is often accompanied by blaming and accusations. When extreme, it can also cause suspicious fears and watchful guarding. Two common examples of jealousy are the fear of losing one's partner to others and the fear of losing one's social position.

David often struggled with jealousy when he noticed another man looking at his wife while they were together in public or when she spent time with her female friends. Sometimes he even accused her of deliberately flirting, even though he had no objective evidence to support his claim. David's father had a very hard life as a child and was a controlling and suspicious man as an adult. This negative model, combined with David's difficulty fitting in with his peers when he was young, produced the jealousy he felt as an adult.

Two of the core beliefs David identified in Chapter 6 were, "A man should be strong and never let others take advantage of him" and "In many ways people are my adversaries. I must always be on guard and fight to make sure no one takes what is mine." Both of these beliefs were things his father had told him many times and acted out in his own life. In addition, David's anger and difficulty with intimacy often caused his wife to withdraw from him emotionally to protect herself. David's isolation and failure to feel close were often expressed as jealousy. In essence, he was projecting what he wanted (to be close to his wife) onto others because he was unable to obtain it himself. Here is a summary sheet that David developed around this issue.

Jealousy in Regard to My Wife

Why This Is an Issue

My father was a tough, domineering man who had a very hard childhood. He was a great businessman, but he didn't know the first thing about relationships. He also tended to be suspicious of others and was bitter about his divorce. I remember him making comments like "You can't trust anyone" and "As soon as you turn your back on a woman, she'll be doing you dirt." Many of my beliefs come from him. My rebellious nature as a kid has also contributed. Because I never listened to others and always had to do things my way or no way (another Dad trait), I've always struggled with relationships. The fact that I didn't experience much intimacy and trust as a kid makes it difficult for me to trust as an adult.

Situations Where This Belief Causes Problems

1. When I see another man looking at my wife or giving her a compliment, I get jealous and sometimes say something mean to my wife or try to ruin the compliment.

2. When my wife goes out with her friends, I get jealous. Sometimes I think that she doesn't care about me. Other times I think that maybe she's thinking of leaving me and that her friends are probably encouraging her.

3. I often think that my wife has deliberately done something to make me angry and I blow up.

Ideas That Can Help Change How I Think

1. My suspicions and jealousy have no foundation in reality. They are old habit patterns that I've copied from my dad. My wife has shown that she loves me by staying with me and encouraging me as I go to counseling.

2. Men like to look at pretty women, just as women like to look at handsome men. I do it all the time. When I see and appreciate a beautiful woman, it doesn't mean that I'm going to run off with her. Likewise, when some woman gives me a compliment, it doesn't mean I'm suddenly smitten with love. I need to think that my wife is at least as mature as I am. Actually, in many areas she is much more mature.

3. I like to get together with my friends. My wife needs to be able to get together with her friends. They probably do sometimes talk about me, but it's probably no different than with me and the guys grousing about our wives.

4. I behave like a small child who doesn't want to let go of his toy. "When I was a child, I talked like a child, I thought like a child, I reasoned like a child. Now that I'm a man, I put childish ways behind me." If I don't put away my childish ways and allow my wife to have friends and independent activities, she will resent me.

5. Often my jealousy is due to my difficulty in being close to my wife. As I learn how to love

her in a more intimate, mature and open way, these feelings will decrease.

6. One of the tenets of my faith is that we should love one another. Learning to do so is essential for my spiritual growth as well as for my personal happiness. This is especially true for loving my wife.

Things I Can Do

1. During my devotional time, I can read scripture that deals with this issue and ask God to heal the brokenness from my past.

2. Even though I feel jealous when a man compliments my wife, I can practice responding with simple statements such as "Yes, my wife does have good taste in clothes" and "Yes, she is beautiful." I can also remind myself of the above rational challenges.

3. I can tell my wife to enjoy her time with her friends. When she returns, instead of interrogating her, I can say, "I'm glad you had a good time." If she doesn't choose to share details, I can allow her some privacy. If she does, I can respond positively and not make derogatory comments or teasing jokes.

4. I can practice giving compliments to her and telling her "I love you." These things are difficult now but will become easier as I practice them.

5. I can practice accurately labeling my feelings and being honest with myself.

6. I can practice sharing my feelings with her. This will also become easier with practice.

7. I can practice listening to my wife and my kids, encouraging them, and showing interest in what they're doing.

SUMMARY OF KEY IDEAS

1. Resentment can be thought of as recurring anger about a past event.
2. Resentment can be released by exploring five areas: (1) Is my resentment worth it? (2) Why did others act the way they did? (3) Is the resentment simply a message that I need to take action? (4) Is my resentment due to distorted thinking? (5) Am I receiving secondary gains from this resentment?
3. Envy is the feeling of discontent that occurs when you want something that someone else has.
4. The assumption underlying envy is that what this person has "should" belong to you but you've lost it to them in some mysterious way. This causes you to believe that life is not fair. These false beliefs usually trigger anger and resentment, and you might take direct or indirect actions to either demean or sabotage the other person's good fortune.
5. The key to reducing envy is to challenge the erroneous assumptions that support it and clarify how you find happiness in life.
6. Jealousy is generated by the belief that you have what you want but might lose it to someone else. This belief is often due to insecurity and a sense that others can't be trusted. When intense, jealousy can cause suspi-

cious fears and watchful guarding.

7. Working to challenge core beliefs that generate jealousy, practicing trust and kindness, and learning to develop intimacy are the basic approaches to overcoming jealousy.

RECOMMENDED ACTIVITIES

Create at Least One Summary Sheet

If you have not yet created a summary sheet, do so this week. If you have already created one, select a new issue that you would like to address, and create a summary sheet for it. Use the section of your journal that you set aside for summary sheets. Be sure to review the instructions for creating summary sheets in Chapter 12.

Label Resentment, Envy, and Jealousy Accurately.

This week, set some time aside to identify times when you experienced resentment, envy, and jealousy. As you consider these times, answer the following questions.

- What events triggered each of these emotions?
- What thoughts were you thinking just before and while you were resentful, envious, or jealous?
- What did you do in response to these emotions?
- If your behavior was inappropriate, what could you do differently in the future?
- What distorted thinking or false beliefs caused you to feel this emotion? What rational challenges could you use to correct your distorted thinking the next time you think this way?

Continue to Create and Use D.E.R. Scripts

Continue to create and use D.E.R. scripts when you are in a conflict situation or have a problem that you want to resolve with others. If this is difficult for you, take several days to review Chapters 10 and 11 before you begin the next chapter.

Continue to Record in Your Journal

Record at least one incident in your journal when you became angry, and analyze it using the same format, shown below, as you used in Chapter 9.

Date:

Incident:

Level of Arousal ___, *Level of Aggression* ___

Thoughts:

Actions:

What emotions other than anger was I feeling?

Five Questions:

1. *What exactly did this person do that triggered my anger?*
2. *What needs or wants caused this person to act in this way?*
3. *What beliefs or aspects of this person's past (hurts, losses, successes, fears, lack of skills, etc.) influenced this behavior?*
4. *Considering the above, how could I have responded in a different and more effective manner? How might a positive role model have behaved?*
5. *Were any negative labels, family role models, or incidents from the past affecting this situation?*

Rational Challenges

14

Managing the Frustrations of Parenting

I F YOU DO not have children, you might think that this chapter doesn't apply to you. It does. Most of the ideas it contains apply to adult relationships as well as to parent-child relationships. In addition, it can help you identify parenting approaches that you experienced as a child, along with their effects on you. If you have children, you can do this too, but your main focus should be identifying those areas where un-realistic expectations generate inappropriate anger and self-defeating behaviors. This will not only reduce the amount of anger your children trigger, it will also make you a more ef-fective parent and your children more enjoyable.

CHILDREN ARE NOT MINIATURE ADULTS

One of the most common errors adults make with children is to treat them as if they were miniature adults. Children are different from adults in many important ways. First of all, they do not have the experience that adults have. Everything is new and mysterious to them. While children often are very good at learning by observing others, adults often expect them to know things that they have no way of knowing simply because they are a certain age. As a child, David often heard phrases such as, "At your age, you should know that," or "You're old enough to know better." However, no one ever took the time to teach him the things he was "supposed" to know. Instead, he was left on his own to try to figure them out.

One day when David, as an adult, was unloading the dishwasher, he noticed that a glass was not clean because his six-year-old son had not placed it in the rack properly. In the past, David would have accused his son of being lazy, or worse, of deliberately disobeying him. Poor performance on chores was an area where David frequently had angry encounters with his son. Now, because we had recently discussed that children need training, David took a moment to cool down, before calling his son to him with a friendly voice. Using "I messages," he said, "I see that some of the dishes didn't get washed thoroughly. Let's take out the clean ones, and I'll show you how to load the dirty ones so the water is able to reach everything." During the next few days, David made a point to stay in the kitchen, control his temper, and remain friendly while his son loaded the dishes. Whenever he saw his son loading them improperly, he pointed it out with a friendly voice and recommended a better way. In a very short time, his son had mastered this skill and was feeling good about his ability to do it well. David was also feeling good about being able to interact with his son in a positive way and teach him a skill without criticism and anger.

Another important difference between children and adults is that children do not have the reasoning ability of adults. Because of the way the brain develops during childhood, many simple concepts that are obvious to an adult are often beyond a child's ability to understand. In fact, some of the more subtle, higher reasoning processes don't begin to develop until the early teenage years.

Especially important in this regard is the fact that children are concrete learners: that is, they learn through physical experiences. A young child does not learn about gravity by hearing verbal explanations about it. Instead, he or she learns by crawling, climbing, throwing, and dropping things. Unfortunately, parents often expect their children to behave just because they have verbally explained to them what their expectations are and what consequences will occur if they don't behave. Young children, however, only understand limits only when they have pushed against them and experienced the consequences of violating them. After they understand a limit, they retest it periodically to see if it's still there. As a general principle, easygoing children test less and strong-willed children test more.

As we have seen, distorted thinking and should/must rules can lead to inappropriate anger (see Chapter 4). By changing her unrealistic expectation that "children should behave after you tell them once," Sharon was able to reduce much of her anger and resentment over her children's normal testing of limits.

MOST THINGS CAN WAIT

Anger, as we have seen, produces energy and motivation in response to a threat (see Chapter 2), the more intense the anger, the greater the motivation to respond to the threat. Taking time-outs is important because anger tends to interfere with our ability to think and make good decisions (see Chapter 2). Unfortunately, when we are angry, we tend to want to resolve problems now, even though it's not likely that we will resolve them effectively. One of life's realities is that very few everyday situations need to be addressed immediately. Most can wait. In fact, by delaying action until you are calm and able to use all of your reasoning ability, you usually choose more effective actions.

When Sharon and David came home after an exhausting day and found their children misbehaving, they learned to delay addressing the problem behaviors. They would say things such as "Go to your room. We'll talk about this later." They found this approach helped them take more reasonable and effective actions. When a new and surprising misbehavior occurred, they would just do what was needed to establish order and then wait until the next day before responding further. This gave them time to think more calmly and develop an appropriate long-term response to the problem. Practicing this type of "time-out" greatly reduced both their inappropriate anger and their inappropriate actions making them much more effective parents.

MINIMIZE ACTIONS THAT DISCOURAGE

When people try to motivate others, they frequently have good intentions but use methods that achieve poor results.

This, in turn, can discourage them and, with children, contribute to a poor self-image. One way to become more effective in all of your relationships is to learn how to encourage others. This reduces the amount of anger you experience due to poor relationship skills.

The first step in becoming a source of encouragement is to minimize the amount of discouragement you do. Here are four common types of discouragement that both children and adults use:

Criticism and Humiliation

People often criticize and humiliate as a way to get others to do what they want them to do. However, if you think of times when you were humiliated or criticized, it's easy to see how counterproductive this method can be and how it can cause a person to resist your efforts or give up. One common form of humiliation is name-calling. In Chapter 8, we explored common negative labels that are used with children. Another common form of humiliation is inappropriate teasing. Be sensitive to times and issues that your children, friends, or partner finds difficult. For example, a child preparing for his or her first piano recital is usually very nervous. Making jokes about people laughing at mistakes and similar frightening comments can be devastating. This would be a time to offer support and encouragement. The same applies to times when your partner is having difficulties.

Asking for Perfection

Parents want their children to master the skills needed to be successful adults, but when they think of their children as miniature adults, they frequently expect them to complete tasks as an adult would. The frustration and negative feelings this expectation generates in a child can be tremendous.

Many good books are available that describe child development. If you are not sure what is appropriate for your children, I recommend that you read a couple of books like this or attend a parenting class to gain more realistic ideas about what to expect from your children.

Asking for perfection doesn't apply only to children. People often expect other adults to live up to unrealistically high expectations. Considering how you would perform in circumstances similar to those of another adult can provide a good reality check on whether your expectations are realistic. Additionally, if you are highly skilled or knowledgeable in a certain area, remember to lower your expectations for those who are less skilled or knowledgeable. While this seems obvious, it's surprising how often people just don't do it.

Overprotection

Parents want to protect their children and keep them safe from harm. Unfortunately, overprotection during childhood can become a major source of dysfunction in adulthood. One source of Carmen's two core beliefs, "The world is dangerous" and "I am not as capable as others" was her parent's overprotection. This message, although indirect, was powerful. Children need to be allowed to test their wings and take reasonable risks such as climbing on playground equipment and using age-appropriate cooking equipment. Only by doing something do they gain confidence in their ability to take care of themselves and meet successfully the various challenges life presents. A good general principle is, "Never do for children what they can do for themselves."

Making Comparisons

In order to encourage their children to try to do as well as other children, adults often compare them with their siblings or friends. Unfortunately, this is usually very counterproductive and can lead to a poor self-image. Think for a moment of how you would feel if your partner was always pointing out how others were doing things better than you. Even if they always added, "You can do that too," you would probably have negative feelings and would not want to cooperate. You might even feel like abandoning the activity where the comparison was being made.

BECOMING A SOURCE OF ENCOURAGEMENT

Here are several ways in which you can encourage others. Place a check by those that are difficult for you.

Say Thank You

Showing appreciation for the positive things that others do is one of the simplest yet most effective forms of encouragement. Because Sharon and David both grew up in households where little appreciation was shown, they rarely expressed appreciation to others. Both of them made a conscious decision to say thank you to someone at least once each day for two weeks, and it soon became a regular part of their vocabulary.

Give Genuine Compliments

A genuine compliment is a comment about a small specific thing that someone has done or some quality of that person. In contrast, global praise tends to be general and excessive. The difference is most easily seen by contrasting the two as is done below.

Global Praise: You always look so great.
Genuine Compliment: I like the color of that shirt.

Global Praise: You did a great job cleaning the house.

Genuine Compliment: Thank you for vacuuming and picking up. It looks much better.

Global Praise: You're a fantastic cook.

Genuine Compliment: I enjoyed the lasagna. The sauce was delicious.

Global Praise: You're such a good person.

Genuine Compliment: Thank you for taking time to drop by. I was feeling a little lonely and your visit really brightened my day.

Global praise, while positive, is so absolute that it's difficult to accept. To some, the excessively high standard of performance it implies can also feel like a burden. At the same time, you aren't quite sure what it was that you did that is being appreciated. In contrast, genuine compliments tell you exactly what was appreciated. Because they deal with small, specific actions, they are also easier to accept as true. The other important feature of genuine compliments is that they tend to cause a person to repeat the action that was complimented.

Often someone like Alex, who is a perfectionist and always aware of what's wrong, has difficulty noticing positive things. He decided to practice giving at least one genuine complement each day for three weeks. At first, this was difficult for him, and several days would go by without any compliments. Slowly, as he redoubled his effort, he soon became comfortable giving compliments. He found that he was not only developing a more positive attitude, but that people were being friendlier with him.

Have Regular Special Time with Each Child

Special time is one-on-one time, when one parent does something enjoyable with one child. If you do not spend regular special time with each of your children, you are missing the opportunity to create memories that you and your children will cherish. You are also not taking advantage of the best means for building a positive relationship and for encouraging your children. Spending regular special time with children is one of the most powerful ways to let them know you love them and they are important. Unfortunately, when you are having an ongoing conflict with a child or partner, special time can be difficult. Instead, the focus shifts to punishing or avoiding this person. The key to breaking this vicious cycle is to reconnect through positive activities. In addition, whenever a child or parent is experiencing personal difficulties in life, additional special time is needed and will greatly increase the bond between you.

Recognize Improvement and Effort

When someone is struggling to learn something new, comment positively on small steps this person is making in the right direction. Examples: "That looks much better." "It didn't take you as long to do it this time." "You're improving."

Give Hope

Think of times when someone gave hope that helped you continue in the face of adversity. What a blessing it is to do the same for others. Examples: "I know you can do it." "Keep on trying. You've almost got it."

Emphasize Process Not Product

Emphasizing process is especially useful with people who are perfectionists and feel that their performance rarely meets their expectations. Examples: "You're sure putting a lot of effort into that." "It's good to see you enjoy doing that."

Identify Similarities Between Yourself and Your Child

During times of trouble, one of the most encouraging things to hear is how someone else struggled with the same issue and came through it successfully. Examples: "I had a tough time with that when I was your age too." "That hurt a lot when it happened to me, but I eventually moved on with my life." "I've felt that way."

Show Sympathy but Avoid Pity

Showing sympathy is showing that you understand and feel sorrow for the misfortune or suffering that someone has experienced. Pity is feeling sorry for the person because of a misfortune or suffering. Here's an example of pity: "Oh you poor thing. How awful!" Here are examples of sympathy: "I can see that you had a rough time." "It's sad when that happens." "How frustrating." Pity tends to see someone as a helpless victim. Sympathy views them as able to deal with misfortune and sadness. Pity conveys the message that a child will be overwhelmed by sad events. Sympathy conveys the message that the child will hurt when sad events occur but will eventually recover and move on.

TEACHABLE AND UNTEACHABLE TIMES

Curiously, parents often try to teach their children important lessons at times when they are least able to learn them. A lecture when a child is upset and unable to process logical information is useless. Worse yet, the result in both is often frustration and anger. For example, when a child breaks a favorite toy and is crying, a lecture on the proper handling of toys will not be heard. Likewise, a lecture on door safety is not heard when a child is crying because of accidentally shutting a door on his or her finger.

In both these examples, the parent wants the child to learn a valuable lesson. Unfortunately, strong emotions prevent children from hearing logical information. In addition, the strong emotion that parents usually feel at these times tends to make them use one or more of the forms of discouragement previously discussed. The same holds true for adults: We are not teachable when we're upset. We need to calm down in order to process new information fully.

Once a person has calmed down, avoid lecturing or scolding the child, and use the problem solving approach described in Chapter 11. With younger children, you can simplify this approach into three questions:

- What happened?
- Why do you think that happened?
- How could you do things differently next time?

When you want to discuss a problem that concerns you directly, such as poorly done household chores, find a time when both you and your child are feeling relaxed and in a good mood, such as after school, when the child is having a snack, or after dinner. Avoid times when the child is upset or might be tired and uncooperative, such as just before bedtime.

While special time should focus on positive activities, it can also become a time when you pass values and traditions on to your children. Avoid talking about problems with homework and chores, but do talk about positive things that the child has done or about life issues that are important to the child. Here are some examples.

- I liked the way you were able to work things out with Jim this afternoon. (This comment was made while playing cards with a child who has difficulty resolving problems with his friends.)

- Why do you think the boy in that movie we watched was so unhappy? (This comment, said while baking cookies, led to a short discussion on how people find happiness.)

LOWER YOUR ACTION POINT

Carmen, although she was generally fairly nonassertive, could become very angry and aggressive with her children. When one of her children was misbehaving, she would give a friendly warning or reminder. If the child continued to mis-behave, the level of her anger would rise, and she would say

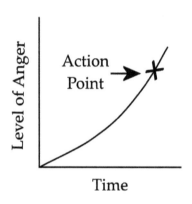

things such as "How many times have I told you . . . ," "Why aren't you listening?" and "Haven't I already told you . . ." Because she tended to suppress her anger, it had to rise to a fairly high level before she would take action. This process is diagramed at the right.

By warning them gently, Carmen was trying too hard to be nice to her children, and be-cause she did not follow through on her warnings with actions, her children had learned to ig-nore them. Since she took action only when she became very an-gry, her children became "par-ent deaf" when she spoke in a

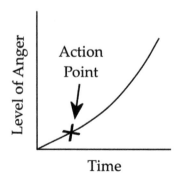

normal voice. Without realizing it, she had taught her children that the only time her directions would be backed with action was when she was angry.

The solution for this situation, although initially difficult for Carmen, was simple. She needed to lower her action point and take action that backed up her words while she was still calm. This is diagramed at the right. By taking action when she was calmer, she was able to enforce consequences in a more reasonable manner.

Alex found this same principle applied to many situations in his life. When his girlfriend or a coworker did something that bothered him, he found that by speaking up while his anger was at a low level, he was able to use the various assertive skills he was learning much more effectively.

NATURAL AND LOGICAL CONSEQUENCES

A natural consequence is an undesirable outcome that occurs in the absence of parental intervention that teaches a child a lesson. A child breaks a favorite toy by mishandling it, for example, or becomes cold because of forgetting his or her coat. In these types of situations, a child can learn important lessons as long as the parent does not interfere by scolding, lecturing, or trying to "fix" the situation. All the parent needs to do is be sympathetic, use listening skills, and, if appropriate, do some problem solving with the child.

Soon after learning this principle, Carmen received a phone call from school. One of her children had forgotten his lunch. Her response was "I really can't take off from work to bring it to you, but it will keep in the refrigerator. You can have it when you get home." In the past, she would have taken thirty minutes off work to bring her son his lunch. Then she would have to make up the time she missed during her own lunchtime. Once she began using this new approach, she was surprised at how quickly her son began to remember his lunch on his own. She had learned an important principle: "Children continue to forget whenever there is an adult to remember for them."

Unfortunately, many undesirable things that children do have no natural consequence (such as tracking mud onto a floor you just cleaned) or have unacceptable consequences (such as being hit by a car due to running into the street). In these cases, the parent needs to create a logical consequence. When developing logical consequences, remember the three R's; they need to be reasonable, respectful, and related to the misbehavior.

The easiest way to develop a logical consequence to use for a specific misbehavior is to imagine what would happen if you, as an adult, did that behavior. If you threw food while eating at a friend's house, you would probably be asked to leave. Thus, for a young child showing poor table manners, a logical consequence would be to have the child leave the table. Similarly, if you left a bike outside, it might be stolen; so, a logical consequence for a child who continues to forget to put away a bike would be to remove the bike for a few days.

Logical consequences are most effective when applied to recurring misbehaviors. With young children, state what you want and the logical consequence of not doing it just prior to when the misbehavior usually occurs. When Carmen took her preschooler to a nearby park, he would throw sand at the other children. To solve this problem, Carmen began to set this limit as they were arriving at the park: "If you want to play in sandbox, you need to keep the sand on the ground and not throw it. If you throw sand, we will go home." At first, the child immediately began throwing sand at another child as he had always done. When the child had done this in the past, Carmen would give endless warnings and eventually spank him when they got home. Now, however, she took him by the hand and returned home, saying in a calm voice, "You cannot play at the park if you throw sand at the other children. It looks like you have chosen to go home. We'll try again after naptime."

Notice how her reply put the responsibility of having to go home on the child, along with the promise that they would "try again." To her delight, she only had to take him home twice. By taking action rather than giving endless reminders, scolding, and yelling, she was now using a form of training that matched the concrete way in which young children learn.

When you set up a logical consequence with older children, use a modified D.E.R. script where the request includes both your request and the consequence of not meeting the request. When Sharon's children were leaving candy wrappers in the living room, she addressed the problem this way: "During the past several days, I've noticed that there have been lots of candy wrappers left in the living room when I come home. I'm concerned that we might have a problem with ants again. If you cannot put your wrappers in the trash where they belong, there will be no candy in the house for a week." It only took one application of this consequence for the children to change their behavior.

Much more could be said about logical consequences, but it's beyond the scope of this book to go into any more detail. If this is a new concept for you or if you have difficulty applying it, many excellent parenting books are available that have examples of logical consequences for just about every situation you might encounter.

GET OUT OF THE "CRIME AND PUNISHMENT" CYCLE

Many parents use punishment as their main tool for training children. While logical consequences are an important part of parenting, you will not be effective if they are your primary tool. As children grow older, they eventually realize that with enough determination and resistance, no one can make them do something they don't want to do. Strong-willed children (like David when he was young) often learn this at an early age. The result is tremendous anger and fighting between parents and children.

The most effective way to influence children as they get older is through your relationship with them. If it's strong and positive, they will naturally want to please you and respond more readily to your guidance. If the relationship is severely damaged, you have little or no influence over them. Having regular special time with them when they are young, and emphasizing encouragement, are the best ways to develop strong, positive relationships with your children. Repairing a damaged relationship with older children is more difficult and takes time and effort, but encouragement and special time are the best way to accomplish it.

Identifying the reason for a child's misbehavior is also useful. Younger children often misbehave simply due to fatigue, hunger, or illness; when this is the case, addressing the cause is much more effective than punishing the crime. David was on vacation with his family when his children were beginning to become quarrelsome. He realized that it was past their normal lunchtime, so he said, "I'm hungry. Is anyone else ready for lunch?" His children quickly stopped fighting and began discussing what they wanted to eat.

Another useful concept is to identify a "theme" for each of

your children. A theme is the area where a child struggles the most while growing up. The easiest way to identify a child's theme is to think of the misbehaviors that are most troublesome with that child. For example, if the child does not cooperate well, the theme you need to stress is cooperation. If the child has many fears, the theme is learning to be strong and courageous. If the child is selfish, the theme is thinking of others.

Surprisingly, many themes are due not to poor childrearing practices but to inborn genetic tendencies. They are not your fault. They are just a reflection of the child's personality. You will probably not resolve such problem areas in a week or even a few months. Instead, you will most likely work with the child on his or her themes throughout the time he or she is in your house. This does not mean you are constantly focused on the child's themes. Instead, as the child grows, the problems connected to a given theme come and go, changing and developing variations. Hopefully, real progress will have been made by the time the child is launched into the world. Viewing your child in this more realistic way helps you remain calm when your child's theme resurfaces from time to time.

Sidestepping Power Struggles

Power struggles are a natural part of parenting. As a child grows and develops, the need to see how much power he or she has is normal. Easygoing children test limits less frequently, strong willed children test more frequently. If you or your partner has a need to be powerful, as Sharon and David did, the chances are that at least one of your children will also display this characteristic. Unfortunately, when dealing with power-hungry children, adults themselves often become very childish.

Reducing Power Struggles

Here are several things you can do to reduce the frequency and intensity of power struggles.

Have Special Time

Effective parenting is always based on establishing a positive relationship with the child. Having regular special time is the best way to develop a positive relationship. When you are having difficulties with a child, your anger and disappointment can make it difficult to have special time. This is usually when special time is especially important. If you are struggling with a child, write about your negative feelings toward him or her in your journal, or discuss them with someone you trust. Talking to people with older children can give you perspective and hope.

Set Reasonable Yet Firm Limits

You need to decide what behavior you can and can't live with, what you can and can't control, and what choices you are willing to give your children. You also need to be able to define problem behaviors clearly and specifically—exactly what does the child do that concerns or bothers you?

Give the Child Positive Power

When children have positive ways to feel powerful, they are less likely to seek power through negative ways. Here are three general ways to give children positive power:

- Allow the child positive choices you can live with. Example: "The leaves need to be raked up before you go to your friend's Saturday morning. When would you like to do it?" Notice that an unspoken consequence has been built into this chore: if the leaves aren't raked by Saturday morning, you will do it before going to your friend's house.

- Be willing to compromise through joint, mutual problem solving. Nothing makes a child feel more powerful than solving a problem. Either use the five-step process described in Chapter 11 or the simplified three-question version described earlier in this chapter.

- Redirect the child's energy into constructive channels. This can be done through sports, hobbies, and chores.

Show Respect:

"Do unto others as you would have others do unto you." Neither the parent nor the child should be a slave or a tyrant. This is especially true when carrying out logical consequences. Do not give long lectures or make derogatory remarks. Instead, enforce limits with as few words as possible.

Recognize the Parent's Role in Power Struggles:

Realize that a child who wants to be powerful often has a parent who is controlling and over focused on being powerful.

Responding to a Power Struggle

Here are some specific guidelines on how to respond when a power struggle begins.

Control Your Anger
If you are overly angry, take a brief time-out, so you can cool down and decide what is most important right now.

Focus on What Is Needed to Maintain Order
Power struggles are unteachable times. Do only what is necessary to maintain order. Leave everything else to a later time. If a child needs to be in his or her room, just send him or her there. If a child needs to go to school, focus on getting him or her out the door and nothing more.

Do the Unexpected or Withdraw
A parent who has been continually battling a child about picking up toys before bedtime might say, "Let's just leave everything and get ready for bed." This parent might then develop a logical consequence and explain it to the child the next day: "Either you can pick up the toys, or I will do so after you go to bed. If I pick up the toys, they will go into a bag and be placed in the garage for a week."

Implement Logical Consequences as Calmly as Possible
Focus on only one consequence at a time. Delay dealing with less important issues until after you have accomplished your primary goal.

Let the Child Save Face
After you have invoked a logical consequence, the child might mutter or slam the door. Ignore it. The old idea that a child "should do what I say and smile when he or she does it" is not valid. When you get a traffic ticket, you are unhappy. Allow the child to be unhappy.

Remember Recurring Patterns
Power struggles occur most frequently when either the parent or the child is tired, hungry, ill, experiencing extra stress, or feeling powerless. If you have noticed that power struggles arise when the child comes home from school or that he or she has problems with cleaning up toys just before bedtime, consider how you can sidestep these types of situations. You might make a snack available as soon as the child comes home, or you might have pickup time earlier.

SUGGESTIONS FOR VERY YOUNG CHILDREN

Here are some additional suggestions for very young children

Environmental Control (Babyproofing)
Move expensive or easily broken items out of reach rather than constantly saying no and punishing.

Remember That Fatigue, Hunger, and Illness Are the Three Most Common Sources of Misbehavior
Do not delay a young child's mealtime, nap, or bedtime and expect cooperation.

Try to Maintain a Routine
Regular mealtimes, naps, bedtimes, and play times make a child's world more predictable and reduce misbehavior.

Distraction/Redirection
When a child is upset or doing something you don't like, point out something interesting or begin a simple game.

Positive Attitude
"Act as if" you expect the child to be cooperative, and ignore negative comments. Use positive words and mannerisms.

Set Limits with Simple Language
Avoid repeating explanations that the child has either already heard or is too young to understand.

Time Out
A common consequence for young children is to send the child to his or her room for a time out. It's often helpful, for both you and the child, to set a timer to signal the end of the time-out.

Reverse Time Out
Instead of sending a child to his or her room, you withdraw.

Again, many good books are available that explain each of these parenting techniques in detail. If you are unfamiliar or unskilled with them, I encourage you to read one or two books or attend a parenting class to pick up new ideas on how to solve recurring problem behaviors.

SUMMARY OF KEY IDEAS

1. Children are not miniature adults. They don't have the experience or the reasoning powers of adults. They think in concrete terms.
2. Most problems with children do not have to be solved immediately. Waiting until you are calm and logical often makes you much more effective.
3. Parents often try to motivate children with methods

that are discouraging and generate a poor self-image. Reducing discouragement and increasing encouragement builds a closer relationship.

4. People are unteachable when they are experiencing strong negative emotions. Wait until everyone is calm and friendly.

5. Being willing to take action that backs up your words while you are still calm (lowering your action point) makes you more effective because you are responding with all of your reasoning abilities.

6. The quality of your relationship with a child is the key to your effectiveness. The stronger and more positive your relationship, the more effective you will be as the child grows older.

7. Natural and logical consequences are essential parts of effective parenting.

8. While power contests are a normal part of child development, you can sidestep many of them in several ways.

Recommended Activities

If You Do Not Have Children

- List the ideas in this chapter that apply to your relationship with your partner, friends, and coworkers. Review this list at the beginning of each day for one week.

- List poor parenting approaches that your parents used, along with any irrational beliefs that might have developed as a result of these approaches.

- Review the section titled "Becoming a Source of Encouragement." Identify those forms of discouragement you use. Write these on a card and review them at the beginning of each day for a two-week period. Make a conscious effort to avoid using them. Next, identify two forms of encouragement that you would like to practice. Write them on the same card, and review them at the beginning of each day for a two-week period. Make a conscious effort to use both forms of encouragement at least once each day.

If You Have Children

- Identify the forms of discouragement you wish to reduce, along with the forms of encouragement you wish to increase. Write them on a card. Make a conscious effort to avoid using the forms of discouragement. Practice using the forms of encouragement at least once each day for two weeks.
- If logical consequences are new to you, develop a logical consequence for one recurring misbehavior.
- If you are not already doing so, begin spending special time with each child.
- Make a list of the specific ideas and skills you would like to work on. In the weeks to come, review this chapter periodically, and work on one skill at a time for a period of one to two weeks.
- Consider reading a parenting book or attending a parenting class. This is especially important if you feel you have not been effective with your children. In order to change your behavior, you need to have a clear idea of the new behavior you want to substitute for the old one.

Continue to Create and Use D.E.R. Scripts

Continue to create and use D.E.R. scripts when you are in conflict situations or have a problem with others that you wish to resolve. If this is difficult for you, take several days to review Chapters 10 and 11 before you begin the next chapter.

Revise Your Summary Sheets

This chapter contains many different suggestions on actions you can take with children. Most of them also apply to adults. Review the "Things I Can Do" section of each summary sheet you've created, and add any ideas in this chapter that apply.

15

Making Peace with Intimacy

T HE NEED TO experience intimacy is one of the most basic and strongest needs we have. Unfortunately, when intimacy becomes paired with pain, it can become very frightening. As we have already seen, much of the inappropriate anger that people experience is due to their defending against childhood pain. While these painful childhood associations can make experiencing intimacy difficult, the rewards of reducing their influence are well worth the effort. Indeed, making peace with intimacy is one of the most powerful ways to tame the beast.

SUBSTITUTES FOR INTIMACY

Painful childhood associations with intimacy can interfere

with one's ability to form relationships and feel intimate with others. As a result, normal activities can become substitutes for intimacy, such as sex, work, drugs, fame, power, and accomplishment. David, for example, having grown up in a critical and emotionally distant family, found it difficult to give his wife genuine compliments, hold her hand, and do many of the other little things commonly associated with intimacy. Instead, his main way of feeling close to her was through sex. His experience with sports gave him a way to experience intimacy with other men when he talked about sports with them. Since all of his eggs were in these two baskets, he guarded both of them fiercely. The dialogue between David and his wife recorded in Chapter 11 shows how difficult it was for him to hear her request to spend more time together. Instead, he defended his right to spend time watching sports on television.

David's association of pain with intimacy also interfered with his relationship with his children. Because young children usually are nonthreatening, David found it easy to hug, talk to, and play with his children when they were young. However, as his children grew, it became increasingly difficult for him to give compliments and express warmth. Instead, he found himself relating to them more and more in the critical manner of the parents who raised him.

Sharon also found it difficult to express intimacy verbally or to allow herself to be vulnerable. She did have a wider range of physical intimacy that was "safe." In addition to sex, she enjoyed holding hands, hugging, and cuddling. Indeed, lack of this type of physical intimacy was a big source of conflict in her marriage and one of the reasons for her divorce.

Another substitute for intimacy was the recognition Sharon received for her accomplishments at work. While everyone enjoys receiving recognition, Sharon's need for it had become exaggerated because she used it to meet her need for relationship and connection. This increased her fear of making mistakes, since errors might cause disapproval and a loss of recognition.

Alex used the emotional intensity experienced in the early stages of a relationship as his primary way of experiencing intimacy. He was good at playing the role of suitor, and he enjoyed the intoxicating emotions associated with infatuation. The fact that he did not have to disclose much about himself during the initial phase of a relationship helped to make it safe. However, as infatuation shifted to the deeper intimacy of a more lasting relationship, he would start to feel restless. Messages of danger, triggered by his painful childhood associations with intimacy, became louder. He would eventually find something wrong with the relationship and move on to the emotional high of a new pursuit.

Substituting less satisfying activities for intimacy is similar to drinking salt water in an attempt to quench your thirst. At first, the salt water seems to satisfy your thirst, but the salt actually causes the body to lose water. After a short time, you are actually thirstier and craving more to drink.

Because the various substitutes don't really satisfy the need for true intimacy, they leave you feeling emptier than when you started. This causes you to try to meet this need with even more of the substitute. The only way out is to recognize what is happening and learn how to meet your need for intimacy in a healthy and direct way. Doing so not only reduces your distorted thinking, inappropriate anger, and self-defeating behavior, it also assists you in leading a happier and more satisfying life.

WHAT IS INTIMACY LIKE?

Emotional intimacy is based on the belief that you have a strong connection to another person and that you are safe with this person. You can be vulnerable without fear of ridicule, and you can express your emotions, hopes, dreams, and fears without censoring them. You trust that he or she will not hurt you when you expose this confidential and vulnerable side of yourself.

Those who grow up in families where their parents were warm and trustworthy, like Carmen, experienced this kind of intimacy as a natural part of childhood. It's easy for them to expect others to behave in this way. Those whose parents were cold and distant, like Sharon and David's parents, or used things said in confidence as a weapon, like Alex's parents, find this type of intimacy very uncomfortable. Still, with an understanding of what is happening and with time, you can learn to enjoy intimacy and feel safe with another person.

Three things are necessary in order to be intimate with another person. First, the other person must both desire this type of intimacy and have the capacity to be intimate.

When David and I first began working together, one of his wife's complaints was that he was "distant." However, when he began to control his anger and act in more loving ways, she became more distant herself. She came in for several sessions with David, and we explored why this was occurring. We found two reasons. First, she didn't trust that the changes she was seeing in David would last. However, when she constructed her own genogram, a second reason soon became evident. Like David, she came from a family that was disengaged and distant. Intimacy was just as frightening for her as it was for him. As long as she considered David as the only one with a problem, she did not have to look at her own difficulties with intimacy.

The second requirement for intimacy is being comfortable with intimacy. When a parent continually thwarts a child's attempts to be close, a strong association between the pain of rejection and intimacy develops. As the child becomes an adult, a strong unconscious defense against becoming too intimate develops. Then, whenever the painful emotions associated with intimacy are experienced, an automatic conditioned response is triggered that causes the person to do something that creates a "safe" emotional distance. Since this is an unconscious association, people tend to be confused by their behavior and say things such as, "I don't know why I back off" or "I don't know why I get so uncomfortable when this is something I really want."

Fortunately, it's possible to go through a desensitization process and overcome the unconscious fear of intimacy that a lack of intimacy in childhood has caused. This is done by learning to experience and be comfortable with intimacy in stages. This is a form of systematic desensitization used to overcome other types of deeply ingrained fears.

Both David and his wife found the "What's happening? What's real?" technique (described in Chapter 8) useful in overcoming their discomfort with intimacy. Whenever David found himself becoming uncomfortable during a time of closeness, he would tell himself, "It feels like those old warning signs from childhood are going off. My wife is not my mother or father. She is a different person who is on my side and who is a safe person." Sometimes he would also share with his wife what he was experiencing. While this was difficult for him, it was another step toward becoming more open and intimate. All his life he had hidden these types of feelings both from himself and from others. He was now learning that he no longer had to run away from them. He was also learning that there was someone he could trust, and over time, he found it easier to share his feelings with his wife.

As David's wife also began to trust him and become more comfortable with intimacy, their relationship changed in ways that neither of them had expected. They found that their ability to communicate honestly and to feel like a team rather than adversaries increased. Their ability to resolve conflict increased. Indeed, finding the type of love that truly satisfies was one of the most powerful tools David discovered for taming the beast. After all, much of the beast's ranting was simply the cry of a hurt child retaliating against a painful childhood world that no longer existed.

The third requirement for intimacy is the ability to think and act in a realistic and mature way. We will explore this area in detail in the following section.

Eight Qualities That Increase Intimacy

The behaviors and skills necessary for an intimate relationship do not come naturally — they must be learned. Therefore, the key to change is to notice old patterns as soon as they start and choose new responses that move you toward your goal. Eight specific qualities are characteristic of the realistic and mature thinking essential for intimate relationships. Fortunately, you probably already have several of them and only need to work on a few of them. Place a check by those qualities that are comfortable and reflect your current behavior and a star by those you need to practice.

Accept Responsibility for My Actions.

If you want an intimate, mature, adult relationship, you need to be a mature adult who is willing to be vulnerable. Instead of waiting for your partner to change, identify what you yourself need to do differently. If you are weak in this area, you need to address (1) the various forms of distorted thinking described in Chapter 4, (2) the tendency to blame, and (3) the four erroneous assumptions described in Chapter 6. If accepting responsibility for your actions is still difficult for you, review these chapters and identify areas of work you still need to do in each one.

Identify Needs Clearly and Take Direct, Positive Action to Meet Them.

If you are unable to identify accurately your own needs and take positive steps to meet them, it's unreasonable to expect your partner to do it for you. It also is unreasonable to expect your partner to fulfill all your needs. No human can successfully meet all of the needs of another. One of the challenges that everyone faces is finding ways to satisfy the needs that our partners are unable to meet.

Carmen's husband loved her deeply, but he just didn't understand why "talking about feelings" was so important to her. He tried to be empathetic and listen, but because of his personality, she would frequently become frustrated with his clumsiness. As she and I discussed this problem, she realized that she was expecting her husband to react toward her the same way she responded to him. She was a very emotional and sensitive person, while he was very practical and easygoing. In fact, his emotional steadiness was one of the qualities that attracted her to him when they first met and one that she had always admired. As she thought about it, she realized that she needed to spend more time with friends who responded more as she did.

Carmen's recognition of her need to find sensitive friends does not mean that she stopped asking her husband to communicate his feelings. In fact, his ability to do so did increase as she encouraged him. However, she came to understand and accept that the differences in their personalities meant he was unable to fully meet her need in this area. Having friends she could talk to not only helped her meet her need, but also made times when her husband did talk about himself more satisfying.

If you expect your partner to meet all of your needs, you place him or her in an impossible situation. Take some time this week to identify friends or relatives whose strengths or interests can compensate for qualities your partner lacks. A word of caution: It's best to choose same-sex friends when doing this. If you do have a close friendship with someone of the opposite sex who is near your age who is filling a need your mate lacks, do not place yourself in compromising situations, such as working together late or spending time alone with this person at his or her residence. People who don't follow these simple commonsense guidelines often find themselves turning to this person for intimacy when their own relationship is going through a difficult period. The disastrous results of these types of affairs are all too common today.

Let Go of the Past and Focus on the Present.

When I am counseling couples, the first rule I establish is: When discussing current problems do not talk about past problems and hurts. Unfortunately, many people become so attached to the past that they are unable to separate it from the present. It becomes a lens through which they see current events. This causes them to distort the present so it looks like the past, which virtually guarantees that nothing positive will occur.

If you dwell frequently on the past or return to past hurts when dealing with current conflicts, you need to work in two areas. First, separate the present from the past. Many people mistakenly believe they are controlled by the past—that once something strongly influences their life it will continue to determine their feelings and behavior for the rest of their lives.

When Alex was angry with someone, his self-talk often included statements such as "I'll never be able to forget what he did" or "I can never trust her again." Such statements are usually false overgeneralizations. While you might not be able to forget negative experiences, you can choose to think about other, more positive things rather than dwell on them. Likewise, just because something holds true in some circumstances, it doesn't mean that it's equally true under all conditions. When a person lets you down, caution in the future is usually warranted. However, it doesn't necessarily mean that this person will always let you down. Allowing yourself to remain too strongly influenced by past events can also cause you to stop trying. In fact, the irrational belief that the past determines the future can become a self-fulfilling prophecy.

The second area to work on is developing the belief that today is your point of power. Considering the past objectively can help you avoid repeating mistakes. Working to change how you think and act today is the key to future change. If dwelling on the past is a problem for you, create a summary sheet for this issue.

Communicate My Feelings with Honesty and Openness.

If you are a mystery to your partner, true intimacy is impossible. Hiding your emotional life from your partner forces him or her to guess at what you are experiencing. Since people often guess incorrectly, much misunderstanding and discord can result. In Chapter 9, we saw how people use anger to defend themselves from emotional pain and the importance of learning to identify your emotions accurately. As you learn to identify your feelings accurately, sharing what you experience through "I messages" (described in Chapter 10) is a powerful way to help your partner understand you more fully.

In addition to being able to identify and communicate your feelings, you also need to understand and accept the different emotional responses of your partner. Because of the many temperamental and emotional differences between men and women in general and the specific differences between any two individuals, it's natural that your partner will see events and your relationship differently from you. Sometimes, the needs of one of you will be met while the other will be disappointed. What is ideal for one could be boredom for the other. For honest and open communication to work, it must be a two-way street. You must courageously ask how your partner feels and not just focus on what you feel. When your partner shares differences and hard-to-hear truths, you must be ready to hear them with acceptance rather than with blame or retaliation.

Listen Empathetically When Feelings Are Being Expressed.

The first step in learning to listen empathetically is to stop talking and pay close attention to what the other person is saying. Asking questions, focusing on problem solving, and providing information are a normal part of everyday conversation. However, doing this when someone is experiencing strong negative emotions tends to cause a person to stop talking.

One day, David's wife was telling him how swamped she was at work. He genuinely wanted to help her figure out a way to get caught up, so he asked, "How did you get so far behind?" He was puzzled when she abruptly cut him off, saying, "You never try to understand," and walked away. While his question was well intentioned, David later learned that she felt that he was blaming her for her problem. When someone asks you questions while you are upset, it's common to feel accused or put on the spot.

David's question also prevented his wife from saying what was really bothering her. She was actually upset about something a coworker had said. When talking about being swamped with work, she was stating a "presenting problem" that was not really her main concern. People often do this to see if it's safe to discuss the real problem. David had not listened long enough to be sure that he was hearing her real concern, so he addressed something that was really not important to her. His wife, in turn, interpreted this response as an unwillingness to be heard. When someone is emotionally upset, the only questions that tend to be non-threatening are "open-ended" ones such as "Do you want to talk about it?" and "I'd really like to hear about what's going on."

A second common mistake many people make when listening is to try to begin solving a problem while the other person's negative emotions are still interfering with his or her ability to think logically. Knowing someone understands how you feel reduces the intensity of your negative emotions, which, in turn, allows you to think more logically. Therefore, when someone is experiencing strong negative emotions, it's important to allow for the expression of feelings about the problem before you try to solve it. This helps the person to calm down and switch to the logical thinking required for problem solving.

Another problem with giving information or problem solving is that people who are describing a difficult situation or event often do not want you to offer a solution or advice. Instead, they might simply want someone to know what they have experienced and connect with them emotionally in their difficulty. Connecting with a person experiencing pain on an emotional level like this can be a very intense form of intimacy. Unfortunately, people like Sharon and David find this intense intimacy uncomfortable, so they switch to a logical activity such as giving advice or trying to solve whatever problem they can identify. When David's wife started talking about some difficulty she experienced, he found it helpful to ask her, "Do you want help in resolving this, or do you just want me to listen?"

When you are dealing with a sensitive issue that generates negative emotions, it's best to refrain from trying to solve the problem or provide information until:

- You're reasonably certain you're dealing with the real problem. (You've listened well first.)
- You're certain the other person wants you to help rather than just listen to his or her experience.
- You sense that the other person is ready for your help and is accepting you as a consultant.

When someone is experiencing negative emotions, the basic skill to use in order to listen empathically is called feeling confirmation. It's the process of making guesses about what emotion the speaker is experiencing and then commenting on it. Feeling confirmation is the second of two basic skills used in active listening. The first, paraphrasing, is used to make sure you understand the factual information you are hearing and to let the speaker know you have accurately heard what was said (see Chapter 11). Feeling confirmation focuses on the speaker's emotional response. After you have guessed what the speaker might be feeling, comment on it in one of three ways:

- Make a personal statement about how you would feel in the same situation.
  Examples: "That would have really scared me." "I would have been angry at that."
- Make a statement that uses words like "seem" or "sound" to indicate it's only your perception.
  Examples: "You seem excited." "You sound sad."
- Ask a "soft" question, using words like "aren't," "didn't," or "weren't."
  Examples: "Weren't you worried?" "Didn't that make you angry?"

Remember that when people are hurt, they tend to close the door to communication as a form of self-protection. Being empathetic encourages them to open the door. In addition to using feeling confirmation, a touch on the hand or shoulder and a quieter tone of voice makes you safer. If intimacy has been difficult for you, you might need to practice this for some time before it becomes comfortable. While it took David a few months of conscious practice, he found that feeling confirmation became not only comfortable, but a natural part of how he communicated.

Whenever you want to resolve a conflict or problem that you know will trigger strong negative emotions in the other person, deliver your D.E.R. script, then be ready to switch to listening with feeling confirmation. Proceed with problem solving only when you sense that the other person's strong emotions have lessened. In the following example, notice that David begins with a short D.E.R. script, and then switches to active listening that emphasizes feeling confirmation.

David: "During the last two weeks I've been trying very hard to give you at least one compliment each day, but you haven't acknowledged my efforts. It's discouraging to be working hard and not have it acknowledged. I'd appreciate at least some recognition of my efforts to change."

Wife:"You know how hectic things have been at work. I don't know which way is up."

David: "It has seemed like you've been pretty overwhelmed the past few weeks."

Wife:"The conversion to the new computer system has everyone confused and behind in their work. It's been all I can do just to get through the day."

David: "I guess I'd be pretty distracted if I were facing that."

Wife:"That's exactly how I've been feeling, but I have noticed that you have been different."

David: "I really appreciate hearing that. It means a lot when someone sees the effort I'm making."

Wife:"I do see it. Sometimes I'm just too tired or distracted to say anything."

David: "I can see that you've been really tired, but I would appreciate some encouragement from you. Maybe we could practice giving compliments at dinner."

Wife:"You know, I think that's a good idea."

Choose to Encourage Your Partner.

It's amazing how stingy people can be with encouragement. While encouragement alone cannot transform the person receiving it, it can boost other person's self-confidence and help him or her develop a more positive self-image. It's also an excellent way to show someone you care for them. If you tend to withhold your encouragement, review the section in Chapter 14 that describes how to encourage others and begin practicing these behaviors. In addition to the forms of encouragement suggested there, become comfortable with the following phrases and use them often.

"I love you."
"I like your . . ."
"I like how you . . ."
"I appreciate . . ."
"I enjoyed . . ."
"I value . . ."
"I respect . . ."
"How can I help?"

If you come from a discouraging childhood, it could take time to become comfortable giving encouragement to your partner and friends, but the rewards you reap are well worth the effort.

Choose Thoughts, Words, and Actions That Support the Positive Goals of the Relationship.

If you are in a relationship with someone who is immature, self-centered, vengeful, or violent, this section might not apply. However, if your partner has generally shown that he or she cares for you and wants to be in a loving relationship with you, it's important to remind yourself that your partner is really on your side and would not intentionally harm you. Most of your partner's hurtful behavior is generated by time tunneling or viewing your actions as a coded message that you don't love him or her (see Chapters 7 and 9). It's likely that your partner is struggling just as much as you are with his or her own issues.

When your partner does something that is hurtful, take a time-out before you respond. Once you've calmed down, use the exercise titled, "Take a Walk in Their Shoes" in Chapter 6 to gain some understanding of what caused the hurtful behavior. Then use a D.E.R. script to tell your partner exactly what he or she did that was hurtful. You will then probably need to switch to active listening. Use lots of feeling confirmation and paraphrasing to find out what was behind the hurtful behaviors. Once you have identified the problem, you can then work with your partner on resolving this issue and becoming more loving toward each other in the future.

Another important way to support the positive goals of your relationship actively, is to consider your friends. Are they mature, and do they have intimate relationships? If not, they will reinforce irrational and immature ways of thinking in you. If you are struggling with intimacy, it's important to identify one or two individuals you know who are comfortable with intimacy, and spend time with them. It's impossible to work out relationship issues in isolation. The only way you can become comfortable with intimacy is to experience it within a relationship. Spending time with people who know how to have healthy relationships will help you to become comfortable with intimacy yourself.

When Conflicts Arise, Engage in Constructive Problem Solving.

When couples are struggling with intimacy and conflict, it's often necessary for them to adopt a very structured approach when discussing a problem. This simple method has helped many couples develop a friendlier approach to conflict resolution. Let's assume that you want to initiate a problem solving session with your partner.

1. Before you talk to your partner, create a D.E.R. script for the problem you want to resolve.
2. When your script is ready, tell your partner that you

want to have a problem solving session. Then set a time that is convenient for both of you and when you both will be calm, relaxed, and alert.

3. At the appointed time, begin the session by reading your D.E.R. script aloud.

4. After you have read the script, your partner paraphrases it. If you do not feel that your partner heard the script accurately, restate the problem parts and have your partner paraphrase them back until you believe you have been heard accurately.

5. Your partner responds to the script. The response should be kept relatively short.

6. As your partner responds, you paraphrase his or her response. If your partner does not believe that you have heard his or her position accurately, your partner restates his or her position while you again paraphrase it. Continue this until your partner believes that you have heard his or her position accurately.

7. Once each has heard the other accurately, it's time to brainstorm possible solutions for the problem. Do not go on to the next step until several possible solutions have been suggested.

8. Each possible solution is evaluated, and the best one is chosen. If none is mutually agreeable, return to brainstorming.

9. Once you both have agreed upon a solution, you both restate it to make sure you both have the same understanding of it.

This is a specific application of the five-step approach for resolving conflict that I described in Chapter 11. Be sure to review this section before beginning to use this approach.

Often, you can resolve potential conflicts before they become problems by checking periodically to see how things are going between you and your partner. This is especially true whenever a major stress occurs in your life, such as changing jobs, the birth of a baby, launching a child into adulthood, or retirement. The stress that accompanies transitional periods like these tends to increase distorted thinking.

Finally, do not let problems go unresolved for long periods of time. This lesson was especially difficult for Alex to learn. However, as he learned to speak up and deal with issues that were bothering him more quickly, he found that he had much more time and energy for constructive activities. It also reduced the amount of overgeneralizing and magnification he did.

FOUR COMMON AREAS OF CONFLICT

The following areas are common sources of conflict in many relationships. Place a check by those that create conflict between you and your partner. If more than one area creates conflict, do not try to resolve them all at once. Since it's easy to become overwhelmed, select one area to work on and spend at least two to four weeks on it. This gives you and your partner time to discuss the problem, experiment with different solutions, and become comfortable with the changes you've made. Once you have done so, move on to the next area.

If a particular area is very difficult for you and your partner to discuss, seek help with a therapist experienced in working with couples. You might also find it helpful to read one or two books dealing with that area.

Sex
In order to enjoy a satisfying sexual relationship, you need to be able to discuss it with your partner. To begin a discussion

of how the two of you express your sexuality with each other, here are several questions you can use:

1. Is it easy to talk about sex with each other?
2. Can each of you ask for what you want?
3. When something pleasing happens in sex, can you tell each other about it?
4. When something disappointing happens, can you discuss it without shame or guilt?
5. Are you pleased with the frequency of your sexual activity?
6. How are you and your partner's interests in sex different?
7. Do you feel that there is enough touching, kissing, and hugging in your relationship?
8. Do each of you feel comfortable initiating sex? If not, why not?
9. Are you satisfied with the ways in which you are sexual with each other? If you would like to have more variety in sexual activities, what specifically would you enjoy?

Since many common misconceptions can interfere with this special form of intimacy, you might find it useful to read one of the many good books available on healthy sexuality.

Money

Money can be a powerful symbol for many other things in a relationship. For example, having money can represent power and a conflict over money is actually over who has power and control in the relationship. Spending money might also represent love. When money is a major factor in a person's self-image, the lack of money can cause him or her to feel inadequate and interfere with a relationship. Common problems with money include unwise use of credit cards, refusing to stick to a budget, spending sprees, gambling, and overspending for housing, clothing, recreation, furniture, or personal hobbies.

As with everything else in your life, the first step in gaining control over money is to make an honest assessment of how you currently use it. If you are misusing money in any way, you need to take responsibility for your actions. Then you need to decide what specific actions to take to change the situation. If you are unable to do so, many helpful resources are available in the form of books as well as personal consumer credit counseling services.

Here are several questions with which you can begin a discussion of how you and your partner use money.

1. How do you view the money that you and your partner make? Does your personal income belong only to you, or is it "our" money? Does the same apply to your partner's income?
2. Can you say exactly where your money is spent each month? Does your partner know?
3. Do each of you have at least some separate personal money you can spend freely?
4. If one person handles most of the bookkeeping, is the way in which he or she is doing it satisfactory with the other? If not, what changes would you like to see? What responsibility would you be willing to take to see that these changes are made?
5. Do either of you spend money when you are angry or sad?
6. Do either of you spend money impulsively?
7. Do you ever feel guilty or bad when you spend money? If so, when? Why do you feel this way?

8. How often do you and your partner quarrel about money? What issues are behind these conflicts?
9. Have you and your partner agreed on a savings program? If not, how would you develop one?
10. Do you have an emergency savings fund that could support you for at least three months? If not, how could you create one?
11. What changes would you like to see in how you or your partner handles money?

Recreation

Recreation is essential for good mental and physical health. It reduces physical tension, increases stress tolerance, and revitalizes your sense of humor. While everyone needs some time by themselves, it's also important to spend time with your loved ones if you are going to have a truly intimate relationship. How much alone time as opposed to couple time a person needs varies greatly from couple to couple. Finding a balance that is satisfying for both you and your partner is an essential requirement for intimacy. Here are several questions you can use to begin a discussion of how the two of you spend your free time and pursue recreation.

1. What recreational activities are most enjoyable for you?
2. How much time do you think should be spent on each of the following?
   - Hobbies involving only one partner.
   - Social activities involving only one partner.
   - Fun activities involving both of you.
3. How often do the two of you enjoy each other's company?
4. Are you satisfied with the way you spend time to-

gether? If not, what would you like to do differently?

5. How much free time does watching television absorb? Would you like to make any changes in this area?

Religion

Your religious beliefs can have a profound impact on your relationship. Here are several questions you can use to begin a discussion of religion in your relationship.

1. What religious beliefs did each of your parents have? What beliefs did your partner's parents have? Were these beliefs incorporated into their daily life—did they live them?
2. Were either of your or your partner's parents affiliated with a particular religious group? Were you or your partner included? If so, how?
3. Did your parents have prejudices against people with different religious backgrounds or beliefs? If so, what were they and how were they demonstrated? Do you do this?
4. Was religion used as a weapon to control your behavior? If so, how? Do you do this?
5. Was religion used to provide you with a sense of security, appreciation, and wonder of life? If so, how?
6. What are your current spiritual/religious beliefs?
7. Do they provide you with satisfactory answers for the pain, suffering, and unfairness that are part of life? How?
8. Is there anything you would like to do differently on your own in this area of your life? If so, what?
9. Is there anything you would like to do differently with your partner in this area of your life? If so, what?

SUMMARY OF KEY IDEAS

1. Learning to be comfortable within an intimate relationship is one of the most powerful ways to tame the beast, since much of the inappropriate anger that people experience comes from defending against childhood pain associated with intimacy.

2. A person who has a strong association between childhood pain and intimacy often substitutes sex, work, drugs, fame, power, or accomplishment for intimacy.

3. Emotional intimacy is based on the belief that you have a strong connection to another person and that you are safe with this person. You are able to be vulnerable and express your emotions, hopes, dreams, and fears without censoring them.

4. In order to have an intimate relationship, you need to have a partner who also desires this type of intimacy and who has the capacity to develop an intimate relationship.

5. People who grow up in families where intimacy was lacking need to desensitize to the experience of intimacy. The "What's happening? What's real?" technique can help with the desensitization process.

6. True intimacy can be achieved only when a person has the ability to think and act in a realistic and mature way. This chapter describes eight characteristics of emotional maturity.

7. Feeling confirmation is the process of making guesses about what emotion a speaker is experiencing and then commenting on it. Feeling confirmation conveys empathy and can help to dissipate negative emotions. This can prepare the way for effective problem solving.

8. Four areas of conflict that commonly distance couples are sex, money, recreation, and religion.

RECOMMENDED ACTIVITIES

Evaluate Where You Currently Stand

The first step in developing a more intimate relationship is to make an objective evaluation of where you currently stand. Take some time during the week to answer the following questions in your journal:

1. What qualities in your partner initially attracted you to him or her? How do these same qualities either please you or cause difficulty for you now?
2. What aspects of yourself that you like does your partner allow or encourage you to exercise?
3. In what ways does your partner remind you of things you like about your mother or father?
4. In what ways does your partner remind you of things you don't like about your mother or father?
5. What scares you the most about getting close to your partner? What might happen if you worked through these fears and really let him or her get close to you?
6. What negative patterns would you like to change in your relationship? Where do you need to improve?
7. What positive patterns or characteristics would you like to see develop or keep if they are already present?

As you identify specific fears and negative beliefs, develop a summary sheet for each one.

What If My Partner Is Resistant?

Some who are reading this book have partners who do not

want to discuss the issues in this chapter. If this is true of your partner, you first need to face the fact that he or she is a non-negotiator in this area. Review the approaches for dealing with a nonnegotiator that I discussed in Chapter 11. Decide which topic in this chapter would be least threatening to your partner, and try to win cooperation in working together on that one.

If your partner continues to be a nonnegotiator in the area of improving your relationship, you have to decide whether you want to continue the relationship. If you decide to continue it, you need to accept the fact that your partner may never change. In order to make up for the areas where your partner is weak, you need to develop a strong support network of friends and activities that can meet at least some of your needs for intimacy and nurturing. Many find that church groups, common interest groups (such as hiking, biking, or quilting clubs) and service groups (like Red Cross volunteers or Senior Gleaners) can help to meet these needs.

If your partner's lack of cooperation becomes a major issue for you, I strongly recommend that you find a qualified counselor. A good counselor can help you sort through the issues you are facing and identify alternatives you might not be able to see on your own.

Desensitizing to Intimacy

If you are uncomfortable with intimacy, you need to go through a process of desensitization where you gradually learn to enjoy it. As you desensitize, you need to manage the anxiety that intimacy can cause. Write several coping self-statements you can use when you feel uncomfortable to remind yourself of what is happening. They should encourage you to continue the behaviors that lead to intimacy. Here are several examples for three common problem situations:

Statements That Can Be Used When You Are Feeling Uncomfortable During a Tender Moment with Your Partner

- "The discomfort I'm feeling is a reaction to the past. I'm safe here with this person. Don't run away. Just let the discomfort be there, and refocus on my partner."
- "This discomfort is only an old message from the past. It's a danger signal that was real when I grew up, but that is not valid here and now. It will slowly fade as I practice staying in the present with my partner and separate the present from the past."
- "It's okay to feel anxious/scared/vulnerable. I don't need to run away and cover it up. My partner is safe and will not hurt me. Share what I'm experiencing with my partner, as this type of vulnerability can bring us even closer together."

Statements That Can Be Used When Experiencing Discomfort While Watching an Intimate Scene on TV at a Play, or in a Movie

- "I don't have to be strong and in control right now. I can allow myself to experience these feelings."
- "Don't run away from this experience. This scene is triggering old fears. I'm safe here. It's common for people with my background to experience these feelings."
- "It's normal to experience this emotion. I don't need to protect myself or hide it."

Statements That Can Be Used When Resolving a Conflict with Your Partner

- "My partner feels like my parent right now. He/she is not my parent. He/she loves me and is on my side. He/she will not punish me as my parents did. He/she is willing to work this out."

- "I'm not a child trapped in a house where I'm going to be hurt. That was long ago and far away. I'm an adult now. My partner is different from my parents. He/she loves me and is willing to work on this problem in an adult way."
- "While my partner is unhappy with me right now because of this problem, he/she is not my parent. He/she is able to control emotions and express them in an appropriate way. He/she wants to resolve this conflict constructively."

Connection Time

If you want to have an intimate relationship, you need to spend time together. Connection time is time that you set aside to connect with your partner. It's not a time for resolving problems or working out conflicts. Here is a simple structure you can use.

1. Agree on a time when you can meet for ten minutes each day during the next two weeks.
2. Decide who is going to speak first. It can be the same person each time, or you can alternate.
3. The person who speaks first has five minutes to talk about anything he/she wants: work, friends, family, sex, chores he/she plans to do—anything. The only restriction is that neither of you bring up a problem that involves the other person. Do conflict resolution at a different time.
4. While the first person talks, the other person listens. Practice using paraphrasing (Chapter 11) and feeling confirmation (this chapter).
5. After five minutes the listener says, "Thank you."
6. When the first person's five minutes are up, reverse roles and the second person speaks.

After you have practiced this exercise for two weeks, experiment with other forms of connection time. A few possible variations include taking a walk together, sitting and holding hands, playing a game, and reading to each other. Be as creative as you wish. The idea is to create a time you can spend together doing something enjoyable.

Practice Feeling Confirmation

If feeling confirmation is a new way of listening for you, or if it's uncomfortable, find at least one situation each day during the next week where you can practice it. The easiest way to become skilled with feeling confirmation is to first use it in situations where the other person is experiencing positive emotions. For example, try using feeling confirmation when a friend has had something good happen or when your partner has just done something he or she is proud of. When you practice feeling confirmation in situations like this, notice how it invites increased conversation. After you become comfortable using feeling confirmation in positive situations, you are ready to use it during situations where there are negative emotions.

Practice Encouraging Your Partner

If encouragement is not comfortable for you or is something you do not do regularly, you need to practice it in a structured manner. Select a time during the day when you and your partner can give each other encouragement. Some couples use this time as an opening for their connection time. Others make it part of their mealtime. State something about your partner that is positive. Possible opening phrases might include:

"Something I appreciated about you today was . . ."
"Thank you for . . ."
"I enjoyed . . ."

"I liked the way you . . ."

The person receiving the encouragement responds with a simple "Thank you." This is especially important if you find encouragement uncomfortable. Encouraging each other in this way will help you experience greater cooperation and a greater sense of belonging and togetherness.

Identify Specific Areas of Work You Need to Do
This chapter listed eight specific ways to increase the amount of intimacy you experience. Identify those you need to address. If there are several areas that you need to work on, select the one that is most important and spend two weeks doing the activities recommended. Then move on to the next. Once you've worked on each one in this manner, repeat the cycle.

Address Specific Areas of Conflict
You cannot be intimate with someone when you are angry about an ongoing conflict. This chapter listed four common areas of conflict that couples face: sex, money, recreation, and religion. Identify the ones that are currently creating problems in your relationship. Then set a time when you both have an hour together to discuss one of the four areas. This has to be a time you both agree on. It also has to be a time when you both will be free from distractions. Do not select a time when either of you will be tired or hungry. Before the meeting, each of you should read through and answer the questions provided for that area of conflict individually. When you meet, begin by reading the questions together and sharing your responses. If things become too heated to continue, take a break and set another time to get together. If you simply cannot discuss or resolve the issue, find a counselor who specializes in couples counseling to assist you.

16

On Your Own

NOW THAT YOU'VE reached the final chapter, you
might be wondering, "What next?" The answer to this
question depends upon where you are currently and how
you've worked through this book. If you read through the
book like a novel looking for information and doing only
a few of the exercises, you've probably learned a few new
things, but you're probably still reacting to situations in the
same way as when you started. The work done by David,
Sharon, Alex, and Carmen took place over many months and
entailed much effort on their part. While it was hard, each of
them was richly rewarded.

Sharon found that she was controlling her temper much
more effectively when dealing with her children. She also
developed much better relationships at work. As is common

some of her problems with anger resurfaced periodically. When they did, she reviewed her summary sheets and was soon back on track. Over time, the old patterns recurred less frequently. A few years after our initial therapy work, when her children reached their teens, Sharon returned for several sessions. By then she had remarried and was facing new challenges. After addressing the new issues of a blended family and the normal conflict of raising adolescents, she was once again managing her anger effectively.

Like Sharon, David was also able to control his temper much more effectively. He was especially pleased with the change that had taken place in his relationship with his children. Instead of condemning their mistakes and barking orders at them like a dictator, he learned to hold his tongue and become more encouraging. As a result, his children were much more willing to share their lives with him. For the first time in his life, he said that he felt that he was able to fill his role as a father in a satisfying way. This does not mean that there were no problems. Like Sharon, he did occasionally slip back into old behaviors, especially when he encountered stress at work or other unexpected problems. He also came in for therapy several times during the years following our initial work to reinforce his skills and address additional problems. Much of this work centered on increasing intimacy with his wife.

Carmen grew in many ways during our anger work. She was able to be much more assertive at work, which increased her confidence in her ability to handle life's problems. Being able to deal with conflicts also helped her manage her conflicts with her children much more effectively. About a year and half after we finished working together, Carmen reported that she was in a management training program at work and doing well. Depression, she said, was no longer a problem. Sometimes, she would catch herself sitting, staring, and feeling blue, but when this happened, she would realize that she needed to set limits in some area of her life and focus on taking action. Then she began to feel better.

About a year after we finished our initial work, Alex came in for a short round of premarital counseling with a woman he had met during our initial work. He had continued working on identifying what he was feeling and what actions he needed to take. As a result, he was able to communicate what he was feeling and what he wanted in a much more direct and positive manner. His fiancée reported that he only occasionally stewed over something. When he did, they eventually talked it out and life returned to normal again.

THREE PLANS

This section describes three different plans for how to proceed after you have worked through this book. Read all three before you decide how you want to proceed. Since no plan can fit everyone who reads the book, feel free to modify the one you select to fit your unique personality. You could even find it useful to combine parts of two plans together.

Plan 1: For Those Who Feel That They Have Made Little or No Progress

The main reason that people have made little progress by now is that they read the book without doing any of the exercises. As was previously stated, information and insight alone usually do not change deep-seated habit patterns. You need to apply information and insight to your life in a systematic way. If you have done few or none of the exercises, return to the first chapter and begin working through the book as it was designed to be used. Of special importance is the anger journal, a very powerful tool for change.

If you have been working through the book systematically on your own but have had poor results, you might need additional help. I recommend that you find a trained therapist you can work with. When selecting a therapist, be sure to follow the guidelines given in Appendix 1. This is especially true if you experienced physical, sexual, or emotional abuse as a child, or come from a family where there was substance abuse. A good therapist will be able to identify those blocks that have prevented you from making the progress you desire.

Plan 2: For Those Who Have Made Progress but for Whom Anger Is Still a Major Problem

Those who fall into this group, often just need additional time and work to achieve the results they desire. Like many people, you might choose to work through this book two or three times. Each time you do, you will gain new insights and an increased ability to apply the skills. All of the ideas and skills in this book are interconnected so that understanding the information in the final chapters helps you understand the information in the beginning chapters in ways that were not possible when you first worked through them. Likewise, having some ability to use the skills in the final chapters strengthens your ability to apply those presented in the earlier chapters.

If after working through the book a second time you still have important areas where you feel that you are stuck, you probably need help. Use the guidelines given in Appendix 1 to select a therapist who can help you.

If you experienced physical, sexual, or emotional abuse as a child, or come from a family where there was substance abuse, you might find it valuable to seek individual counseling or become involved in a support group that addresses your specific issues. Appendix 2 provides guidelines for locating a local support organization that is right for you.

Plan 3: For Those Who Have Achieved the Results They Wanted

Congratulations! It's now time to make the skills you've learned so automatic that you no longer have to work on them consciously. This usually takes time, but it does happen. Here are a few ways in which you can reinforce your new behaviors so they will last the rest of your life.

Schedule a monthly review of the lessons for the next six months.

Select one day each month for the next six months, such as the first Saturday of the month, for a review session. On that day, spend at least one hour reviewing the work you have done. A good place to begin is to review your summary sheets. Pay special attention to the second section of each sheet titled "Situations Where This Belief Causes Problems." Identify any that are still a problem. If there is more than one, identify the problem behavior that is most troublesome. Spend the next week focusing on it by reviewing the summary sheet that you created each morning. It's also useful to review the sections of your journal that address this behavior and the beliefs that support it. If several behaviors are still a problem, focus on a different one each week until you have rotated through all of them.

At the first sign of old behaviors, review your new skills.

While you may be doing well now, some of the old patterns will probably return when you encounter an unusual stress such as an illness, a work-related problem, or an unusual family problem. Do not be surprised or alarmed when this occurs. Instead, look at the brief return of old patterns as a message that you have important life issues to address. Spend a few weeks reviewing the sections of the book or doing an activity that addresses the specific pattern. This is also a time to pull out your journal and write about incidents where you have repeated old patterns. Be sure to analyze your self-talk and create rational challenges for any distorted thinking you did. Then spend at least one week reviewing the summary sheet you created that applies to the belief that underlies this specific behavior. If you do not have such a summary sheet, create one. In addition, take time to write about the life situation that triggered the return of the old pattern.

Reread this book three to six months from now.

Rereading this book in six months is one of the best ways to review the work you have done. As you do so, review the work you did in your journal. When you identify an area where you need additional work, devote a week or two to the chapter and the recommended activities that deal with it.

Do supplemental reading.

Every two or three months over the next year, read at least one book dealing with an area on which you feel you need additional work. Remember to take your time as you read these books. It also helps to read each chapter twice: once for the big picture, and once for detail. This is the best way to absorb the information and skills presented in a self-help book. Continue this practice for at least a year.

Attend lectures, classes, or workshops that reinforce what you have learned.

In most large communities, many different personal growth classes and workshops are held at churches, hospitals, colleges, the adult education division of local school districts, and counseling centers. While many excellent programs are available throughout the country, some are of dubious quality. Therefore, check on the credentials and experience of the person presenting the workshop. Stay away from programs that promise a quick fix. If it sounds too good to be true, it probably is.

It has been a tremendous privilege for me to play a role in your growth. With all my heart, I wish you the best as you work to tame the beast of anger.

Appendix I

Guidelines for Selecting a Therapist

I F YOU DECIDE to seek help, take time to choose your therapist carefully. The following guidelines are designed to help you find a therapist who is a good match for both your personality and the problem you're struggling with.

How Do I Start?
Your initial objective is to get recommendations for at least three therapists. If you have friends or acquaintances who have been in therapy or might work with or know a therapist, ask them for the therapist's name. Another good place to start would be to call a therapist who has presented a class or lecture that you enjoyed.

If you have no personal contact with a therapist or with someone who is familiar with therapists in your area, ask your primary care physician or health insurance company for three referrals. If there is a women's shelter in your area, it will have a list of anger management programs and therapists who specialize in dealing with anger. You might also want to visit a self-help group on anger and ask for recommendations from the group members.

When doing an internet search, begin with "anger management." Be sure to add the name of your city when searching. You could also try "anger management counseling" or simply "anger counseling."

Here is a list of the current types of therapists you'll probably find:

- *Psychologists:* These individuals usually have a doctorate (Ph.D.) in psychology.
- *Marriage and Family Therapists:* They usually have a master's (M.A. or M.S.) in counseling or psychology. Sometimes they have a doctorate (Ph.D.).
- *Social Workers:* These individuals have training similar to marriage and family therapists.
- *Psychiatrists:* These are medical doctors (M.D.) who, after their basic training in medicine, specialize in psychiatry. Because psychiatrists are trained as medical doctors, they tend to view psychological problems as medical problems and usually focus on determining which medication could alleviate a person's symptoms. Since many psychiatrists work only with medications, other types of therapists may be more likely to use the approaches described in this book.

What Should I Ask?

After you get the names of at least three possible therapists, take time to interview each one by phone before you set an appointment. Just as medical doctors specialize in different types of medical conditions, therapists also have areas of specialty. If you need a specific type of surgery, you want a surgeon who has performed the procedure hundreds of times. Likewise, the best therapist for you will be one who has worked with many people experiencing problems like yours.

When you interview a prospective therapist, begin by giving them a brief summary of your problem. Describe the specific problem behaviors you want to change, and explain how often they occur. Here is an example of what David might have said to a prospective therapist:

David: "I'm calling because I'm seeking a therapist who specializes in anger management problems. I can be very critical and sometimes I explode over trivial matters."

After you have given the prospective therapist a short summary of your condition, ask the following questions:

- Are you licensed? (Many states do not license one or more types of therapists)
- What kind of training have you had to work with my . type of problem?
- How much experience have you had with this type of problem?
- How many people have you treated with this type of problem in the past year?
- What is your basic approach? How would you work with me?
- How successful have you been?
- How long does therapy usually take?
- How much does treatment cost, and is any of it reimbursable by health insurance?

Which Approach Is Best?

Each of the many different therapeutic approaches has its own set of terms and limitations. Cognitive therapy involves learning specific techniques for changing the way you think. The discussion of distorted thinking in Chapters 4 and 6 and the rational challenges in the later chapters are examples of a cognitive approach. A behavioral approach focuses on actions you can take. The "Situations Where This Creates a Problem" and "Things I Can Do" sections of the summary sheets in this book illustrate a behavioral approach. A psychodynamic approach focuses on the interaction of an individual's conscious and unconscious mental or emotional processes. Chapters 7, 8, and 9, where you explore core beliefs from childhood, illustrate a psychodynamic approach.

An exciting new approach that I have found useful when combined with a cognitive-behavioral-psychodynamic approach is called eye movement desensitization and reprocessing (EMDR) or simply, eye movement therapy. Unfortunately, it might be difficult to find someone who has adequate training in this method. Although eye movement therapy seems deceptively simple, using it effectively requires a high degree of skill. Therapists often use the same terms but with different meanings. So, be sure to ask the therapist to explain when a term is used that you do not understand.

How Do I Evaluate the Therapist Once I Start?

After two or three sessions, take some time to decide whether the therapist you've chosen has the knowledge, skill, approach, personality, and style that seem right for you. Ask yourself the following questions:

- Am I comfortable with my therapist?
- Can I speak freely with my therapist?

- Does what the therapist says make sense and seem relevant to my problems?
- Does the therapist speak in a way that is easy for me to understand?
- Does the therapist take time to explain things I don't understand?
- Does the therapist treat me as an adult rather than as a child or someone who is beneath him/her?
- Do I feel comfortable disagreeing with the therapist?
- Does the therapist take time to establish a set of goals for my therapy that I can understand?

Changing deeply ingrained habits often takes a year or more. It does not necessarily require weekly therapy sessions; many people take periodic breaks from formal therapy to practice and master the skills they've learned. They then return when difficulties arise that they cannot resolve on their own. People with very traumatic childhoods often work weekly for an extended period of time. While therapy takes time, you should be able to see clear progress. If you feel that you have made no progress and that your therapy has no clear direction after four sessions, you probably need to try someone else.

Before you switch to a new therapist, tell your current therapist you are considering going to someone new because you feel your therapy is not going anywhere. It could be that you are making progress but are simply not seeing it. If you have tried several different therapists with little progress, you might need to reevaluate your efforts. Have you made a real commitment to the therapeutic process and done the work you were asked to do? If not, return to the therapist who seemed most effective.

Appendix II

Locating a Self-Help Group

S ELF-HELP GROUPS AND short-term structured programs provide a valuable resource for people struggling
with anger management. If you're in therapy, these groups
and programs can provide excellent supplement or follow-
up to professional treatment. You'll also find them valuable
if professional treatment is either not available or not afford-
able. Even people who do not feel their anger management
problems are severe enough to warrant professional treatment often find self-help groups a valuable resource.

The first place to look for a local self-help group is online.
Start your search with the term, "anger management." Be
sure to add the name of the town you live in. You can also try
"anger group" and "anger class." Again, be sure to add the
name of your city. If there are no results for your search, try

using the names of larger nearby cities. The local chapter of the Mental Health Association or a woman's shelter in your area would probably have a listing of self-help groups and short-term structured programs for effective anger management. If you want a group with a spiritual focus, contact the larger churches in your area to see if they sponsor groups that address your concern.

If you are unable to locate any agencies that can refer you to local self-help groups, try searching for Mental Health Clinics, Psychiatrists, Psychologists, Marriage and Family Counselors, and Social Workers. Again, add the name of your city for local referrals.

After you have the names of several possible groups, identify the one that is best for you. As when selecting a therapist, find a group that matches your needs and personality. If there are several chapters of a particular group in your area, attend more than one so you get the flavor of each one. Attend at least three meetings of a particular group before you decide whether it's right for you.

If any of the following areas apply to you, you might also want to consider attending a group that deals with that area.

Substance Abuse

Anger management problems are often related to substance abuse problems. Whenever this is the case, it's always necessary to deal with the substance abuse problem before progress can be made with the anger management problems. If you are currently abusing any legal or illegal drug, you need to be in treatment. You also need to become active with Alcoholics Anonymous, Narcotics Anonymous, Pill Addicts Anonymous, or one of the other groups for substance abusers.

Effects of a Dysfunctional Family

A dysfunctional family is one in which children have experienced one or more of the six types of child abuse described in Chapter 2. Groups that deal with issues common to people from dysfunctional families vary greatly. Often they focus on a specific type of abuse, such as sexual abuse or physical abuse.

A Current Unhealthy Relationship

If you currently live with or have a close relationship with someone who is a substance abuser or who abuses you mentally or physically, you will probably need help to deal with the situation. This help might have to be professional therapy. In addition, self-help groups can provide you with both the strength and the courage to act effectively, along with practical suggestions for how to handle a difficult situation. Al-Anon, the companion organization to AA is a good example of a national organization of such groups. Most large communities have local shelters for battered women that sponsor regional and local groups.

Effects of a Major Illness or Physical Disability

If you have a major illness or physical disability, addressing the issues surrounding it may be necessary in order to manage your anger effectively. Most major illnesses and physical disabilities have their own national or regional self-help organizations. These organizations can usually provide the latest information regarding the treatment of a particular problem and help a person accept and cope with the difficulties associated with his or her problem.

About the Author

R ENEAU PEURIFOY holds a master's degree in counseling and attended Fuller Theological Seminary. He is the author of several books including *Anxiety, Phobias, and Panic: Taking Charge and Conquering Fear, Overcoming Anxiety: From Short-Term Fixes to Long-Term Recovery* and *Why Did God Give Us Emotions?* Peurifoy is a frequent guest speaker for organizations  including the Anxiety Disorders Association of America (ADAA), the nation's primary organization for anxiety-related problems. Peurifoy was in private practice for twenty years as a marriage and family therapist specializing in anxiety disorders. He retired from private practice in 2000 to teach at Heald College in Sacramento, California. In 2015, he retired from teaching and received a ministerial credential from the Church of God headquartered in Anderson, Indiana. He now is spending his time writing, speaking, and seeing people with anxiety-related problems as a pastoral counselor.

Additional Books by Reneau Peurifoy

Anxiety, Phobias & Panic

Mr. Peurifoy's first work, now revised and in its third edition, was based on a program that was developed by the author over a period of eight years and which has become the standard for therapists and treatment centers around the world.

One of the unique features of this work is the way it's organized into a series of easy-to-follow lessons. This structured approach is the reason *Anxiety, Phobias & Panic* is used in treatment centers and self-help groups around the world. One of the most helpful aspects of *Anxiety, Phobias & Panic* is the list of recommended activities at the end of each lesson. The book is full of practical exercises showing the reader how to apply the concepts and ideas it presents. Instructions for the exercises are given step-by-step, in simple language.

Overcoming Anxiety

Overcoming Anxiety presents a unique approach to managing anxiety, offering readers a comprehensive and far-reaching philosophy that stresses lasting preventive measures over superficial — and often just temporary — antidotes. This groundbreaking book shows sufferers how to shift their focus from the messenger, or the symptoms of anxiety, to the message — the core cause of anxiety.

Like his first book, *Overcoming Anxiety* is structured as a series of lessons. However, the lessons are intertwined with three case histories drawn from the author's extensive clinical experience. By following these individuals through the process of recovery, you learn not only how to identify and challenge negative thinking patterns, but also how to achieve control and change destructive and dysfunctional behavior. Each chapter ends with a set of recommended activities. Also included is an extensive resource guide.

Overcoming Anxiety can be used as a stand-alone program for learning how to personalize the valuable healing strategies set forth, paving the way for a more complete, lifelong recovery from the troubling afflictions of anxiety disorders. It's also a valuable follow-up for those who have read *Anxiety, Phobias & Panic* and would like additional skills.

Why Did God Give Us Emotions?

Why Did God Give Us Emotions? takes a detailed look at the many sources of our emotional responses and the role our emotions play in our thoughts, actions, relationships with others, and our relationship with God from a Christian perspective. Peurifoy holds a master's degree in counseling, has attended Fuller Theological Seminary, is a credentialed pastor, and has spent over twenty years in private practice and teaching. With the gift of making seemingly complicated issues easy to understand, Peurifoy states: "From the very start

I had two goals: I wanted to look at what science has learned about emotions from a biblical perspective, and I wanted to do it in a way that would strengthen the reader's walk with God."

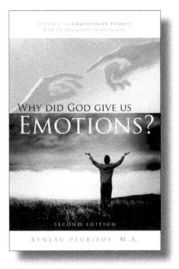

Why Did God Give Us Emotions? is essential reading for both those struggling with emotional issues as well as for the general reader who wants to not only understand their emotions more fully, but who is also seeking skills for managing emotions more effectively. Pastors and counselors will find both the insights offered and the recommended activities at the end of each chapter to be a valuable resource for many years to come. The group discussion questions at the end of the book also make it an ideal vehicle for small group study.

.

CPSIA information can be obtained
at www.ICGtesting.com
Printed in the USA
LVHW050007060619
620339LV00001B/94/P